By What Authority?

BY WHAT AUTHORITY?

Confronting Churches
Who No Longer Believe
Their Own Message

Hoffman House
PRESS

Cover art: Mary Ann Simmons. Mary Ann Simmons is a portrait artist working in watercolor, has owned two art galleries and currently resides in Minneapolis, Minnesota. She can be reached at: artistmaryann@gmail.com.

Photographs: Larry Meyers. Meyers has lived most of his life in eastern Washington. A self-taught photographer concentrating on landscapes in black and white, he enjoys walking around towns and the countryside throughout the United States in order to find subject matter. After teaching mathematics and photography in Richland, Washington, for thirty-eight years, he retired in 2002 and now resides in Spokane.

ISBN-13: 978-0-9801835-0-4

Copyright © 2008 WordAlone Network

First Edition: April 2008

Printed in the United States of America

Published by

Hoffman House Press, LLC
Post Office Box 161
505 Fourth Street South
Hoffman, Minnesota 56339

The WordAlone Network

The WordAlone Network was organized in March 2000 as a Lutheran grassroots network of congregations and individuals in the Evangelical Lutheran Church in America (ELCA) committed to the authority of the Word manifest in Jesus the Christ as proclaimed in Scripture and safeguarded through the work of the Holy Spirit. WordAlone advocates reform and renewal of the church, representative governance, theological integrity, and freedom from a mandated historic episcopate.

WordAlone's primary concern is that the ELCA is losing its Christ-centered focus. ELCA churches and members are turning to authorities other than the authority of God's Word, revealed in his risen Son, Jesus Christ, and in his inspired Word in the Holy Scriptures. The other authorities—human experience, wisdom and tradition—are used to turn aside the authority of God's Word. The weaknesses within the ELCA—ecumenical agreements that compromise on significant biblical and confessional truths, the teaching and preaching of universalism, a decline in the proper mission of the church (global missions and new mission starts) and the push for approval of sexual relationships outside of marriage to name just a few—are symptoms of the deeper problem with the ELCA, the crisis over the authority of God's Word.

WordAlone's membership includes ELCA members in all sixty-four geographic synods, more than 6,000 individual members (of whom more then 1,000 are ELCA pastors), and more than 230 congregations.

WordAlone in its first eight years has launched several ministries, including a new Lutheran church, Lutheran Congregations in Mission for Christ (LCMC), a new institution for theological education, the Institute for Lutheran Theology (ILT), a new Lutheran agency dedicated to hymnody and liturgical renewal, Reclaim, a new Lutheran confessional publishing house, Sola Publishing, and with other Lutheran reform groups has helped launch Lutheran CORE.

ꙮ • ꙮ

Table of Contents

Foreword ix
Note to the Reader xiii

Section One
The Problem

Chapter 1   A Senior Warden's Farewell Warning to a "Comfortable"
             Congregation *Bill Boniface* 1
Chapter 2   Who's Really in Charge? *Al Quie* 17
Chapter 3   "Radical Lutheranism": Travels in the Middle of the
             Road *Jaynan Clark Egland* 25
Chapter 4   We Have No King But Jesus *Nathan Hanson* 29
Chapter 5   Who's Your Daddy? *Paul Owens* 37
Chapter 6   Authority and Power in the ELCA *Robert Benne* 43
Chapter 7   When Parents Falter, Children Speak *James C.
             Bangsund* 53
Chapter 8   ELCA Denies Seminarian's Rights *Steven Broers* 63
Chapter 9   The Piper's Flute: Hearing the True Voice in the
             Heresy *Meredith Schultz* 69

Section Two
The Theology

Chapter 10   Two Kinds of Authority: Law and Gospel
Steven Paulson 79

Chapter 11   Biblical Authority: Scriptures Claims for Itself
David N. Glesne 103

Chapter 12   Scriptural Authority in the Lutheran Confessions
James Arne Nestingen 117

Chapter 13   What Belongs and What Does Not *Jeffray Greene* ... 127

Chapter 14   Scripture Authorizes Women *Frederick W. Baltz* 139

Chapter 15   Authority Over What? *Mark C. Mattes* 153

Chapter 16   By What Authority? The World Mission of the
Church *Charles Lindquist* 165

Chapter 17   Something You Should Know *V.F. (Bud)
Thompson* 179

Chapter 18   Technology, Thinking, and Theology *Lothar
Schwabe* 187

Chapter 19   Norms for Life and Living *Hans Schwarz* 197

Section Three
The Solutions

Chapter 20   Do People Fear the Living God? *Mark C. Chavez* ... 207

Chapter 21   The Practical and Functional Authority of
Scripture *Steven E. King* 225

Chapter 22   Mission: By What Authority: Ponderings from
China Service Ventures *Paul Varo Martinson* 233

Chapter 23   Inerrancy is Not a Four-letter Word *David Lahren* ... 245

Chapter 24   No Middle Ground *Gary Diers* 253

Chapter 25   Word Alone: Every Night in Every Home
Rich Melheim 259

Chapter 26   The Lord Found Me *Louis M. Hesse* 269

Foreword

The Last Word

ON A HOT AUGUST AFTERNOON IN 1999, I sat sobbing on a curb near the Hard Rock Café in downtown Denver. I cried as one who's lost a loved one, sharing my grief and curb space with other pastors, lay leaders, professors, even a bishop. We experienced a few moments that day of complete disillusionment, like abandoned orphans. In the café the music played on and in the street traffic rumbled in a steady flow, but my understanding of "church" had just been changed forever.

In an assembly hall not far away, the debate was ended. The Evangelical Lutheran Church of America (ELCA) rendered its decision embracing full communion with Episcopalians (ECUSA, now TEC) and I was confronted with my own idolatry.

For too long I had served in the denomination in its global mission department and on synod councils and committees, so long that I had confused the institution with "the church." A once mainline now sideline denomination struggling against its ever-increasing deterioration and impending death by insignificants had just sold its birthright for an ecumenical bowl of porridge. Certainly the "church" on its firm foundation was still there for us and hidden among us, but the idolatry blinded my eyes. I had come to love the ELCA and had elevated it to the status of church in my heart and faith.

We who had adamantly confessed that the church is "where the Word is preached and the sacraments are administered rightly" now were called on to believe and live by that confession. Surely there were others who knew that none of this was about "loving the Episcopalians," or "fearing change" but rather went to the heart of the many problems this denomination and all the others are experiencing. The question needed to be answered, "By what authority do you do these things?" How can we as Lutherans adopt as regular practice an understanding of ordination and apostolic succession that is not only not scriptural but is on a collision course with our Lutheran confessions written 500 years ago?

In recent years as a denomination, we had already changed our paradigm for global mission and adopted accompaniment ministry as our calling not primary evangelism, after all, we are reminded, the name of Jesus is offensive in many areas. In this world of pluralism and relativism many think that is just an okay route to follow; however, who then is doing the mission of the church as commissioned by Jesus himself in Matthew 28: 18-20 (NIV)?

"And Jesus came and said to them, 'All authority in heaven and on earth has been given to me. Go therefore and make disciples of all nations, baptizing them in the name of the Father and of the Son and of the Holy Spirit, and teaching them to obey everything that I have commanded you. And remember, I am with you always, to the end of the age.'"

If the church is not going to name the name and go out to make disciples, who is? Government? Social service agencies? Hardly. As important as it is to feed the hungry and clothe the naked and shelter the homeless as our good Lord directed us to do, we must know in our hearts that you can give a starving man bread to fill his empty belly but if you do not deliver to him "the Bread of Life" is he not still starving? You can drill new fresh water wells for the thirsty but if you do not tell them the stories of "the Living Water" will they not still thirst to death? You can build fine shelters and houses but if you never tell them about their Father's house with many rooms being prepared for them are they not still vulnerable to the elements, and alone without hope? All witness to "mission" that builds on the sands of this sinful world and not on the Rock named Jesus is doomed.

When mission becomes development, when inclusive language becomes more important than the naming of the Triune God as Father, Son and Holy Spirit, when theological education teaches biblical interpretation that stands over the Word and dismisses its independent authority over all our lives, when relating to other Christians ecumenically becomes more pressing than proclaiming to the nonbelievers, when ministry standards for clergy and our entire understanding of marriage and sexuality are up for a vote then one needs to ask, "By what authority are you doing these things?"

This question was directed at Jesus himself by the chief priests and elders in the temple (Mt. 21:23-27, Lk. 20:1-8). Mark adds the scribes to the inquirers (Mk 11:27-33). They questioned him as the one who healed and gave the gift of forgiveness. Jesus just answered their question with a question and they were left confused and plotting. He had to go . . . some way, some how. They regarded him as a loose cannon, out preaching and teaching and healing and forgiving. They chose to kill him rather than answer his questions because his asking left them naked as the emperor in his new transparent, imaginary clothes. Exposed and vulnerable.

When Truth itself in bodily form authoritatively addresses us as individuals and collectively as the assembly of believers called "church" there is certainly a death coming. However, let us be assured that this time it will not be Jesus for he eternally resides among us as the Crucified One who wears the scars of our sin and opposition to his authority and "soul" sovereignty.

What you have before you in this book is a "potpourri" of essays written by concerned confessional Christians, mostly Lutherans, who are lay leaders, pastors and professors within the denominational institution asking the true "church" question of the institutional denominations made by human hands, "By what authority do you do these things?" Does the Word of God in three forms: Jesus the Living Word, the preached Word and the written Word still stand as the sole authority for all of faith and life for this denomination that calls itself Christian? The writers in these pages have each struggled to put on paper their concerns and their witness at this time in these circumstances. They share with you here their reason, emotion, and faith in today's climate of accommodation of the "church" to the world, where it conforms to society instead of engaging in the ministry of transformation by the renewal of the Holy Spirit.

This is supposed to be called the "Foreword," rather than "The Last Word." However, with the difficulty of launching this book I resorted to my preaching preparation aid in times of "slow starts" and wrote the end first, then went back to get there. It sometimes helps to go to where you want to end up. As you turn through the pages in whatever order, finally arriving at the last page, you might find yourself pondering the clear reality that "when all is said and done . . . there is a lot that has been said, but there is much more left to be done!" If so, then the writers have succeed in their confession by motivating yet one more Christian to leave the silent majority and join the vocal minority attempting to witness by speaking the Word not waiting to see or for someone else to "do something." What are any of us waiting for? After all, Jesus was the one who astounded the crowds "for he taught them as one having authority and not as their scribes." (Mt. 7:29)

When all authority in heaven and earth has been given to him alone (Mt. 28:18), how can we do other than to proclaim his name boldly in the face of adversity? His cross is ever before us as is the light streaming from the door of his empty tomb and some day every knee will bow before him and know what "Authority" really looks like!

Christ Jesus, the Alpha and Omega is definitely "the Last Word." In His Grace and Truth,

Jaynan Clark Egland
President/CEO WordAlone Network

Note to the Reader

Why should you read this book?

This is a book about the end of traditional Christianity as practiced in modern times. Not a futuristic end, but an end already accomplished, or partially accomplished in a majority of countries, cities, and churches. Protestant or Catholic, the affliction is universal in most traditional churches.

Strange as it seems, many Christians haven't noticed. But others were so concerned they've gathered in these pages the wisdom of alert pastors, theologians, laity, young seminarians and evangelicals. They all have a story to tell you in their own voices, and it's a story so urgent and timely it opens your eyes in ways few might imagine.

May you have "ears to hear" and mouths to proclaim the Way, the Truth, and the Life.

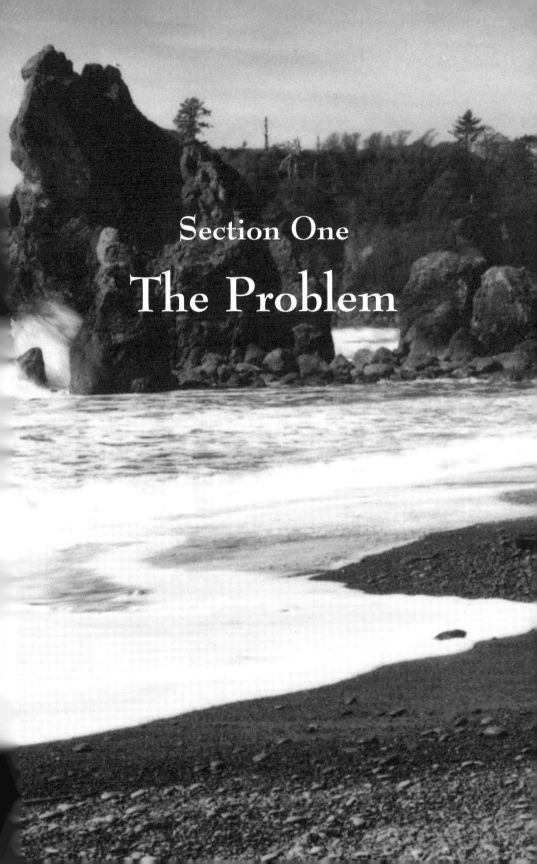

Section One
The Problem

A lifelong Episcopalian and twice parish senior warden, Bill Boniface graduated with a Bachelor of Science from Annapolis in 1972 and later earned a Master of Science from the George Washington University.

During a career as a Navy pilot spanning thirty years, he served in a variety of challenging operational squadron and ship assignments and staffs around the world and as Iraq Country Director and Deputy Director of Near East/South Asia Affairs in the Office of the Undersecretary of Defense for Policy following the first Gulf War. He later taught at the College of the Holy Cross in Worcester, Massachusetts as a professor and Chair of the Naval Science Department. He served his final assignment based in Italy as Chief of Staff for NATO's air anti-submarine and reconnaissance force in NATO's Southern Region.

Retiring from the Navy in the summer of 2002, he returned home from overseas to the small Episcopal country parish he had left as senior warden nine years earlier and resumed an active role in parish affairs. Controversial decisions arising from the Episcopal Church's General Convention in Minneapolis the following summer, however, put him suddenly and unexpectedly at odds with the denomination he had spent his entire life in. In the ensuing months, he actively sought to inform and educate his congregation in the danger that new direction posed for faithful Christians everywhere. Again elected as senior warden, he repeatedly urged the vestry to open a dialogue with the parishioners to learn the facts and discern a healthy way forward for the parish.

The vestry's staunch refusal to engage the vital issues in spite of an obviously growing denominational crisis ultimately resulted in his decision to leave the parish. He delivered the following remarks to the congregation at the annual parish meeting on his and his wife's last day in the parish.

Over the next two years he personally developed and led Episcopal Witness, an active lay outreach ministry whose goal was to reach out to uninformed or unengaged Episcopalians to make them aware of the danger the Episcopal Church's new theology presents to them and their children. When his new parish voted to leave the Episcopal Church in December 2006, his more than five decades as an Episcopalian came to an end. Today, Bill remains an Anglican as a member of a Virginia parish in the Convocation of Anglicans in North America (CANA), a part of the Anglican Church of Nigeria. Today, Bill and his wife of thirty-five years, Susan, reside in Hershey, Pennsylvania, where they

are houseparents for twelve teenaged boys from socially disadvantaged backgrounds.

A Senior Warden's Farewell Warning to a "Comfortable" Congregation

Bill Boniface

Editor's Note: *The term senior warden, as it occurs here, refers to the lay person serving as a rector's (pastor's) most valued assistant.*

Expanded Excerpts from the Senior Warden's Report given at the St. Thomas' Parish (Croom, Maryland) Annual Parish Meeting February 2005

The Danger to Our Church

AS YOU'RE ALL AWARE, I'M SURE, this is sadly my wife's and my last day at St. Thomas'. Never in my wildest dreams when we came back to this little church after many years away and made the decision to remain in Upper Marlboro for the foreseeable future did I think we'd ever become part of that large group of folks known as "former St. Thomas' parishioners."

But now I have to talk to you from the heart in a little different way. Families know that to let disagreements go without addressing them slowly destroys the bond of love and trust that holds them together. Ignoring serious disagreements only means that a price will have to be paid some time in the future. And if I didn't think the Episcopal Church's current disagreement would ever force St. Thomas' to pay a huge price in the future—in fact, the price of its very survival—I'd step away from this podium this very moment and simply walk away with the happiness of this gathering to warm me. That would be so easy. But I couldn't ever look you—or even worse, Christ—in the eye again if I did that.

I believe all the responsibilities of a Senior Warden are important, but I think his or her primary responsibility—along with the vestry—is to first and foremost guard the faith. We're a church, after all. We're here because of the faith. Without it, there would be no need for buildings or church suppers or altar guilds. For the vestry, it's like the meaning behind a doctor's Hippocratic oath, simply do no harm.

And so I'm going to share with you why two members of your parish family who love and cherish each and every one of you as friends and have made St. Thomas' parish our home would drive away today for the last time and start all over again in another Episcopal parish across the Potomac River.

It's not about what anyone's done here. No one's done anything to us. Everyone has been loving and kind. No one here is pushing an agenda on us; the rector isn't being dishonest with us, and there are no disputes between parishioners that make us want to leave. Most people would say everything is calm. And it is.

But it's what's behind that calm that should scare the living daylights out of you—not just you, but your children and grandchildren.

As your Senior Warden, I've been like a seismologist who watches for earthquake activity and detects an undersea earthquake with a reading of 8.9 on the Richter scale. Because I've studied it closely from as many angles as possible, I know what an earthquake of that magnitude will mean—not today, but soon—to people who live on the shoreline and for all the people out on the beaches. It will be a tsunami, and it will destroy everything and everyone in its path.

My friends, there has been an earthquake deep in the depths of the Episcopal Church—and there's a tsunami coming that will affect St. Thomas' whether we close our eyes and turn our beach chairs the other way or not. For well over a year, I've been trying to warn you in the most subtle way I can that we need to seek higher ground. I've done so cautiously, in a way that wouldn't generate a controversy that would divide the parish, as has been so often the case in the past. We're a parish family, and I've openly and honestly discussed the danger with our rector and many others for some time now. I decided it was best to approach the vestry in a manner more like a mild intervention than a debate. In that conversation, it became clear to me that St. Thomas' is hopeful that the tsunami racing toward the parish will somehow simply pass us by.

As we all have an obligation to protect our families, I decided that even as I will continue to warn of impending disaster, it's my responsibility to take my own family to higher ground. It always upsets me when I see parents on news reports when a huge hurricane is approaching who have "decided to stay and ride it out," their tiny children visible in the background, hoping in all their innocence that mom and dad weren't going to let them be killed.

To ignore the wave that's heading toward us and picking up force and height every day is simply unthinkable to me. Even if we want to disregard it for our own lives—and many of us here today have already had the chance to live full ones—why would you risk your children and grandchildren?

The desire to "remain comfortable" by refusing to recognize the disagreement that exists or trying hard not to face up to it even if you know it does, can't possibly give us comfort. It is reality and the facing up to it that gives us comfort. Comfort doesn't bring us reality.

So, what is this great "tsunami" rolling toward us? It's a radical agenda that has as its primary target not St. Thomas' parish, not the Episcopal Church—these will just be "collateral damage" in its wake—but the concept of Church itself. If this tsunami can get far enough

3

inland, your children and grandchildren or their children and grandchildren are unlikely to care about—much less be a part of—any church during their lifetimes.

So what makes me so wise as to offer such an assertion? Nothing special. I've studied the situation, prayed on it, sought to understand every aspect of it and, finally, been fortunate enough to get a sneak peek at the "playbook" of those who caused the earthquake in the first place. To put it another way, I've seen "the man behind the curtain."

I know why and how the strings are being pulled and can turn the pages to see what's coming next. Like people who pick up the Bible for the first time, get bored reading all the names in Genesis and turn instead to the more "exciting" part—Revelation—I quickly thumbed my way to the back of the playbook. I saw the final play, then I started looking backward at the pages of strategies and tactics that would make it possible.

This is not a playbook that's knowingly being used on us by anyone in the parish. The brilliance of the strategy is that in it each of us can find something that seems to make sense, something we can support, something that we can even advocate, but no one in our own little parish family is forcing anything down our throats. All of us, after all, have shown that we're really just trying to be good Christians.

But that's where the benign and unknowing acceptance of the strategy ends. Forces in our diocese are hard at work with the playbook carefully tucked under suit jackets and vestments, working each small part to create the synergy to achieve the ultimate goal. In countless dioceses, and indeed all the way to the Presiding Bishop's office of our national church headquarters, the strategy is being carefully played out like a chess game. The tsunami is being strengthened day after day, even as our children's choir rehearses, the ladies in the Altar Guild place flowers on the altar, and as good people are educated for ministry.

You don't just see it here. Go down the road to other small Episcopal parishes. I've visited many churches throughout the diocese, and I see much the same in most small country parishes. Everyone is holding their breaths that the great wave won't engulf them and, as they close their eyes, their numbers dwindle, the money goes away, and they will most surely be overtaken. And they'll eventually be dots on a map of historical parishes people will visit on a touring bus, but where all the parishioners have long gone.

Then there are courageous parishes—even small ones—that have seen the storm brewing and taken prudent measures so that when it passes, they'll be able to survive it and go on worshiping God when it's run its course. All Saints in Chevy Chase, Christ Church in Accokeek, Christ Church in Port Republic, and Truro Church in Fairfax are just a few among them. They've "gone to higher ground." Not as individuals, but as parishes.

What is this "higher ground?" It's members of a congregation standing together arm in arm in faith to guard the faith from the ravaging onslaught against it. It's certainly what I've wished St. Thomas' could be—like a beacon of faith in the countryside—standing first for the faith against all harm that might come to it. It's a fight I would gladly lead were there a congregation to follow.

If there is one fight in our lives we should all be a part of before we take up permanent residency out there in our cemetery, it's the fight for Christ and the faith. Many of our folks fight great fights for land rights or other worthy causes. But when it comes to standing up boldly against the most serious assault on our church since the English Reformation, these same people are notably absent. Surely Christ should have at least equal status to real estate and land policies.

Does the Danger Really Exist?

Some of you doubt the very notion that there's a serious and divisive situation in the Episcopal Church today. Please don't rely on me or any one person to sway you. Make your own decision from the following facts and then decide on your own whether this is serious enough:

•Over 40,000 faithful Episcopalians left the Church last year (didn't just change congregations, but left it altogether).

•100 entire congregations have left together to form new churches or worship under the protection of foreign Anglican primates or bishops.

•Eleven dioceses have formed a Network within the Episcopal Church structure in opposition to the direction their Church is going. These dioceses represent 1,100 clergy, 735 congregations, and 176,000 faithful communicants.

•Cathedrals and multi-million-dollar retreat centers are being closed down and sold to raise money for the Episcopal Church due to losses of parishioners who took their money with them.

•The Washington Diocese alone is tapping $1.9 million from a trust fund just to continue operating ($1.4 million this budget year alone).

•In the Diocese of Newark (New Jersey), where there is reputedly the strongest support of any diocese for the Episcopal Church's new agenda, forty parishes are projected to close this year.

•Twenty-two of the other thirty-seven provinces in our Anglican Communion have declared impaired or broken communion with the Episcopal Church.

•Fifteen of these twenty-two provinces now officially recognize only the Network—not the Episcopal Church—as the voice of Anglicanism in the U.S. These fifteen provinces represent fifty-five million Anglicans.

•Faithful priests all over the country are being deposed and inhibited by their bishops for speaking against the church's "new direction."

•The Episcopal Church is suing a number of Episcopal congregations for their church property in a number of states that won't go along with the new "doctrine."

•Two parishes in the Washington Diocese have joined the Network in opposition to the church's policies and thirteen vestries in the Diocese of Maryland have joined together as "confessing vestries" whose congregations refuse to follow the church's new policies.

While it's quiet in our small corner of the countryside, you're free to render your own judgments as to whether these facts represent business as usual in the Church or something more. I myself contend that the tremendous damage already recorded was merely the first and smallest wave of the tsunami that will eventually engulf us. Whole dioceses, parishes, entire congregations, and thousands of individuals like my wife and me are "going to higher ground" to preserve the faith against the onslaught.

What the Crisis Isn't About

So what is behind this? A radical agenda orchestrated by supposedly "gay rights" activists that seeks far more than just rights. Who in this congregation is not for equal rights for all people? Who in this congregation wants any among us to have fewer rights than we? I can tell you from experience that all those dioceses and parishes who are standing in opposition to the Episcopal Church's new direction aren't against those things. And I seriously doubt that any of us are.

But it's not about equal rights. That's simply the strategic soundbyte. It's about taking human experience and desire, laying it up next to Holy Scripture, and asserting that it's the Holy Scripture that's in error and has been for these almost two thousand years. That behaviors—not just sexual orientations, which are completely neutral—are not only acceptable, but that bishops and priests should now both affirm and call down God's blessing upon them.

Most changes—like women's ordination—come about by the presentation of theological arguments that at least attempt to show how they line up with Holy Scripture. No such case has been made for the Episcopal Church's "new thing." They simply did it "with good intentions" by a vote at a convention.

Those other sins remain, of course, "but we're voting this particular one to no longer be a sin." The real eye-opener here is this: Most of our bishops consider the Bible pretty much irrelevant today except to use it for sermon filler. They see the Bible, as one of our bishops described it, as "a book of poetry with a lot of history in it."

You should know that at that same convention in Minneapolis in 2003, sixty percent of the Episcopal church's bishops voted against—yes, against—a resolution to reaffirm the beliefs of their ordination vows and the agreements of belief of the Anglican Communion signed by our presiding bishops over the years. Reaffirming beliefs would have been a good way to at least try to help calm the crisis. Not being willing to reaffirm them—as the Church's leadership—speaks volumes for where our denomination is heading.

I'm proud to stand up each week and reaffirm my belief through the words of the Nicene Creed. Can you imagine what it would be like if the lay reader asked you to stand up and together reaffirm our faith through that creed and sixty percent of your congregation remained quietly seated? Welcome to the Episcopal Church of the "anti-war, free love" '60's-generation bishops. They are the perfect group upon which to work a dangerous and radical agenda because they believe their degrees on their walls confer upon them wisdom not held by a bunch of "simple-minded" Apostles. Those Apostles may have walked on earth with Christ, but we are now told how "unenlightened" they were and that "they just didn't understand all of this back then."

As a friend of mine used to say, "I was born on a Tuesday, but not last Tuesday." I'll take what the Apostles said any day. And, yes, Regis, that's my "final answer."

The Real Agenda

This well-organized but radical fringe has a goal that goes well beyond anything any of my own gay friends have ever voiced support for

—the ultimate demise of the Church itself. Not just the Episcopal Church—but all churches.

In some ways, it's similar to the dichotomy faced by so many Muslims today. Most Muslims simply want to find favor with Allah and live normal and peaceful lives, but intertwined throughout their communities is a radical style of fundamentalism that seeks a larger goal far beyond theirs that threatens all they hope for and puts all of them collectively in a negative light.

Why this goal to get rid of the churches? Because when society has completed its transition to open acceptance of all types of sexual behaviors, the Church will be the only place left where doctrine and discipline stand in the way of people being free to follow any norms they desire.

The Church simply has to go if people are going to be free to follow their human desires anywhere they lead without admonition.

The best way to beat down opposition to this dangerous agenda is to paint all those who recognize it and are determined to stand in their way as "anti-gay" or "homophobic"—a strategy used all over society today and increasingly in our Church to demonize opposition. How many times have you heard that our Church's controversy is about nothing but sex? Or that we're all wound around the axle over "homosexuality."

But we're all adults here. Let's look at the facts: We live, work and worship together with people of all types and of differing sexual orientations. In the almost eight years my wife and I have attended St. Thomas', no one to my knowledge has cared one iota who is black or white, old or young, gay or straight. As I said at the beginning, we're all a family of Christians. And Christians by definition accept all people who come to God. They love one another. Otherwise, they really have no business being called "Christians."

Whether our behaviors will find favor with God when the Day of Judgment arrives is unknown. We only have the Word to go by, and we can follow what Scripture says or not. It's a personal thing, and we're all in the same boat. I personally hope for my sake that God is a merci-

10

ful one—or at least has a sense of humor when I arrive! One thing I do know is that I will personally pin my hopes for salvation on what the Apostles passed down, not on a vote at General Convention, past or future, whether they vote away and affirm my own sins or not.

Another popular way to quell dissent is to repeatedly encourage everyone "to get back to the things that are really important." We should all "focus on other things." Nonsense. These are hugely important issues, and we can address them and still do all the other "important" things. These pleas are simply a way of saying "take your eye off the ball and, quick, look over there . . . !"

The strategy being worked on us depends on two lines of attack, one against society in general, and one against the churches. The strategy against society—like a guerilla war—began subtly and picked up more and more steam as it achieved success over the past four decades. In this case, it's been over forty years of one small success after another. The strategy is so brilliant that we should all wish this bunch was directing our war on terrorism today.

The strategy to soften up the society is necessary to lay the groundwork for the strategy against the church, simply because people in churches live in that society.

The Strategy against Society

Here's the strategy for the society at large:

•Teach the children from an early age through schools and other organizations that making judgments—especially moral ones—is a bad thing (everyone should be unconditionally accepted).

•Preach and model moral relativism (what you think is good or bad depends on the situation) at every opportunity; there are no absolutes when it comes to good or evil.

•Where debate has been traditionally encouraged, particularly in high schools and colleges, launch a program of "political correctness" to stifle it, stating values or viewpoints other than the "correct" position is not only discouraged, but prohibited.

• Give support to hate-crimes legislation, then expand it to include hate speech to quiet open dissent, where people may actually be arrested for voicing their views in public; only protect open speech that supports the radical agenda.

• Finally, push every vestige of Judaic-Christian influence or presence from the public square with an endless barrage of lawsuits and intimidation; this dovetails perfectly with the education of our children, each successful suit against religion being useful as "precedent" to show that religion and values are provable negative influences on society.

Moving the Strategy into the Church

This strategy, which has been highly successful, sets the stage for people's thinking about the church. Here are some key points to their strategy for the churches:

• Find a church of relatively small membership but wide recognition with the most liberal philosophy and the most "flexible" theology: The Episcopal Church.

• Flood that church with as many radical activists as possible, including ordaining priests.

• Build those numbers over years, and combine with activist laity to achieve strategic placements on national church councils and diocesan staffs.

• Seize the property of parishes nationwide by passing a canon putting all of them in trust to the Church's national body; this will assure exceptional leverage against parishes who try to stand up against revisionist doctrine.

• Find the state with the lowest "churched" population of all fifty states in the nation—a "weakest link"—and vote in an activist priest as bishop. New Hampshire.

• Force a vote at General Convention to approve his consecration and at the same time another to approve "blessing rites" for non-celibate homosexual partners in spite of the Theology Committee of the House of Bishops recommending strongly against it and almost the entire Anglican Communion pleading with the Episcopal Church not to do it.

• Label those who oppose these moves as "uninclusive" and "un-Christian," regardless of whether grounds for either assertion exist.

• Paint African and other "Two-Thirds World" Anglicans as "simple" and "backward" as reasons for their opposition; like the Apostles, they're too "simple" to understand that the Bible really is just a "book of poetry."

• Force those who disagree—clergy and laity—either out of the Episcopal Church altogether or into submission (use jobs and pensions for leverage against clergy; use parish properties as leverage against laity).

• Weaken belief in Holy Scripture:
    – Teach that Jesus is not the only way to God.
    – Teach that the Gospel has simply been misunderstood all these years.
    – Teach that other religions are equally valid; Christianity holds no sway over others.
    – Affirm all "feelings" and behaviors.
    – Teach that transformation by Jesus is unnecessary; what you want to do is paramount.

• Ultimately point to the fallacy of the whole Bible, not just selected portions.

Eventually, belief will be sufficiently weakened to support the activist's ideology that not only do human desire and experience trump Holy Scripture, but that lacking a valid foundation, belief in Jesus is illogical. Transformation from what? Redemption from what? Neither is any longer necessary. "Come as you are, stay as you are" will be the prevailing call. Jesus—and His death for our sins—becomes irrelevant.

The failure of the Episcopal Church or its decline into near irrelevance will be the jumping off point for elevated attacks on other churches until there no longer exists a moral authority which will challenge the elevation of human desire and experience.

So, am I saying our rector is part of this agenda? I think only in the sense that, like so many other clergy, he's been trained and educated over the decades to passionately believe in the nice part of the agenda that appears so benign. He's a decent and gentle person, and I think he has a strong faith. I'm sure he doesn't recognize the dangers of the larger agenda and would deny loudly that it's there.

But sometimes when you're in the "belly of the beast" everything seems pretty normal. It's only when someone makes noise fighting the beast from the outside that you realize you may not be where you thought you were. That's our rector's predicament. It's also that of many of our other priests.

Reason for Hope

As brilliant as this strategy is, however, thousands of faithful Episcopalians are increasingly seeing through it and are coming together to counter it.

It's true that "All it takes for evil to prevail is for good men to do nothing," and what keeps my heart steeled for the fight is the knowledge that a lot of good men and women recognize the danger and are not just standing by and "doing nothing."

I think Martin Luther had it just right when he said:

> If I profess with the loudest voice and clearest exposition every portion of the truth of God except precisely that little point which the world and the devil are at that moment attacking, I am not professing Christ, no matter how boldly I may be professing Christ.
> Where the battle rages, there the loyalty of the soldier is proved. To be steady on all battlefields besides is mere flight and disgrace if he flinches at that point.

I plan to be where the battle rages. I hope in all sincerity that St. Thomas' will in time realize the danger, go to higher ground and keep this beautiful little parish from becoming nothing more than a historical site in years to come. It's a battle I'd proudly stand beside you in.

Don't just take what I've written here or any one person's viewpoint to decide which way you want to look at the problem. There is a massive amount of information on both sides of the issue, and if you really care what happens to your parish—and your children and grandchildren—go out and find it. I know of nothing that's more important.

In Christ's love and in His promise of hope.

Al Quie, the third child of Nettie and Albert Knute Quie, was born September 18, 1923, at Longfurrow Farm near Dennison and Nerstrand, Minnesota. Like most farm children, Al learned to do chores at a young age. He was given his first pony when he was eight years old.

Al graduated from Northfield High School in 1942, and shortly after became a pilot in the U.S. Navy during World War II. He graduated from St. Olaf College with a degree in political science in 1950 and married his college sweetheart, Gretchen Hansen, of Minneapolis, on June 5, 1948. The two have five children, fourteen grandchildren and one great grandchild.

In 1954, while operating the family farm, Al was elected to the Minnesota State Senate. He served there until February 1958, when he was elected to the United States Congress, representing Minnesota's First Congressional District. Al was successful in his bid for governor of Minnesota in 1978.

After twenty-eight years in public service, Al decided not to run for re-election as governor. That is when he was able to take time to fulfill his life-long dream of riding horseback along the Continental Divide from Canada to Mexico.

Al has served on many boards including Prison Fellowship Ministries, Lutheran Brotherhood Mutual Funds, Lutheran Health Systems, Tentmakers, Vesper Society, Nobel Peace Prize Forum, Search Institute, Council on Crime and Justice, Urban Ventures, AGORA, the Commission on Excellence in Education that wrote "A Nation at Risk," and WordAlone. Several of these are currently on

his agenda. He also is a sought-after speaker, and serves as mentor to many individuals.

Al is a member of Minnetonka Lutheran Church and has been a voting member of the Evangelical Lutheran Church in America Church-Wide Assemblies.

ঞ 2 ৎ

Who's Really in Charge?
Al Quie

O N OCTOBER 4, 2007, I WAS IN ALGOA PRISON outside Jefferson City, Missouri. Together in the room with me were the prison's superintendent, guards, prisoners, Innerchange Freedom Initiative (IFI) staff at Algoa, members of the IFI Board of which I was chair, our attorney, and a member of the Missouri legislature.

During the discussion, the legislator said she had trouble explaining the difference between the faith-based IFI and other programs in the prison that have the same purposes—changing lives to result in less recidivism, the conquering of addiction, and the fostering of more responsible behavior. A prisoner immediately raised his hand. As we all looked at him, he said, "One word," then paused slightly and added, "Jesus."

To all of us who had been discussing the question of authority the afternoon before, a huge smile came over our faces. It was clear to a criminal that Jesus had transformed him. The prison authorities were looking for programs. Many church people thought religion and faith in Christ were the same. Some of us remembered that it was Jesus who said, "All authority in heaven and on earth have been given unto me."

To a follower of Jesus Christ and the invisible church, there is one ultimate authority. In the visible church there is conflict over authority because people need some kind of governance to maintain order and give direction. Power gets exercised. Good and evil are in existence and at odds. The good unifies; evil divides. For the secular world governance is essential. Anarchy does not work. Since history began, we read of governance, family, tribal, community, state, national and "world" governance. Today monarchies hardly exist. Totalitarian (dictator) governments have dramatically reduced in number. Democratic republics have increased since the Soviet Union collapsed. The United States is one of the oldest democracies. (Iceland is the oldest.) Theocracy ideas are being thrust forward and new democracies are finding it is not as easy as anticipated.

Let's look at governance. Since we belong to a denomination, the Evangelical Lutheran Church in America (ELCA), located in a representative democracy, here is what I think is part of our problem. In our democracy the ultimate authority is in the hands of the people, exercised through the ballot box no matter what their religion, race, color, gender, or political persuasion. Voters select their representatives for all levels of government, and the representatives are answerable to the voters. It has been operative for over 200 years.

In the Church of Jesus Christ, the invisible Church, the ultimate authority is Jesus Christ. Christ picks his representatives. Christ's representatives are all his followers. Their ultimate authority in the church life, church government, and secular life and secular government is Jesus Christ even though they themselves are part of the ultimate authority of secular government. Read Ephesians 4: 11 (NIV). "He gave the apostales, the prophets, and evangelicals, the pastors and teachers to equip the saints for the work of ministry, for the building of the body of Christ—" The believers are Christ's representatives, the "priesthood of all believers."

The problem with the ELCA is that we have confused denomination governance with the "church." To me the church is the congregation. The ELCA constitution states that there are three expressions of the church: church-wide, synod, and congregation.

Therefore, in ELCA governance, members of a congregation elect some of their members to be "members" of their synod assembly but members of a congregation do not elect representatives to the synod council, the Synod Assembly does that. "Members" of Synod Assemblies elect "members" to the Church-Wide Assembly but not representatives to the church-wide council, CWA "members" do that. So the governance of the ELCA operates with some oligarchy principles (government by a small group of people). While the congregation members experience representative democracy in secular governance—the ability to vote directly to elect representatives—it is denied them in the ELCA.

Jesus Christ trusts those who believe in him to represent him. We are citizens in this country where we, along with non-believers, are trusted to select people to represent us at all levels of government, state and national as well as local. Why can't the ELCA take the same risk as Jesus and the citizens of this country?

Governing in a denomination both congregational and inter-congregational is important. We remember from the Gospels that it was the religious leaders and the secular rulers who had Jesus killed so we have a right to be suspicious of both. As we read history, remember events in our lifetime, and watch it unfold now, we see that governments and leaders of belief systems have killed a lot of people besides our Lord and Savior.

The important part is that Jesus has risen and gone back to where he came from. The Holy Spirit now dwells in the hearts of those who believe in Jesus and, therefore, become obedient to him. All who are in Christ will also rise again. Communication with God, which we call prayer, ministering to each other and whoever God lays at our gate, proclamation of the Gospel (what God has done, is doing and will do through his Risen Son, Jesus Christ), reading and meditating on the Scriptures where we learn the nature and character of God plus the human condition, watching as the hand of God is revealed to us, and even partaking in the body and blood of Jesus in remembrance of him, all enhance our yielding to the Holy Spirit in obedience.

Let me go back to Ephesians 4:11, about the leaders equipping the lay people. While in Congress I heard a sermon from an LCA pastor and friend saying that Jesus was not born to a virgin since it could not be verified. Later having dinner with an ALC pastor in my district, he told me there was no such thing as resurrection. When we died, we were just dead. You can imagine the shock for me who just took these truths for granted.

Every Sunday, all my life, I had been repeating with other people as we gathered together that we believed that Jesus was born of the virgin Mary and that he rose from the dead. People in the two churches where those two pastors served repeated the Creed as well. None of my non-Christian friends had ever challenged me on this. I had read intellectuals, not in the church, who had challenged these truths, but that had not bothered me.

What this shock caused me to do was to study, meditate, listen to God and marvel at the words of institution at the Lord's Supper. Most of all, to my amazement, my faith was not shaken. It gave me a new understanding about faith, trust, and realizing the truth, which is Jesus Christ. Well, after studying, I went back, entering into disputation with my pastor friends. The first changed his mind, not the second. The first had faith and saw that he had been only given part of the story by a seminary professor. The second had lost faith in what St. Paul said was essential, the resurrection of Jesus Christ. That is what grieved me when he died.

Lastly, I wish to share what I perceive as observing the hand of God. First, my grandfather, who was influenced by what he learned about the evils of slavery, enlisted in the Union Army, recruited other young Norwegian immigrants and was wounded in the Battle of Antietam, September 1862, sixty-one years before I was born. As a child, listening to his offspring tell the stories of their father, I was filled with awe and wondered what caused him to do this.

Also as a child, I witnessed the hungry hobos who came to our house from the railroad over a mile away. Hobos were fed in our dining room, which was only used on our farm at Thanksgiving, Christmas, Easter and when our minister, Reverend Rosenquist and his family came to dinner. Dad said, if he were a "tramp" that is the way he wanted to be treated. As I learned Bible stories about Jesus telling the story about the rich man and Lazarus and the man of small stature, Zacchaeus, who climbed up a tree so he could see Jesus, and Jesus, realizing that the only reason the man was up there was because the Father sent him, called him saying he would dine with him that day, I began to realize I was hearing about and seeing the hand of God as Jesus did. Blackaby writes about this in the book *Experiencing God*.

The Holy Spirit keeps calling, enlightening and sanctifying us. Recently, I came to the end of a year visiting a group of men in prison. One person from the beginning caught my attention. He sat with arms folded across his chest looking at me it seemed with suspicion and he seemed always to be testing me. After a while it became obvious that he always sat with his back against the wall. He was on my heart and in my prayers, so I decided that the next time I went to the prison, I would arrive early, sit down beside him and talk firmly to him, at least to get him out of that back seat against the wall. With resolve I entered the room and to my surprise he was sitting in a front chair closest to the door. Greeting him, I said with joy, "You have changed." He told me he always protected his back, but now somebody else was protecting his back. "I trust Jesus to protect my back."

Since seeing him before, he had asked for and received baptism. Jesus taught me a lesson again. It is not you, Albert. It is me who transforms people. The Bible is the most authoritative book we have, but with faith, Jesus is our authority. The Bible brings the One God, Father, Son and Holy Spirit to us.

The church is struggling with its voice. As the culture has changed to make sex, the most intimate human activity, an acceptable recreation, the church and its leaders are struggling to please those who believe that God now finds homosexual practice acceptable too and not lose too many of those of us who still believe such practices are unacceptable if one is obedient to God.

If believers are the temple of God and the Holy Spirit dwells in us, can we in the church continue to be quiet even about heterosexual activity? Sex without love, out of wedlock sex relations, intentional single parent families, fatherless homes, infidelity. When the church is quiet, it indicates acceptance. God made us sexual beings, capable of sex other than procreation. If we accept that in becoming like Jesus, we act justly like God and love mercy like God. If we are like Jesus, we don't tell God what to do but pray that we might humbly and obediently follow Jesus.

Also, we cannot expect God to change his mind because so many people have changed their moral standards. Jesus is amazing, much more relentless in his demands than even the religious leaders of his time (Be perfect, even as I am perfect) and he handles disobedience differently too. He died that we might live. He does expect faith from which obedience will flow.

The divisions in theology have been growing all through the enlightenment and even more so in these post modern times.

22

Denominations have always had differences with each other, but now there are huge differences within denominations. Therefore, the "saints" mentioned in Ephesians 4 are being poorly equipped by the divided voices of "the apostles, the prophets, the evangelists, and the pastors and teachers" being sent out. Whose authority is guiding them?

By What Authority?

Jaynan Clark Egland is President/CEO of the WordAlone Network and a member of the board of directors from 2000 to 2006. She also served on the synod council (Eastern Washington/Idaho Synod) and is a member of the advisory council of Lutheran Community Services (LCS).

Jaynan was born and raised on a farm in southeastern Minnesota. She attended school in Lyle, Minnesota. Growing up, Jaynan loved the outdoors, enjoyed farm work, building grain bins, and entered the "office" world as the bookkeeper/receptionist for her dentist in Austin, Minnesota, a job she kept while attending the local community college for two years. A transfer to Arizona State University in Tempe, Arizona, took her into the world of business with a double major in Marketing and Advertising. As a field sales engineer for Texas Instruments, Inc., Jaynan sold the insides of computers to a world that did not yet have home computers.

In 1981, she entered Luther Northwestern Theological Seminary in St. Paul, Minnesota. God graciously called her to the upper northwest corner of North Dakota for an incredible internship year at First Lutheran Church in Williston. During that year, she had an opportunity to preach in rural churches without pastors and to direct programming at the Upper Missouri Bible Camp in Epping.

After receiving her M.Div. degree in 1985, Jaynan's first call was as a missionary in Tanzania, East Africa, among the Maasai tribe. She returned to the United States in 1991 and has served Immanuel Lutheran Church, Cresco, Iowa; Trinity Lutheran Church, Bonners Ferry, Idaho; and Prince of Peace Lutheran Church in Spokane, Washington. During the mid-1990s, Jaynan enjoyed on-leave from call status in Hawaii as she cared for her four young children full time.

Jaynan was an early participant in the WordAlone movement and a delegate to the 1999 ELCA churchwide assembly, at which she spoke out in opposition to Called to Common Mission, the full communion agreement with the Episcopal Church.

She was elected to the Board of Directors at the March 2000 Constituting Convention of WordAlone and served for six years on the board. She has served as president of the WordAlone Network since fall 2001.

Jaynan's pride and joy are her four children, three boys and one girl. She loves to volunteer in the kid's schools on a weekly basis and be the "treat mom." The family enjoys their home out in the woods (Nine Mile Falls area) where they engage in many outdoor activities such as snowboarding,

wakeboarding and hiking, claiming they would rather wear out their bodies than rust out.

ॐ 3 ॐ

"Radical Lutheranism"
Travels in the Middle of the Road
Jaynan Clark Egland

"My foot stands on level ground . . ." —Psalm 26 (NRSV)

BECAUSE I'VE BEEN A RUNNER for thirty-five years, there appears to be, according to my doctor, some wear and tear on my middle-aged body. A couple of physicals ago he observed that I am a "legal runner." By this comment he meant that my "pictures" show that I probably run against the traffic routinely, and, therefore, my left foot is repeatedly striking on the curvature of the road that slips into the ditch. It is true. Therefore, my hip and knee show the effects of being too far to one side.

I remember the grin on his face when he said, "Never quote me on this because if you get hit I'll be blamed for your accidental death. But living way out in the boonies as you do, you should run down the middle of the road where it is the flattest and most level. That is the most natural place for you to be because you aren't hanging off one edge or the other."

It is, of course, the most dangerous place to travel. There is a rather high likelihood that one is going to collide with on-coming traffic, get hit from behind and thus be good ol' road kill. The middle of the

25

road is the place of death and life, so it seems. As it is on the highway for the runner so it should be for the Lutheran church.

Lutherans cannot, by definition and pure identity, travel on the right or the left extreme edges. On the edge we find ourselves either in the ditch of relativism, reductionism, revisionism, or the ditch of legalism and literalism. Neither fits with our confessions. The "isms" define the ditches and extreme edges, slippery slopes. Neither are "the way" traveled by Lutherans for 500 years.

"Radical Lutheranism" finds itself in the middle of the road—always in danger, always moving forward, always experiencing death—and dependent on daily divine resurrection. There are no fences to ride in the

middle of the road. There is no "going with the flow" with the world or even the institutional churches that race by on our left and right.

"Radical Lutheranism" is not a catchy slogan or creative line that should be recklessly used. Theologian Dr. Gerhard Forde coined that phrase to center us, not push us to one side or other. In his writings, sermons, and lectures, Forde explored the radicality of God's grace revealed in Jesus Christ and how the chief article (Article IV of the Augsburg Confession) on justification captured that good news. His life of teaching and preaching as a theologian of the cross left him in the very middle of the road—misunderstood by those on his left and his right.

Some continue to attack his understanding of the life of the forgiven Christian. Others use his words in a construct of antinomianism that is absolutely foreign to his understanding of the law and the Gospel. Too many times I have listened to the present presiding bishop of the ELCA, Mark Hanson, misquote Dr. Forde and use this rich and descriptive term "radical Lutheranism" as a cheer to rally support for a new ministry of recklessness. I don't recall this bishop relating it at all to repentance. I can't remember his mentioning the reality of sin and the need for forgiveness. I just remember thinking as I heard his eloquent speeches, "Was he saying that when Jesus died on the cross with arms outstretched it was a big group hug for everybody so 'don't worry, be happy'?"

There was nothing "radical" about what the presiding bishop said by way of "conviction of the heart," only radical in how extremely un-Lutheran this ideology really was. I intentionally use "ideology" not "theology" because theology is about God and ideology is about a concept.

When any person stands in authority over the Word in order to interpret it rather than prostrates oneself under the authority of the Word so that the Word interprets the sinner, then the radicality of the Lutheran Christian message is lost. Perhaps that is why our Lutheran Christian birthright is so easily frittered away these days or apologized for in attempts to be more appealing, contemporary or ecumenical.

Radical Lutherans live not on the fence or in the ditch but travel on the centerline. Too often we are road kill under the careening wheels of contemporary thoughts and ideals and agendas, but the centerline it is—for life and for death and for life again as the repentant, forgiven, radical Lutherans we are called to be.

Nathan Hanson is a pastor's son, born in Hardin, Montana, in 1955. His father served in Montana (Hardin and Glendive), Minnesota (Crookston) and in Texas (Odessa and Winters). A 1978 graduate of Concordia College in Moorhead, Minnesota, Nathan taught for two years in the same state at Farmington Middle School as a sixth-grade teacher. It was in the classroom where he discovered the children in his charge were more interested in personal and spiritual relationships than any subject matter they could be graded on. He applied for admittance to Luther Seminary in St. Paul, and was a student there from 1980 until his ordination in the ELCA in 1984.

Nathan is currently pastor of the three Lutheran churches that comprise Moe Lutheran Parish of Hudson, South Dakota. Prior congregations served were in Minnesota (Bear River), Texas (Oslo), and Idaho (American Falls). In all of his service as a pastor, he has intentionally steered clear of urban and suburban climes. It is his contention God's nurture and care is clearly expressed in the rural scene, and in turn, faithfulness of hearty country believers is what holds the whole world together.

Nathan and his wife, Ruth Halvorson, were married in 1982, and have three children: Ezekiel, Samuel, and Anna. Critical to his ministry out past city limits, Ruth has been a great spiritual and pastoral presence to the congregations they have served. Her capacity as an artist and calligrapher has expanded their life and ministry together. Nathan's grandfather, his father, four uncles and one brother have all served

as pastors in various Lutheran churches that have amalgamated to form the ELCA.

≈ 4 ≈

We Have No King But Jesus

Nathan Hanson

REPRESENTATION IS DIFFICULT. Perhaps you have had to represent your child in a dispute with a teacher. Maybe you've had to represent your firm in a bidding war with another business. Most all of us have had someone else represent our perspective in politics. Many of us have had to represent a position or possibility. All of us have had to suffer a lack of reliable representation of some fashion.

Representation is a natural phenomenon and characteristic of the human community. Nobody can be everywhere at one and the same time. Time travel would not resolve this, nor would clones adjust for the necessity of representation. Our busy lives (easier now than ever they have been, but busy yet) need representation.

The problem of representation is one that has plagued the Christian faith since the Garden of Eden. Adam and Eve were not always eye-to-eye on Who was in charge. Moses was not always a hit with the people of Israel. Walk through the Pentateuch, and you'll find grumblings and murmurings throughout. In Numbers, Miriam and Aaron, Moses' kin, challenge God's choice of Moses to lead them. Again, in Numbers, Korah, Dathan and Abiram challenge God's choice of leader. This time, it is a contingent of leaders, well-known among the people.

God is not impressed, and the earth swallows all three . . . the rest are burned to death. God is not interested in appeasing human demands. God is God, and knows BEST the who, what, when, where and how to bring faith.

The representation of God to the people is the preaching and the teaching of God's word. Notice, I said it is God's word; not our word, but God's word. The authority of God's word is not limited to what *we* deem is credible. That's a ridiculous notion in the first place, because God's grace is itself so incredible to us. God is *the* Creator, making of this former world of cloud and void a real Something Else. With a word, the Father makes all that is, seen and unseen. God knows how this world works, and how the balance of all things is correlative.

You may be an able preacher, but if you defy what God says, you will not thrive. You may be a profound instructor, but teaching without the authority of God's word is hollow. Convolution in argument doesn't win the points and favor with God that it does with humans. We may admire rhetorical twists and turns. If, however, what you deliver is counter to God's witness as cited in Holy Writ, you're doomed. You, and your "disciples" with you.

Currently, our seminaries boast that many of their students have read the Bible. Why do you suppose this basic prerequisite warrants print? Is it because that's truly an honorable enterprise for someone who plans to adhere to its teaching? Is it because this book, for the remainder of their lives, is source of life and meaning for them? That's rather like boasting about a pilot flying an airbus holding 550 people claiming his or her prowess comes at the cost of once reading through the attendant Minimum Equipment List. No thanks to first class on that flight.

We are vainly trying to fill our seminaries with people to pay the bills. That is *not* the same as teaching people who are called by God to serve the people of God. People who are "called" into the ministry represent the word of God faithfully to believers. Support of tenured professors must rest on the fidelity of the faith being properly and constantly impressed upon all they serve in the student body. If you are planning on serving the church because some magazine wrote that being a clergy person was "a good profession" that is not a call from God. That is not even true in the first place. Noble as some secular rag would cite the professional ministry to be, such an analysis hardly reflects confidence in the call of Christ, namely "Whoever would be great among you must be your servant." (Matthew 20:26b NSV)

Another heresy rampant even among ELCA pastors and theologians today is that God is subject to our demands. On the floor of the churchwide assembly held in Orlando in 2005, one voting member had the audacity to declare that we have a right to demand of God what we want of Him.

Sorry, Charlie. We may have the right to demand, but God is not bound by our intransigence. There is no support for such unbridled "freedom" anywhere in the Bible. Even if you believe this to be true, but know better than to cite such heresy, the hearers of the Word will know, and they will abandon such "faith" for the fetter it really is.

This is where the BF Goodrich Premium Radial tire meets the road. The decline in numbers of people (and dollars!) in the Lutheran Church, ELCA, is because our preaching and our teaching isn't reaching. Our preaching and teaching aren't reaching because we don't demand of our preachers and teachers that they believe, obey and teach what God says. Further, we don't demand that these teachers and preachers be any good at what they do. It is a symptom of what is going on in the church at large to see what is happening at the seminary level. To wit: Attending any seminary costs a lot of money. Students have to put up that money. Students, good and bad, have to be sent into the world as pastors because the church is drying up. The "final solution"? Pass everyone. The students get to proceed with their new "calling." The seminary gets money from the student. "Satisfied customers" will encourage others to give to their respective alma mater. The people get pastors for their churches.

The only One left out of the loop is God, Who we seem to believe is preoccupied elsewhere.

This is not the faith that Martin Luther hoped to extend to his world. It isn't what God expects of us to extend to our world. Obedience is not an option, it is a demand Jesus makes of all the disciples. Choose to leave Jesus, and He releases you to the Hell of self-righteousness, forever. Really and truly.

Representation of God to people relies on God's Holy Word for direction, correction, and hope. God chooses the witness of the Word, and the incompetents he summons into service. Representation of the people to God relies on truth, a pursuit of justice and extension of mercy. If we are to encourage truth, we have to have a recognizable standard for that truth. Once again, we turn to the Word of God, and hold it as the truth. Unvarnished, sticky, splintery and heavy as it may prove to be, it is the truth.

We live in a day where words as printed are challenged as not meaning what they read. For example, the parties who challenge the authority of the Constitution of the United States of America. We have (at least) two points of view of this Constitution. One side will insist the document means what it says, and says what it means. The opposite perspective will insist the document is living, and open to every interpretation. The former finds the directions and applications provided as limiting, and helpful. The latter will complain the document as too limiting and hurtful. The problem develops when you manipulate the words into definitions that were not intended.

So, too, the problem of Biblical interpretation in our day. The Bible is often held to be too limiting, and sometimes hurtful when we study. God has spoken, but we are very sensitive these days, and our ears yearn for something sweeter. That there may be something sweeter is a myth, promoted by those who don't believe in God. Honestly. It is God, in Whose mercy we are warned of Hell, who offers the way *out* of our lost end. Without the warning, we are lost indeed. To choose not to heed the warning is to disbelieve God.

Among parents and teachers, an old adage for instruction has lapsed today. That adage was, "To delay obedience, is to disobey." There is little demand for punctual practice of God's demands to believe upon Jesus Christ. There oughtta be. The pressure comes from the end of all things, when time is no more, and the End has come. In Hebrews you'll read "Good news came to us just as to them, but the message which they heard did not benefit them, because it did not meet with faith in the hearers." (4:3 RSV)

God brings love with real meat to it, and His deliverance is all the difference. If there is no hell, God is a liar, and we are all fools. That God delays marks His mercy to everybody, giving everyone ample time to come to Him. Hence the term, known to every collegian facing a deadline, "grace period." You have a little more time to finish your thesis and get it in for your final grade.

Grace, however, is *not* "indifference" to sinful nature, or disobedience to the Word. Grace will drive you to repentance, with all the scraping and scratching that entails. It was a long and weary walk home to the father for the Prodigal. Jesus was telling the parable; He could have put a limo there, ya know. The lad had to wend his way all the way home to find the father waiting for him.

We aren't very adept at representing what God demands of us as pastors or Christians. Too often these days, I hear church leadership demanding justice for various causes. Here, we often cite the office of ministry is to "comfort the afflicted and afflict the comfortable." That may prove necessary, but our job is not to demand that justice. Ours is to proclaim that God is just, and to seek mercy for all those involved. This, probably, is much more difficult, but it is what we represent. We have to descend from our thrones of "all-knowing" parsons and face the fray honestly.

Way too many pastors damn our leadership in government, slamming their decisions. We haven't the humility to recognize we really don't know what we're talking about. We haven't the data to challenge what is happening. The admonition from Paul is to pray for all those in authority. When's the last time you heard your pastor request such, asking God's guidance for President Bush? When's the last time our own

Mark Hanson or your bishop prayed for any other authority than their own status?

We blow about seeking "justice," but our lips smear those who are striving to do justice. The blather of our pulpits is demeaning to the office, as we demonstrate our jealousy and pride. We could fix everything, ya know . . . just ask, and we could do it . . . we're ordained! How discouraging for those who have gone before, who know the real power of humble service.

We have our hands full with the practice of extending mercy where we can. We're not very good at this. In point of fact, we aren't capable of it. Ordination does not bestow mercy for our dispensation. (It would seem ordination instead bestows a proclivity for judgment without knowledge!) It is only by the power of the Holy Spirit that we can provide mercy anywhere, to anyone.

Notice, it would seem to be a confusion of terms, that mercy would be pursued to bring justice. That is not the case: there is no "seem" about it. We cannot put ourselves in the place of another with any accuracy. We can only assume the role of the penitent, who is yearning for release from sin. We are incapable of assessing sin for others, except as God defines it. We plead mercy, and humbly beseech God to hear us for Jesus' sake. There is no other standard of representation that is effective.

The representation of God to one another is simple: live as if Christ Jesus makes all the difference in the world (this one, and the next). This representation is not easy, but it is simple.

Note the words of Jesus to the rich young ruler. "Sell what you possess and give to the poor, and you will have treasure in heaven; and come follow me." (Matthew 19:21 RSV) No huge delineation of the Law here, simply one line. And that line lost the rich young ruler. It was too much to ask. He believed in his heart that there had to be another truth greater than his need for Jesus' truth. He lost everything that day.

Jesus means more to this world than peace in the Middle East.

Jesus means more to this world than you owning your own home.

Jesus means more to this world than you having good physical or mental health.

Jesus means more than your church's Christmas pageant.

Jesus means more to this world than absolutely anything else.

Absolutely.

That's the word this world yearns to hear. That's the representation that matters more than delegates . . .

Oh, excuse me, that matters more than voting members at the churchwide assembly. That's the stuff and freedom that blows the starch out of a pietistical hierarchy that ordains bishops, and pretends it's an installation. Such offices are neither necessary or providential. There is little humility or service represented in such novel and ancient expressions.

Wanna change? In order to turn around, to REPENT, we need to let the middle management go the way of General Motors. We need to fire the bishops, remove the synodical offices, shrink the national staff and get out into the world with the Word. Perhaps then, when there is no earthly turf to defend, we could find ourselves on equal ground, with only Jesus to look up to. That's the representation that makes sense to me. As R.T. Niles once wrote, "I am but one beggar telling another beggar where to go to find bread." That's all the representation anyone needs.

Go, get out there and feed the flock.

Since August of 2002, Paul Owens has served as lead pastor of St. Paul Lutheran Church, Alpena, Michigan. He is a preacher, a delivery boy of the goods God wants hungry sinners to have. He is on the Advisory Board for FaithInkubators and was a contributor to *The Lutheran Handbook II* and *The Christian Handbook for Pastors*. Once in a while, he stumbles on creative ways to proclaim, like the "Deer Hunter's Blessing"*

Paul is the son of Eugene and Arlene Owens. His older brothers are Craig (Texas) and Peter (Michigan) and his younger sister is Lori Crawford (Michigan). Paul is married to the most beautiful woman in the world: his partner in Christ, Sandi (Kalis). Sandi is a wife and mother who is also employed as a substitute teacher. Their three kids are: Andrew, seventeen, John, fourteen, Mary, eleven—all of whom should keep their rooms cleaner. When only God knows where he is, Paul is probably in a stream somewhere looking for trout on the end of his fly line.

Paul is a 1984 graduate of Kalamazoo College (Michigan), where he majored in theology with a concentration in French.

In 1989, he received a Master's of Divinity from Luther Seminary in St. Paul, Minnesota. In August of that year, he was ordained to the Ministry of Word and Sacrament in the Evangelical Lutheran Church of America.

From 1989 to 1992, he served as associate pastor of First English Lutheran Church in Grosse Pointe Woods, Michigan.

From 1992 to 2000, he served as pastor of Ascension Lutheran Church in

Saginaw, Michigan. During this time he was also dean of the Bay Area Conference of the Evangelical Lutheran Church in America (ELCA).

From 2000 to 2002, he and his wife served as foreign missionaries in Garoua Boulai, Cameroon. In addition to her other duties, Sandi Owens taught at the American School in Garoua Boulai. Paul served as professor of Old Testament and Practical Theology. He also served as a circuit rider

pastor to twenty-eight bush congregations.

(visit <www.stpaul.org>)

↜ 5 ↝

Who's Your Daddy?

Paul Owens

THE AUTHORITY OF JESUS—the living word—is an impossible, sweet truth for sinners like us. In our pride we hate it . . . remember what he says to us: "You look for an opportunity to kill me, because there is no place in you for my word" (John 8). Yet when we find ourselves sweetly convicted by him, we confess that his authority gives us our good, our very lives for now and forever. Since the beginning of time, God's people have had a funny habit of trying to hide from his authority. Once in a while, by sheer grace, we end up living under it. In our generation, one way to notice this is to look at three kinds of churches:

First, "museums." The people of this type of church are out to preserve the past and its artifacts. They usually use past-tense grammar . . . "the way we did it in the past is the way we do it today." They have confused the substance with the containers. There is a large, old Bible that has sat in the pulpit for three generations, and when they open it, they are careful with the pages so as not to damage this collector's item. Preaching in a museum church is something like sitting in history class: it might be boring, it might be very interesting, but it generally stays stuck in the past. Hearers are content to leave with a lesson on ecclesiastical or biblical archaeology, words about stuff that is old—old church fights, dead Bible characters, and venerated saints. For these folks, church is a place they go to and then leave. Out of obligation they might pay a fee to get in to the museum, or pay for an "annual membership." The "board of governors" in a museum church works to keep things orderly and under control. And while the regulars may indeed be very friendly with one another, this type of church is generally a place where children are to be seen and not heard, where they ought not run around nor make a mess.

The second kind of churches are those embarrassed about God. Since they are embarrassed about God, these churches instead spend their time talking about politics, social issues, and meditation techniques. They follow wherever the prevailing culture leads, and they are enamored of the trends of the day. They are enlightened people who see the Bible as a collection of "interesting stories" or fables from the past. It has equal footing with any other book they may choose to read. The Bible may be found on a table in their homes and it even gets read sometimes, usually to dabble in it or maybe to look up something to bolster an argument for a particular cause. Jesus is pretty domesticated for churches who are embarrassed about God. He is viewed as one option among many—all gods are the same and equal—in the words of Ricky Bobby: "Help me, dear Jesus, help me Buddha, help me Oprah Winfrey, help me Tom Cruise!"

The preachers and hearers in these churches aren't quite sure what to do with Jesus when he says, "I am the way, the truth, and the life. No one comes to the Father except through me." For the majority of persons in these churches, contributing a little to the cause helps ease their conscience. It's the right thing to do. And in Sunday School, their children learn lots of techniques for getting along with others and being good people, but the thrilling, wild adventure of God's word often goes unopened to them. We need to keep our children safe, after all, and there is just too much in the Bible that is dangerous and exclusive.

The third type of churches are those where, "It's about God, stupid!" In these congregations, God is on the loose, at work. These folks realize that they are sinners—loved, forgiven, changed, and called by Christ. They realize that Christ has left his church in messy hands: *theirs*. In these churches life is dependable and unpredictable, tragic and wonderful. Things get dirty and broken from use, then get cleaned up and renovated for another go. When they exit the building after worship, these people know that wherever they go, twenty-four/seven, they are the church, the body of Christ with Jesus on their lips and in their actions.

Their church council knows clearly where it stands and is also open to new ideas and healthy argument for the sake of God's kingdom. The leaders listen to the congregation *and* challenge disciples to be with them on the front lines of the battle.

Folks in these churches know it's about God so they open the Bible *a lot*, just about every day at home and always when they gather for worship or learning. They make Bibles and solid Bible story books readily available to folks. When they open their well-worn Bibles, they don't turn off their brains. They see letters and sentences on the page, and they know there is a history to how these particular books were written and gathered into the Bible. When they read the Bible, they also are aware that they are not just dealing with dead letters on a page. The lively, living voice of Jesus is at work speaking to them through these words. Sometimes he offends them and exposes their sin, sometimes his voice is the sweetest balm of all as he frees them for a new future. Always, he gets under their skin and they realize they are far better off when they don't run from him or avoid him.

They believe that God speaks, and they are learning to follow him as disciples. In these churches, where it's about God, many disciples openly practice tithing, many strive to grow in their giving, and one can hear honest, good-humored conversations about the struggle to be a giver instead of hoarder. In these congregations, kids and grandkids are all over the place—running, laughing, crying and spilling. And the wise old senior citizens don't get grumpy about them. In fact, one can often see all four generations engaged in each others' lives in simple, wonderful ways. These congregations know that parents are and always have been the primary teachers of the faith. They also know the importance of other authentic, caring adults and peers. So, Christian education is about forming faith and it happens in the home and at church—all life long—the only "graduates" are the saints who have died in Christ.

As you and I live and die and live again under the authority of our Lord Jesus, the living, breathing Word, it's probably helpful to consider which kind of church we are at any moment. Which kind of church do your calendar, your daily actions, your preaching and listening, and your giving reflect? In the vernacular of many, "Who's your daddy?"

Robert Benne is director of the Center for Religion and Society at Roanoke College in Salem, Virginia. He was Jordan-Trexler Professor of Religion and chair of the Religion and Philosophy Department at Roanoke College for eighteen years. Before that he was professor of Church and Society at the Lutheran School of Theology at Chicago for seventeen years. His graduate degrees are from the University of Chicago. He has written and lectured widely on the relation of Christianity and culture. The two latest of his ten books are entitled *Quality with Soul: How Six Premier Colleges and Universities Keep Faith with their* *Religious Traditions* and *Reasonable Ethics: A Christian Approach to Social, Economic, and Political Concerns.*

42

ം 6 ∞

Authority and Power in the ELCA

Robert Benne

DDLY ENOUGH, I REMEMBER A SOCIOLOGICAL BOOK assigned to us in one of my first classes in the field of Ethics and Society at the Divinity School of the University of Chicago in 1960. It was Paul Harrison's *Authority and Power in the Free Church Tradition: A Social Case Study of the American Baptist Church,* published in 1959. In that book Harrison distinguished between formal authority—who or what officially had the warrant to guide the life of an institution or group—and power—who or what *actually* made the key decisions for the institution or group.

Harrison argued that while Baptists had a radically democratic ideology about how decisions were made, the truth was quite different. The Baptist ideology of formal authority dictated that authority rose from each congregation, but in actuality the headquarters bureaucracy covertly usurped the power to make decisions. Because the ideology masked what really happened, the central bureaucracy of the American Baptist Church actually exercised more power than churches that had a much more hierarchical system of formal authority!

I could now move into a lengthy and warranted discussion about how decisions are made in the Evangelical Lutheran Church in America, in which formal authority is supposed to rest in the Churchwide Assembly, but in which the real power lies elsewhere. Anyone who has attended a Churchwide Assembly will sense that formal authority and actual power are two quite different realities.

But the governance problem is not my focus here. Rather, I would like to focus on the difference between the formal, authoritative principles of the ELCA and the actual emphases of the church. The formal authority so nicely articulated in the Constitution gets transformed by those in power into quite a different agenda. In short, if the ELCA really took its authoritative principles as the direct guide for its life we would have quite a different church. But I am getting ahead of myself.

The Principles of Formal Authority

IF WE LOOK TO THE ELCA's CONSTITUTION, especially Chapters Two, Three, and Four on the Confession of Faith, the Nature of the Church, and the Statement of Purpose, respectively, we find a fine statement of authoritative principles.

Chapter Two begins with the confession of God the Father, Son, and Holy Spirit and moves on to the confession of "Jesus Christ as Lord and Savior and the Gospel as the power of God for the salvation of all who believe." It then locates the specific authority of the church in Jesus Christ as the "Word of God incarnate." It adds that the "the proclamation of God's message to us as both Law and Gospel is the Word of God," and that "the canonical Scriptures of the Old and New Testaments are the written Word of God," which as the "inspired Word of God" are **"the authoritative source and norm of its proclamation, faith, and life."** (boldface added)

Further, since it is clear that we all stand in traditions of interpretation of the Word of God, the Confession of Faith accepts the three ecumenical creeds of the ancient church, as well as the confessional writings of the Lutheran church as authoritative articulations and interpretations of the Christian faith. The Statement concludes with this bold commitment: "This church confesses the Gospel, recorded in the Holy Scriptures and confessed in the ecumenical creeds and the Lutheran confessional writings, as the power of God to create and sustain the Church for God's mission in the world."

Chapter Three clearly articulates the source of authority of this church. "All power in the Church belongs to our Lord Jesus Christ, its head. **All actions of this church are to be carried out under his rule and authority.**" (boldface added)

Chapter Four's Statement of Purpose authoritatively sets forth the priorities of the ELCA: "proclaim God's saving Gospel . . . preserving and transmitting the Gospel faithfully to future generations"; "carry out Christ's great Commission"; "serve in response to God's love to meet human needs"; "worship God in the proclamation of the Word and administration of the sacraments"; "nurture its members in the Word of God"; and "manifest the unity given to the people of God."

Except for the impoverished language about God (God, God's, God, God's) dictated by the ELCA's "inclusive language" madness, one could hardly wish for a better statement of authoritative theological principles.

The Power Principles

THE PRINCIPLES THAT ACTUALLY have power in the ELCA are quite different from those that have formal authority. It is not that ELCA leaders have consciously decided to replace the formally authoritative principles for another set. Indeed, they would vociferously deny that any such thing has taken place. As proof of their fidelity to the formally authoritative principles, they can and will plunge into the traditional language of normative Lutheran theology. They do so repeatedly.

But if one would ask what really interests and excites the leadership, what draws their resources and attention, and what is finally non-negotiable for them, another set of principles are pressed forward with real power. What really guides the ELCA are the principles of "diversity," "inclusivity," and a certain conception of "peace and justice." Those are the phrases we have heard from the beginning of the ELCA. They are, as one student put it in a doctoral dissertation, the ELCA's "god-words." They have been the only "new" ideas in the "new" ELCA. They have increasingly displaced the formal authoritative principles of the church.

"Diversity" seems to have been pioneered by the ELCA. The church was ahead of American society in making diversity a mantra, which everyone must repeat and obey. "Diversity" is made up of what must be "included," and in so doing making the church "inclusive." But what is behind this intense commitment to "diversity" and "inclusivity"? In their most benign meaning, these principles mean getting more people of color, women, and non-European-background persons into the life of the church.

One would think that the main effort toward reaching such diversity would be through evangelizing those diverse populations, but there seems to be relatively little effort at domestic evangelism. Rather, another agenda is at work.

Instead of an agenda devoted to evangelizing many sorts of persons and thus becoming more catholic, the real agenda is based on suspicion—the suspicion that white European-background, heterosexual males have distorted the message and mission of the church and must be dethroned from their hegemony. If we invite the voices of those marginalized by the white male establishment into the central decision-making centers of the church and thus increase diversity, we will cleanse and strengthen the message and mission of the church.

This program is consonant with the agendas of the liberal Protestant churches that the ELCA has so long courted. We have so wanted to be accepted by the Episcopalians, the United Church of Christ, the United Methodist Church, and the Presbyterian Church (USA), and now we are "making it" with the mainline just at the time they are in precipitous decline. Our presiding bishop seems to be drawn to the likes of Episcopal Presiding Bishop Jefferts Shori and United Church of Christ President Thomas. The ELCA takes on more and more of the contours of liberal Protestantism.

The general movement of liberal Protestantism can be clearly traced historically. It had its origin, of course, in the European efforts to "update" Christianity by emphasizing its ethics of love over against its retrograde dogmatic claims. Overwhelmed by the threat posed by the sciences to Christian theological claims, the great liberal thinkers—Kant, Ritschl, Harnack, Troeltsch—proposed that the dogmatic content of the faith be replaced by enlightened ethics, something that by its inwardness was protected from the reductionist claims of science.

On American soil the Social Gospel picked up this ethical thrust, though its first generation—represented by Rauschenbusch—still maintained the classical theological themes of the faith. But its emphasis was focused on ethics. Indeed, Rauschenbusch remarked that, "Thus far Lutheranism has buried its ten talents in a tablecloth of dogmatic theory and it has kept its people from that share in the social awakening which is their duty and right." (Quoted in E. Clifford Nelson's *The Lutherans in America*, p. 11)

For Lutherans there is no such thing as a Social Gospel, there is only the Gospel of Jesus Christ addressed to every person and people by the Church's authoritative preaching, as the statement of faith of the ELCA so clearly states. As a response to the Gospel, Christians individually and corporately are led by the Spirit into the Church and the Christian life, which has both personal and social dimensions. So, while there may be a Christian social ethic, there is no such thing as a Social Gospel, strictly speaking. Likewise, while there may be a Christian ethical agenda that aims at liberating persons and groups from oppressive ideologies and structures, there is no liberation theology *per se*.

The elites of liberal Protestantism—those controlling its seminaries, ecumenical organizations, publishing houses, and headquarters bureaucracies—tend not to make those sorts of Lutheran distinctions. For many years now they seem to have either assumed or become uninterested in the proclamation of the Gospel itself. (What happens at the grass roots level is often quite different.) And they have paid little attention to personal ethics, except as such ethics need revision according to their enlightened agenda.

Their energies have been poured into the social, economic, and political ramifications of Christian teachings, not the central affirmations of the Christian faith itself nor in personal ethics. Not only does this miss the main thing that Christianity is about and, therefore, leads to membership losses as people look for the real thing, but it has serious divisive tendencies.

As one moves from the central affirmations of the Christian faith to its social and political ramifications, one passes through several stages of argument that involve different assessments of the current situation, different analytical judgments, different philosophical principles, different ordering of Christian principles, and very different applications of those normative principles. For example, arguments about whether or not we should have invaded Iraq involve all those complex steps, and Christians of good will and intelligence differ about them. But one would never come to that conclusion if one examined the social and political proclamations of liberal Protestantism. They move with utter confidence directly from the central affirmations—or from selected biblical passages or theological themes—to highly debatable public policy. They are joined in this "straight-line thinking" by some of their counterparts among religious conservatives. As this "straight-line thinking" becomes politically predictable over time, one gets the suspicion that political commitments are more dominant than those of a theological nature.

Internally, liberal Protestantism at the elite level spends its energies purging the life of the church from oppressive ideologies rather than focusing on the proclamation and extension of the Gospel and on Christian personal ethics. Those oppressive ideologies are sexism, heterosexism, racism, monoculturalism, and American imperialism. The maniacal movement toward "diversity" in liberal Protestantism and now in the ELCA is meant to shatter and overcome these oppressive ideologies and practices. (Generally, however, "diversity" does not include persons of conservative cultural and political convictions, especially if they are vocal.) So, for example, many catalogues of interdenominational and mainline Protestant seminaries will include pages and pages of rules to govern "inclusive language," but nary a word commending orthodox Christian belief. Students studying in those divinity schools would find it far more dangerous publicly to use "non-inclusive language" than to deny the Trinity, or to support the Iraq war than to deny the divinity of Christ. Volunteering at a Crisis Pregnancy Center would make a student a pariah. Needless to say, the situation is quite different at the level of local parishes.

In short, the grounding of the church's mission in the Gospel has been practically supplanted by a debatable liberal social and political agenda. There is lack of interest in or squishiness at the Christian center, dogmatism at its periphery. Such is the Social Gospel of liberal Protestantism.

It is my judgment that the elites of the ELCA are moving rapidly toward this liberal Protestant consensus. The ELCA will increasingly take as its major preoccupation the struggle against the oppressive ideologies and structures they believe are contaminating the church and world. That struggle will inevitably beg many questions and tip toward social and political liberalism, so confidently that no other interpretations will be allowed.

Many signs of this elite movement are evident. The highest of our elite—our Presiding Bishop—seems to understand his central calling as making "prophetic" pronouncements on every political issue that looms before us. Most of his pronouncements are uninformed by Lutheran themes. He has taken on the mantle of leader of liberal Protestantism. Meanwhile, efforts to stem the steady loss of membership by increased home missions and disciplined lay theological education seem far down his list of priorities.

The ELCA's priorities seem to fit those of liberal Protestantism. Its actual commitments reflect the liberationist thrust of the older denominations. Once one understands this, it becomes clear what is non-negotiable to the elites of the ELCA and what is adiaphora. The former they fight for tooth and nail. Thus, they stand firmly for: quotas (to fight racism and monoculturalism); unqualified abortion rights (to fight sexism); the homosexual agenda (to fight heterosexism); centralization of power (to fight the benighted masses of the church who are infected with all the "isms"); a relentless purging of masculine language from worship materials (to fight sexism); and a strong commitment to insistently left-wing foreign policy positions on Iraq and Israel (to fight against imperialism).

Thus, we have a church with authoritative Gospel articulations in its formal principles, but its exercise of power moves along quite different lines, one that is gradually bringing disaffection from the church on the part of many of its participants. The disaffected answer by keeping more money at home and being totally uninterested, if not hostile, to the ELCA's initiatives. The principles bearing formal authority for the ELCA have increasingly been displaced by a powerful bureaucracy's agenda.

What, Then, Can Be Done?

I ONCE THOUGHT THAT BY MID-CENTURY the declining liberal Protestant churches will have merged into one large generic church. I still think that is a possibility but it now seems more likely that institutional inertia will keep the denominations going in smaller and weaker, but yet identifiable, communions. The ELCA will continue, as will the Methodists and others as discrete bodies. The Lutheran Church-Missouri Synod will also continue, but at increasing distance from the ELCA.

Is there any chance of renewal of confessional Lutheranism in the ELCA? Anything is possible with God, so we should not give up hope. Even completely dead bones were once brought to life. Since the ELCA is a good-sized body, there are many pastors and laypeople who share a similar analysis as that outlined above, so not every one supports the route to decline. But some of those pastors and laypersons are too isolated and unorganized to act in concert for renewal.

The sad truth is that many ELCA members are either uninterested in what happens beyond the congregation and/or have been taken in by the informational monopoly of the national church. (Just observe the full-court press to promote and sell the new hymnal! No criticisms allowed.) While there is no great affection for, or allegiance to, the ELCA, neither is there any groundswell of discontent—just steady decline in mission support for the churchwide organization and loss of members.

Given this situation, it is very important that independent, confessional Lutheran organizations continue and expand their work. They are the "conscience" of the ELCA and, for that matter, the Lutheran Church-Missouri Synod. The WordAlone Network, Lutheran CORE-Coalition for Reform, Lutheran Churches of the Common Confession, Youth Encounter, the American Lutheran Publicity Bureau, The Society of the Holy Trinity, the many regional groups devoted to reform and renewal, *Lutheran Quarterly*, and *Lutheran Forum* (and its newsletter) are crucial instruments for raising the awareness of clergy and laity and for organizing initiatives for constructive change. Above all, they are important for stimulating the thinking of a rising new generation of Lutherans, who may not be intrigued by the weakening liberal Protestant agenda, and who may be captured by the allure of authentic Lutheranism.

It is my hope and prayer that among that new generation of Lutherans there will be strong leaders who are stirred by the Lutheran construal of the Christian faith and who will move into the leadership positions of the ELCA and its many institutions. God still holds the future open!

James C. Bangsund is a pastor of St Timothy's Lutheran Church in San Jose, California. Prior to arriving at St Timothy's, Bangsund and his wife, the Reverend Judith A. Bangsund, served as ELCA missionaries to Tanzania for twenty-two years. The last thirteen of those years were spent at Makumira University College (MUCo), one faculty of which serves as the primary theological seminary of the Evangelical Lutheran Church in Tanzania (ELCT).

Bangsund received his Ph.D. from Luther Seminary in St Paul, Minnesota, and while at MUCo taught Old Testament and Hebrew. He is the author of *Biblical Hebrew: A Simplified Grammar* (The Research Institute of Makumira University College (RIMUCo, 2001) and *Understanding the Old Testament: An Introduction and Theological Overview* (RIMUCo, 2007).

Bangsund has a rather mixed professional heritage, having started off as an electrical engineer prior to going to seminary. What at first seemed like an unlikely combination turned out to be most felicitous when Bangsund arrived in Tanzania. There he was drawn into developing the MUCo website as well as helping establish a campus telephone system, a computer network, and various large power backup systems.

Now back in the parish in San Jose, he continues to manage the website of the ELCT as well as that of Lutheran Mission

Cooperation and the Evangelical Lutheran Church of the Gambia. It is these continuing international connections that have led to the concerns expressed in this article.

∾ 7 ∾

When Parents Falter, Children Speak

James C. Bangsund

THE ISSUE OF SCRIPTURAL AUTHORITY is of particular concern in our relationships with churches overseas—especially with churches and church leadership in what is sometimes called the "two-thirds world." Prior to returning to parish ministry in the United States at the beginning of 2007, my wife and I served for twenty-two years in Tanzania. The last thirteen years were spent on the faculty of Makumira University College, which is, among other things, the primary theological seminary of the Evangelical Lutheran Church in Tanzania (ELCT). In my teaching of Old Testament (along with Hebrew), I often ran into the problem of the differing approaches to Scripture taken by the ELCT and the Evangelical Lutheran Church in America (ELCA). At times, I felt more at home with the insights and persuasions of the ELCT than those of the ELCA; at times not.

I would like to explore this interesting and sometimes troubled relationship by looking at two internationally focused documents, one produced by the ELCA and the other by the ELCT. I will then conclude with some thoughts on the implications of these documents. This will include reflection upon the unprecedented phenomenon in the Anglican Church wherein some conservative congregations of the (American) Episcopal

Church have placed themselves under the authority of African bishops in order to distance themselves from events taking place in their own church.

Accompaniment: "Global Mission in the Twenty-first Century"

The first of the two documents I wish to explore is the ELCA Global Mission document on "accompaniment," entitled "Global Mission in the Twenty-first Century" (GMTC).[1] In general, this document recognizes the changes which have taken place in global missions in recent decades. It notes, in particular, the transition from the early days of "north to south" dominance and leadership to the present time in which overseas "receiving churches" now most often have their own leadership and determine their own policies. GMTC seeks to redress the former imbalance in such a way as to recognize and advocate for a more egalitarian model of inter-church relationship—one which has been described as "accompaniment." What follows in this first section is, to some extent, a summary of a critique which I was asked to write for *Word & World*, a journal of Luther Seminary, St. Paul, Minnesota.[2]

GMTC is an important document because it contains the seminal thinking of ELCA leaders in global mission. Such documents usually do not have a great deal of impact on the ground overseas, where missionaries are, more often than not, focused upon the contextual issues which surround them. They do, however, give a helpful insight into how the evangelical enterprise is perceived in Chicago, and they do at times make their presence felt in discussions with leaders of churches overseas.

The metaphor used and pursued throughout the document is that of "accompaniment," and the justification for this model is said to be the encounter on the Road to Emmaus (Luke 24:13-32). Just as Jesus accompanied the disciples along the road, so we, as northern and southern churches, accompany one another, sharing the resources and visions which God has given us.

The model is in some ways compelling in that it does replace the older vertical, top-down model of missions with one which is more egalitarian and across-the-table. At the same time, the reader may question whether this is indeed the concern of Luke 24:13-32, the text used as the basis for the "accompaniment" project. The Luke text presents a post-Easter appearance of Jesus, and his relationship to the disciples is here, as elsewhere, not merely that of brothers walking the same path. Rather, the text deals first and foremost with the essence and meaning of the Resurrection. But that meaning has been ignored in the "accompaniment" model, and the story has merely been used as a vehicle to carry new freight. Any who have studied exegesis will recognize the old enemy of eisegesis here.[3]

But there is more. In pursuing the goal of replacing the old vertical, top-down model of missions with the model of accompaniment, the writers of GMTC have also replaced the vertical theology of God breaking in upon us in the Cross and Resurrection of the Christ event with the horizontal theology of us-helping-us. Certainly us-helping-us should be one of the outcomes of an encounter with the Gospel of Jesus Christ, but it is not the Gospel itself, and by itself it cannot become the sole content of that which we share.

We get to the heart of the matter with GMTC's Missiological Statement: "This paper focuses primarily on God, the Giver of Life, as a meaningful metaphor for speaking the gospel in today's global context."[4] The metaphor of "life" dominates the discussion, and it is important to understand just how it works here. We are told that "God is on an incarnational mission to heal, restore, redeem, and liberate life."[5] Luke 4:18-19 ("good news to the poor, . . . release to the captives and recovery of sight to the blind," etc.), follows immediately, and then John 10:10 (Jesus came that we "might have life, and have it abundantly").

The move from Luke 4 to John 10 is exegetically significant. In associating "life" with Luke 4, GMTC rightly notes God's deep concern for "horizontal" matters such as justice and healing. These are not mere temporal concerns, as opposed to "more important" spiritual ones. But the spiritual is real; it is not a matter of either/or. We dare not lift up one at the expense of the other. And this is where the theology of GMTC begins to go flat.

In placing its discussion of John 10:10 immediately after that of Luke 4, GMTC suggests that the meaning of "life" in John10:10 is also horizontal. Yet the surrounding context (v. 9: "I am the door; if any one enters by me, he will be saved"; v. 11: "I am the good shepherd. The good shepherd that lays down his life for the sheep") clearly shows John's vertical intent. This is significant and revealing. Certainly both the vertical and the horizontal are present in Scripture; both are crucial. But GMTC (and thus "accompaniment"), in pursuing a goal, was apparently pre-determined, ends up with a reductionist message in which "life" most frequently, though not exclusively, stands for healthy *human* relationships.

Basic theological vocabulary is also used in ways that are flattened and horizontal. Christ's resurrection is understood to affirm our commitment to stand with the oppressed rather than Christ's victory over sin and death.[6] The words "incarnational" and "cruciform" are frequently used not in reference to the Christ event but rather in terms of our commitment to those who suffer or are oppressed. At risk of being accused of insensitivity to these very real issues, one must note that, whereas these horizontal issues are indeed critical, they must be grounded upon God's vertical breaking in upon us in the Cross and Resurrection. One cannot avoid the conclusion that the "fire in the belly" of GMTC is found in its concern for us-helping-us and not—at least not first and foremost—in the sharing of the vertical in-breaking upon us of God in Christ.

Other things could be said here (and are said in the *Word & World* article mentioned above). For the purposes of this article, however, the point is simply that there at times seems to be a continental divide between the use of Scripture in ELCA Global Missions and its use in the overseas churches with which we are in partnership. And this does not go unnoticed in those communities of faith. I have often been asked, "What has happened to the churches which originally brought us the Gospel?"

The Bukoba Statement

As one might expect, this concern has led to reflection and response overseas. One example is the Bukoba Statement of the Evangelical Lutheran Church in Tanzania (ELCT).[7] The statement deals with the complex interrelationship of Globalization, Homosexuality, and HIV/AIDS. Clearly the first and last of these three have had and are continuing to have a tremendous impact upon Africa.

The first part of the Bukoba Statement deals with the impact of globalization upon the economy and culture of Tanzania. There is concern both for the impact of large western free markets upon the weaker markets of developing countries as well as for the impact of western cultural values (or lack there of—the distinction is clearly in the eye of the beholder) upon the traditional and more conservative cultural values of Tanzania.

The second part of the Bukoba Statement deals with homosexuality, and this is discussed below. The third element of the Bukoba Statement then considers the problem of HIV/AIDS in the light of the impact upon Tanzania of the first two elements. The writers of the statement see a connection: from their perspective, homosexuality has not been a part of Tanzanian culture, but the presence of western diplomats, teachers, business people, and tourists has begun to change that. The rise of HIV/AIDS is seen to be one result of that change.

The heart of the Bukoba Statement is clearly its discussion of the issue of homosexuality. And statements of this type do not arise without a context; the bishops of the ELCT gathered in 2004 to a great extent because of what they were seeing happen at the ELCA Churchwide Assemblies.

That the gay-lesbian-bisexual-transexual (GLBT) debates were perceived by them as, foundationally, an issue of the understanding of the authority of Scripture is made clear by the way this portion of the Bukoba Statement opens with quotations of 2 Tim 3:16-17[8] and 2 Pet 1:20-21.[9] They then note that homosexual acts "are condemned by Holy

Scripture because they go against God's plan (1 Cor 6:9-10; Romans 1:26-27). We thus, are obliged to stand with Holy Scripture which is the sole guidance for decency and ethical human behavior."[10]

The argument which is presented is fairly traditional, involving references to creation in Genesis and various New Testament admonitions. It is in §3.5 that the Statement turns to the churches of the west.

> We deplore distorted explanations by several people who use the term "human rights" to justify homosexuality and sodomy. We find this as a deliberate misuse of a good term "human rights." It should be remembered that those forced to accept these deviated lifestyles also have their rights, which need to be protected.[11]

The observation is significant: rather than upholding the human rights of the GLBT community, the ELCA is seen as endangering those rights by virtue of presenting a hope which is theologically invalid and thus false and dangerous. The tension is palpable between the leadership of the ELCT and the perceived wandering of western churches away from traditional understandings of biblical authority:

> There are theologians who interpret, exegete, and misuse Holy Scripture to support and endorse homosexuality in its many forms. The Conference of Bishops rejects biblical expositions done by some theologians and scholars with intent to affirm and legalize homosexuality. The Bible is the foundation of Christian faith and thus the church has an indisputable authority to rightly and scripturally explain faith based on God's word. The church's expositions do not necessarily have to agree with those of the scholars.[12]

In 2005, letters were written to Bishop Hanson and others of the ELCA expressing the intense concern of the ELCT regarding what they saw as a failure of responsibility to uphold traditional understandings of Scripture and, as a result, of human sexuality.

Some Further Reflection

CLEARLY, THE ISSUE OF AUTHORITY OF SCRIPTURE is one that has great potential of dividing the church—and specifically of separating the ELCA from partner churches in developing countries around the world. These churches in general hold to traditional understandings of Scripture being God's Word and thus being normative and authoritative for Christian faith and life. As these churches become more self-assured (if not yet financially independent), they begin to voice their objection when they see the very churches which brought them God's written Word starting to weaken in their understanding of that Word.

Events of late in the Anglican community have become particularly interesting. In 1998, many were surprised and some stunned when African bishops found their voice and the Lambeth Conference (the highest decision-making body in the Anglican communion) rejected "homosexual practice as incompatible with Scripture."[13] The vote was by no means unanimous, and the Episcopal Church (Anglicanism's presence in the United State) responded in 2003 by consecrating an openly gay bishop, V. Gene Robinson of New Hampshire.

This has led to the most unusual response on the part of a group of conservative Episcopalians who have turned to the Anglican Church of Uganda for ordination of an American bishop, John Guernsey of Virginia, to head up a conservative diocese of more than thirty congregations. These congregations, as a result of sensing slippage in their denomination's understanding of scriptural authority, thus reject the oversight of the American Episcopal Church while yet retaining their Anglican identity under the oversight of an African church.

That there are consequences of the differing understandings of authority of Scripture outlined above is clear. Less clear, perhaps, is *what* those consequences will be. Surely there is danger, within the international Lutheran community, as well as elsewhere, of growing rifts that lead ultimately to schism between churches that were at one time seen as parent and child. But whether seeking oversight from a church in

Uganda can be a long term solution is questionable. At present, the dictum "my enemy's enemy is my friend" is sufficient to make it work, since the issue of homosexuality has become such a dominant and polarizing feature of the ecclesiastical landscape. But eventually a multiplicity of other cultural and even theological issues will likely begin to emerge between these congregations and their intercontinental overseers.

That such a solution will not readily be open for pastors and congregations of an organization such as WordAlone is clear when one considers the specific issues which gave rise to WordAlone. Whereas WordAlone is in agreement with the bishops of Tanzania on the issue of human sexuality, one quickly runs into differences with regard to the office of bishop itself. At least half of the dioceses of Tanzania subscribe to apostolic succession (the historic episcopate), and that number will most likely increase over the years. There are also issues such as stricter views on divorce, a position of abstinence with regard to alcohol, and legalistic (sometimes fundamentalistic) interpretations of Scripture which would give most ELCA pastors and congregations pause in terms of seeking oversight.

Actually, and perhaps ironically, the true solution really does lie in the ELCA Global Mission document "Global Mission in the Twenty-first Century" and its concept of "accompaniment." In spite of its overtly horizontal theology, this document does correctly note the continuing growth and maturation of overseas churches and thus advocates for equality around the table. No longer is the north to dictate to the south (if indeed that is all that was happening even in the past). Rather, we are to be partners engaged in common mission, listening to one another and taking seriously the observations and critiques made by our opposites through whom God is also speaking. And now one of those critiques, which many of our southern partners are hoping will receive a serious hearing, has to do with the fading sense of Scripture's authority in the north.

What happens when children are taught well and then, reaching adulthood, note that their parents are failing to live by the healthy principles which they earlier advocated? Will the older parents listen when their adult children now come to them and remind them of those earlier lessons? A telling test of whether "accompaniment" represents the true convictions of the ELCA will be found in how seriously we receive the critique from our partners on our use and authority of Scripture.

Notes

[1]http://www.elca.org/globalmission/policy/gm21full.pdf .

[2]"Accompaniment: Horizontal at the Expense of Vertical" in *Word and World*, Volume 25, Number 2 (Spring 2005), pp. 207-209.

[3]"Exegesis" is the careful study of a biblical text so as to read *out of* it (ex-) and thus hear what it is saying. "Eisegesis" is when teachers or preachers begin with their own personal opinions or agendas and project them *into* (eis-) the text—and then "discover" them there. Eisegesis is not always deliberate. We can all fall prey to it if we are not careful, since we all come to scripture carrying baggage and are often unaware of this.

[4]GMTC, p. 7.

[5]Ibid.

[6]"The resurrection of Jesus is also God's affirmation of Jesus' way of mission in the world, a way of servanthood and commitment to struggle to bring life for others" (GMTC, p. 8).

[7]Found at http://elct.org/news/2004.05.001.html.

[8]"All Scripture is inspired by God and profitable for teaching, for the proof, rebuking error, correcting faults, and giving instruction for right living. So that the person who serves God may be fully qualified and equipped to do every kind of good deed."

[9]". . . no one can explain by himself a prophecy in the Scriptures. For no prophetic message ever came just from the will of man, but men were under the control of the Holy Spirit as they spoke the message that came from God."

[10]Bukoba Statement §3.2.1.

[11]Bukoba Statement §3.5.2.1

[12]Bukoba Statement §3.6.1 and 3.6.2.

[13]Lambeth Resolution 1.10.

At Luther Seminary, there is a culture of fear surrounding the issue of requesting an exceptional ordination. (An ordination excluding the bishop's application of the "historic episcopate," never part of Lutheran theology until full communion was recently established with the Episcopal church in the U.S.A.) Many graduating seminarians would rather go against their theological convictions and their consciences than deal with the possible repercussions of such a request. Both single graduates and seminary families fear delays in receiving a steady income just when school loans become unavailable and begin entering into repayment. Requesting an exception forces a seminarian, with absolutely no power in the process, to risk an adversarial relationship with their bishop, who has all the power.

Congregations need to be made aware of what is happening in the ELCA when their future pastors confess their convictions with integrity. I have not specifically named my bishop of assignment so that congregations might realize that what has happened in my situation can happen anywhere. Congregations should discuss with their bishops how exceptional ordinations have been dealt with in their synod and how they will be dealt with in the future.

Steven Broers graduated from Luther Seminary in Saint Paul, Minnesota, with a Masters of Divinity degree in the spring of 2007. He is married to Kristy Broers and has two children, Sophia (four) and Malachi (one). Steven also holds a Bachelors of Music degree in double bass performance from the University of Nebraska-Lincoln and a Masters of Music from the University of Cincinnati

College Conservatory of Music. He is a member of the Lutheran Congregations in Mission for Christ and is currently seeking a pastoral call.

ꙮ 8 ꙮ

ELCA Denies Seminarian's Rights

Steven Broers

From my essay defending a request for an "exceptional" ordination by the ELCA – Spring, 2007

When the forgiveness of sins is announced, questions abound: "Who is this who even forgives sins?" "By what authority do you do these things?" Seldom are these questions asked out loud, but they are asked in the heart and mind of every sinner. We cannot help ourselves, we are bound and determined to do it. To believe that a preacher can forgive our best and most treasured sins with a simple announcement seems too easy, arrogant, blasphemous or even cruel when we have spent a lifetime protecting ourselves from just such an event. In Matthew chapter 9, Jesus perceived the doubts of the Pharisees after He had forgiven a paralyzed man, but I believe that every pastor perceives these same doubts both in those he or she preaches to as well as in his or her own heart and mind.

I am a sinner. When I despair, I latch on to whatever is left to hold onto. I use any means necessary to defend myself from having to rely on Jesus Christ and his words alone. Why? Because, when I trust in Jesus Christ, then I admit that I am helpless and passive. To be left completely passive means to die, and I do not like dying. The necessity of being ordained into the pastoral office under the historic episcopate tempts me to put my trust in a bishop or in a tradition of bishops rather than in God's faithfulness to forgive sins. This undermines my faith in the very words I am being called to proclaim.

Perhaps there are some pastors who can fend off the devil and his lies easily, but I do not have the faith to withstand his attacks for long. When doubts come flying into my conscience like arrows I buckle and despair . . . Who am I to forgive sins? By what authority do I do these things? Where do I put my trust? Only when I have nothing left to hope in and have been left utterly defenseless do I realize that the authority of the gospel is in the strong hands of Jesus Christ alone. All I have left are his words, "If you forgive the sins of any they are forgiven. If you retain the sins of any they are retained." "Whoever hears you hears me." I am requesting an exceptional ordination because requiring ordination into the pastoral office under the historic episcopate would undermine my trust in the authority of the gospel and my trust in God's faithfulness to forgive sins.

OU HAVE JUST READ THE OPENING PARAGRAPHS of the essay I was asked to write in order to request an exceptional ordination in the ELCA during the spring of 2007. Two months later, I was informed by my synodical bishop of assignment that my request was denied. A pastor has the same authority to forgive and to retain sins as any other Christian within the priesthood of all believers; however, a pastor is given the authority to announce this forgiveness publicly when a congregation calls him or her to ministry. Who or what gives a bishop his or her authority? By what authority does a bishop grant or deny an exceptional ordination?

Shortly after I was informed that my request was denied, I asked to be reassigned to another synod so that I could ask for an exception somewhere else. A week later, I received a phone call from my regional coordinator. I was informed that there had been a meeting the previous week that dealt, among other things, with my situation. At this meeting, it was decided that I would not be allowed to ask for an exception in another synod. The decision of one bishop would be considered the decision of the entire church. Furthermore, my bishop was not alone in his decision; he said that he had the support of his synod council and presiding bishop Hanson. I thought the regional coordinator summed it up best by explaining that the church was supporting the bishop and not me.

It appeared that I had no options left. I finally agreed to be ordained in the normal ELCA way, and I was thankful that my synodical bishop of assignment agreed to continue the process with me. Unfortunately, after a couple of months, it became clear through conversations with the synod office that they were "limited" in where they could place me as a pastor. The synod wouldn't send me to some churches where people might share my positions because they didn't want to encourage the viewpoints I held. Months after my original request for an exceptional ordination, I decided to stop seeking ordination as an ELCA rostered pastor.

Where do bishops get their authority? As part of the priesthood of all believers, they have the authority to announce the forgiveness of sins when called upon; however, they are called specifically to be administrators for the church who are to see to it that the preaching of law and gospel (or the forgiveness of sins) actually gets done. Therefore, while their authority to forgive sins comes from God and is spiritual, their authority as administrators is temporal.

Since the Called to Common Mission (CCM) agreement, I believe that the ELCA has begun to confuse these two authorities by demanding that a bishop use their temporal authority to authorize something that is spiritual. How does this happen? Constitutional bylaw 7.31.17, concerning exceptional ordinations, was put into place to deal pastorally with consciences, like my own, that would be bound through participation in a normal ordination. However, when a bishop is asked to use their spiritual authority to free a bound conscience, they can choose not to use that authority and demand compliance based on their temporal authority.

I do not believe that the bishop into whose temporal care I was assigned is a bad person. In fact, I believe that he is a very kind person and a good bishop. However, I do believe that he has made poor decisions in my situation. Unfortunately, he is part of a system that encourages and supports his behavior. Throughout the entire process, every policy, meeting and leader appeared to support his authority and never chose to look into what I was really saying and what Lutheran pastors and churches like me have said for years about ministry and the Gospel. Now, I am currently on the active list of pastors seeking call for the Lutheran Congregations in Mission for Christ (LCMC). My bishop was fearful that I would lead a congregation out of the ELCA at a time when I had no such intentions; how ironic that those unfounded assumptions finally helped push me out by making no other call possible.

Many in the ELCA believe that the CCM agreement is in opposition to the authority of the Word of God. The exceptional ordination bylaw was thought to be a pastoral response to consciences bound by submitting to such an agreement. I believed, not too long ago, that by requesting an exceptional ordination I could be ordained with a happy conscience. However, I now believe that requesting an exception was a mistake. Why? Because it could be denied by someone using human authority. Requesting an exception is not finally about asking permission to do something in a different way—it is a confession. It is confessing where one is placing one's trust.

Bishops definitely have authority in the church as administrators with the aim of getting true proclamation done. However, creating an exceptional ordination that can be either granted or denied confuses a bishop's spiritual authority with their temporal authority. This situation is not good for a bishop, a synod, a pastor, a candidate, or a congregation. I realize that there are many bishops who would want to grant an exception, but the system in place appears to place more value in supporting the temporal authority of a bishop at the cost of the spiritual office of ministry by which God grants forgiveness to sinners publicly and regularly. My prayer for the ELCA is that it would support not only the temporal authority of its leaders, but also cling to Jesus Christ who authorizes the spiritual authority to free the bound consciences of all sinners . . . even if they have just graduated from seminary.

The mission and ministry of the Christian church is to proclaim that Jesus Christ, God himself, lived, died and was raised from the dead to defeat sin, death, and the devil for you! Jesus Christ has become your

Lord and Savior. This proclamation is the goal of my ministry. This gospel message is its own authority because God authors faith where and when He pleases when His words are heard. "For I am not ashamed of the gospel; it is the power of God for salvation to everyone who has faith, to the Jew first and also to the Greek. For in it the righteousness of God is revealed through faith for faith; as it is written, 'The one who is righteous will live by faith.'" (Romans 1:16-17)

Meredith Schultz is a junior studying political theory at Patrick Henry College in Purcellville, Virginia. She began studying theology and philosophy during her years as a homeschooler and never looked back. Throughout junior high and high school she participated in competitive Bible quizzing, memorizing over 1,000 Scripture verses in the course of six years.

Through her father's work as a physician, Meredith became involved with Helps International, a non-profit medical relief and development organization reaching the people of Guatemala. Since the age of twelve, she has made eight trips to Central America, serving on medical teams, learning the language, and enjoying the country. Before coming to school, she spent five months in-country as volunteer staff, assisting teams in the field and interpreting for the medical personnel.

An armchair social commentator, she loves the click of the keys beneath her fingers, and hopes to make a career of it someday. When not parsing the works of Plato, Augustine, and DeToqueville, she likes

making bundt cakes, going to coffee with Dad, and enjoying crisp fall days in her native Minnesota.

The Piper's Flute:

Hearing the True Voice in the Heresy

Meredith Schultz

M Y CONSTITUTIONAL LAW PROFESSOR once told our class, "Ask a smart sixth grader what the Constitution means, and you'll probably be on the right track." It's only when you start asking lawyers, justices, and Hollywood starlets that "See spot run" is suddenly up for interpretation. It's only then that "the right to choose" and "gay rights" are counted among the unalienable.

But I'm not talking about the U.S. Constitution; I'm talking about the Word of God. The inspired and inerrant Word of God, the lamplight of the Church, passed down through the ages. The powerful and effective Word of God that convicts the sinner and purifies the soul. The Word of God that the modern church has decided is also up for interpretation.

This isn't just a localized illness—it's an all-out pandemic, crossing denominational lines and international borders. Lutherans aren't the only ones—Methodists, Presbyterians, Episcopalians, and even the Baptists are suffering. I always knew it was happening out there, but ensconced in my small, conservative Christian circles, I was largely unaffected. After all, they weren't ordaining homosexuals in *my* church.

One Sunday I went to the Washington National Cathedral with a friend for the church service. Quite a jaunt from campus, we arrived a few minutes late, just as the service was starting. Frosted and chapped by the brisk January wind, we stepped through the doors and were greeted by the low, soothing notes of "The Church's One Foundation" on the immense organ. One of my favorite hymns. I smiled and let the attendants usher us to empty seats in the front left wing.

A few more hymns, the Nicene Creed, the Lord's Prayer—so far so good. Then the priest rose to give the message. Thoroughly forewarned by my father before coming, I was skeptical about content. Noticing an announcement for *meditation* classes in the bulletin, I rolled my eyes and elbowed my companion. Had they carried out a tribal fertility rite during the offertory I probably wouldn't have batted an eyelash.

The main text was from 1 Corinthians 12, the Apostle Paul's appeal to unify the fractured Corinthian church. In firm, but calming tones, the priest exhorted the parishioners to live in unity with one another, drawing heavily on Paul's famous illustration of parts within the body. "The eye cannot say to the hand, 'I don't need you!' And the head cannot say to the feet, 'I don't need you!' If one part suffers, every part suffers with it; if one part is honored, every part rejoices with it."[1]

I nodded in agreement, sliding to the edge of my seat. A few references to Plato and Augustine later, I was completely engaged. It was all of it good. Had I just picked a lucky Sunday? Or were the Episcopals really not so bad after all?

But then, without warning, my experience took a drastic turn. The priest threw the message into a tailspin, turning all of his pithy quotes, his witty anecdotes, his Scriptural support, into condemnation for the Falls Church Episcopals, freshly separated from the rapidly liberalizing mainline denomination. They were the schismatics, the prodigals, the errant brothers who brought trouble and division to the body of Christ.

And their sin? Failing to accept ordination and marriage of homosexuals within the Church. After all, God loves and accepts all, regardless of sexual orientation. Who are you to hate and reject His precious children?

Photo by William Glaser

I felt a cold draft down the corridor. It wasn't because I didn't know what sort of business the Episcopals were up to. It was because the priest had just flagrantly misused the words of Scripture to support sexual perversion within the walls of the Church.

"Come back to us. We'll leave the light on for you." He ended the service with an exhortation for the wandering sheep to return to the fold. I felt uneasy and disquieted, like a close friend was being maligned in polite conversation, and I couldn't do anything to defend them.

A few minutes later, we filed through the immense doors and back into the winter wind. I am told the foundation stone of that cathedral bears an inscription of John 1:14—"The Word was made flesh, and dwelt among us." The Word—the *logos*—eternal and unchanging God who spoke the universe into existence. Even the grandeur of the columns, the graceful arches and spires, the gilt and glory, were only a fog at fast-approaching dawn. Two millennia have passed since the Word was made incarnate among us. Times have changed, but Truth has not.

Later on, we chuckled about the ordeal over Starbucks, but I was still disturbed—disturbed because of the deception. The priest had drawn me in with compelling intellectual arguments and snippets of Scriptural truth. He had petted and primed me. And then he had gone in for the kill.

Here's the scary thing. Had I not been in a Bible-believing church from my youth, memorized hundreds of verses throughout high school, and studied the details of systematic theology in college, I wouldn't have known the difference. And that's exactly how 99.9 percent of the National Cathedral churchgoers likely were that day. Children traipsing after the Pied Piper. Ignorant sheep being led to the slaughter.

And if not for the grace of God, that could have been me.

The modern church isn't seeking God, it's seeking God made in its own image. A docile, castrated God, who will stroke their conscience and affirm their lifestyle choices. A culturally sensitive, ecumenical God who accepts everything and everyone and, naturally, can be modified at the annual denominational conventions. God is Santa Claus, God is Mother Earth—God is my homeboy.

It's Grocery Cart Christianity—picking and choosing scriptural truths and leaving the undesirables on the shelf. Scripture is just a smorgasbord of soundbytes, to be carefully doled out on Sunday morning according to the speaker's necessity. A verse need not be contextualized within the rest of Scripture, or even within the passage. While we're at it, we might as well get rid of those inconvenient, antiquated ones about gender roles and homosexuality. Do we even need this old thing anyway? Why don't we just slip it on the Barnes and Noble shelf next to *Don Quixote* and start over?

And we're not so very far from that. Last year the Presbyterian Church U.S.A. decided to rename the persons of the Trinity to fit their gender neutral agenda. Finding Father, Son, and Holy Spirit to be too sexist, they proposed alternatives such as "Compassionate mother, beloved child, and life-giving womb," "Rainbow of Promise, Ark of Salvation, and Dove of Peace," and "Lover, Beloved, and Love that binds together Lover and Beloved."[2]

It might be funny if it wasn't blasphemous. I'm sure Moses wasn't laughing while he stood in the heat of the burning bush.

God said to Moses, "I AM WHO I AM. This is what you are to say to the Israelites: I AM has sent me to you." God also said to Moses, "Say to the Israelites, 'The Lord, the God of your fathers—the God of Abraham, the God of Isaac and the God of Jacob—has sent me to you. *This is my name forever, the name by which I am to be remembered from generation to generation.*[3] (emphasis added, NIV)

After devastating the Egyptians and delivering the nation of Israel, he gave his people strict instructions where His name was concerned: "Do not misuse the name of the Lord your God."[4] The Jews took God's name so seriously, they would not even write it in its entirety. Common abuses such as "My God!" or "Jesus!" would have been unthinkable, much less "compassionate mother" or "life-giving womb."

The clay is dictating to the potter. Insignificant man demanding that the Creator of the Universe answer to him. Job learned firsthand. We might all take a lesson from his divine interrogation.

Then the Lord answered Job out of the storm. He said:

> Who is this that darkens my counsel with words without knowledge? Brace yourself like a man; I will question you, and you shall answer me. Where were you when I laid the earth's foundation? Tell me if you understand.[5] (NIV)

> "But who are you, O man, to talk back to God?"[6]

St. Paul warned against the deception of the church in his exhortation to Timothy:

> For the time will come when men will not put up with sound doctrine. Instead, to suit their own desires, they will gather a great number of teachers to say what their itching ears want to hear. They will turn their ears away from the truth and turn aside to myths.[7] (NIV)

Modern Christianity has a great number of teachers to say what her itching ears want to hear. Scholars and seminarians, men wise in their own eyes, who have tamed the Word of God to suit their spoiled audience. Scripture is no longer the lamplight, but the lapdog of the church—weak, emasculated, and eating out of academia's hand.

But they all deceive themselves. Scripture brooks no abuse. Revelation closes with an ominous warning against cut-and-paste operations:

> I warn everyone who hears of the words of the prophecy of this book: If anyone *adds anything* to them, God will add to him the plagues described in this book. And if anyone *takes words away* from this book of prophecy, God will take away from him his **share** in the tree of life and in the holy city, which are described in this book.[8] (emphasis added) (NIV)

If intellectual arguments fail, if scriptural parlay falls on deaf ears, perhaps the church will answer to her conscience. God has engraved truth on the heart of all, so that men are without excuse. Even the most dulled and deluded of men know, in the deepest part of their soul, that one day they will answer to their Creator.

Even the demons believe and tremble.

Why do we need the authority of Scripture? So that we too are not deceived.

And it's not so very complicated. The truth of scripture is pure and simple, accessible to priest and ploughboy alike. If it seems baffling, impossible, and paradoxical, that is the failure of man to understand, not the failure of God to speak. The Holy Spirit illumines man's darkened, fallen mind to the Scriptures. We need only to ask. As the Psalmist says, "The law of the LORD is perfect, reviving the soul. The statutes of the LORD are trustworthy, making wise the simple."

I walked away briskly from the National Cathedral that day, light snow dusting my black wool coat. A few hundred parishioners followed me out, heading home to a hot Sunday dinner, heresy fresh in their itchy ears. The world has many voices, the call of the piper's flute, the voice of the Shepherd. But who to follow?

"My sheep listen to my voice; I know them, and they follow me."[9]

Notes

[1] 1 Corinthians 12:21, 26 (NIV).

[2] Greg Garrison, "Presbyterians to try variations on Trinity," 20 June 2006, http://www.al.com/news/birminghamnews/index.ssf?/base/news/1150795253293730.xml&coll=2.

[3] Exodus 3:14-15 (NIV).

[4] Exodus 20:7 (NIV).

[5] Job 38:1-4 (NIV).

[6] Romans 9:20 (NIV).

[7] 2 Timothy 4:3-4 (NIV).

[8] Revelation 22:18-19 (NIV).

[9] John 10:27 (NIV).

Section Two
The Theology

Steven D. Paulson is professor of Systematic Theology, Luther Seminary, St. Paul, Minnesota.

Paulson joined the Luther Seminary faculty as associate professor of Systematic Theology in the fall of 1998 after serving as assistant professor of religion at Concordia College in Moorhead, Minnesota, where he had been since 1993.

He was pastor of Trinity Lutheran Church in Washington Island, Wisconsin, from 1990 to 1993. His experience also includes two years of work as a research librarian at JKM Library in Chicago and five years as a psychiatric counselor at Fairview Hospitals in Minneapolis.

Paulson is a Summa Cum Laude and Phi Beta Kappa graduate of St. Olaf College, Northfield, Minnesota, and earned the master of divinity degree from Luther Seminary in 1984. He holds both the master of Theology (1988) and doctor of Theology (1992) degrees from Lutheran School of Theology in Chicago.

He has been honored with the Goethe Institute Scholarship (1985) and the North American Ministerial Fellowship (1980-84).

Paulson currently serves on the editorial boards of *Word and World* and both the *Lutheran Quarterly* and *Dialog* and has written articles for both journals. He is the author of *Luther for Armchair Theologians*

and editor of *A More Radical Gospel*, *The Captivation of the Will*, and *The Preached God* all written by Gerhard Forde.

ଛ 10 ଙ

Two Kinds of Authority:
Law and Gospel

Steven D. Paulson

TUDIES COMMISSIONED BY CHURCHES on the authority of Scripture like those underway in the Evangelical Lutheran Church in America (ELCA) are as close to an admission of emptiness as one can get. It is like the emperor who had no clothes commissioning a special royal panel to investigate whether clothes in fact exist at all. If one could successfully doubt the existence of clothes, then perhaps being a naked emperor would not be such an embarrassment— it would simply be a sign of the times. Being naked, then, might make me cold in inclement weather, but at least I would be "relevant" and fit with my time and context, would I not?

When Scripture's authority needs to be authorized by the church, then all is lost, since church is the child of the Word, not its mother. Even the Lutheran Confessions begin to signal this problem of trying to authorize its own authority when they included Martin Chemnitz's suggestion for a preface (but not yet an article!) to the *Formula* called "The Binding Summary, Basis, Rule and Guiding Principle, How All Teaching Is to Be Judged in Accord with God's Word and How the Errors That Have Arisen Are to Be Explained and Decided in Christian Fashion."[1] Scripture is the sole authority concerning errors in teaching and all theological judgments, and so a forming norm that has no norm. But such statements seem to belie the situation that persons and church constantly find themselves in when disagreements arise—the Scripture is used by both sides and claimed as the basis for whatever position is argued, and so this issue of Scripture's authority alone is proved unworkable in reality—a good theory and bad practice. At this point we normally laugh at the slogan Scripture Alone and wink, since we all seem to know that Scripture is never alone, it always has an interpreter, and whoever wins the current interpretation war wins over Scripture. That would actually, and frighteningly, be true, if it were not for the very surprising rug that God pulls out from under our feet as we attempt to become our own lords and gods over Scripture. To our surprise God has not one, but two kinds of authority. One is called Law that shapes the world and our work within it, and the other that permanently interrupts the law's order, called Gospel, by means of uncontainable and unpredictable forgiveness of sin. That means that everything about authority hinges upon whether or not one has a preacher and that preacher actually gives two words, not one.

The Problem

MY THESIS IN THIS ESSAY IS SIMPLE: our single biggest problem when it comes to understanding and using Scripture is the loss of the art of distinguishing law and gospel. At least in bygone days preachers were trying to make the distinction, even when they could not, but today law and gospel is a laughing stock in the church and unknown in the world. Lutherans in particular line up to make fun of this old dinosaur of a past age, exulting in the fact that they have evolved beyond their meager Reformation beginnings to a more enlightened age of ecumenical church unity.

Lutherans presently have awakened to the reality that they can actually base a greater unity of churches on the simple rejection of the distinction of law and gospel, and in doing so discover what was the problem with the Augsburg Confession in the first place. Why did so many reject this most Christian and ecumenical confession of the faith, both Protestant and Roman Catholic, so that it came to be viewed as the cause of disagreement rather than its solution? Melanchthon observed that "the opponents single out the law (because to some extent human reason naturally understands it since reason contains the same judgment divinely written on the mind), and through the law they seek the forgiveness of sins and justification." Instead the evangelical teaching asserts that "All Scripture should be divided into these two main topics: the law and the promises."[2]

Law and gospel is now widely considered a discredited model for preaching or perhaps a failed form of exegesis or even simply a bad "theology." So the only current teaching is to explain why it doesn't "work" anymore—if it ever did. In the middle of the ridicule of the one bright light brought by the evangelical preachers, Rome is burning and teachers are fiddling to some other tune, and the only other tune beside law and gospel is the law alone.

Consequently consciences are terrorized and the big blueprints for building new and better "united" churches go painfully unrealized. Since the very beginning of law and gospel's rediscovery, Lutherans themselves have expressed fear for what the distinction would do to church and world. It was like pure uranium that could unleash either the greatest good or the greatest harm to humankind, who knew exactly what it would be used for if it fell into the wrong hands? So it was safeguarded and hid immediately by those nearest to it. One did not have to wait for the orthodox century to make law and gospel into an abstract idea, or the Pietists to make it into a feeling and process, or the enlightened to make it into a limit that human reason could not surpass—and so we had to content ourselves with earthly matters of human reason, which is to say, the law alone. One could listen to what happened in the second generation of Lutherans according to the fifth article of the Formula of Concord:

"The distinction between law and gospel is a particularly glorious light. It serves to divide God's Word properly and to explain correctly and make understandable the writings of the holy prophets and apostles. Therefore, we must diligently preserve this distinction, so as not to mix these two teachings together and make the gospel into a law. For this obscures the merit of Christ and robs troubled consciences of the comfort that they otherwise have in the holy gospel when it is preached clearly and purely. With the help of this distinction these consciences can sustain themselves in their greatest spiritual struggles against the terror of the law."[3]

Then immediately upon making the great confession the Formula tells the rest of the story, "A dispute occurred in this regard among some theologians of the Augsburg Confession." The way ahead once dispute arose in the church is either to blunt this distinction and hope that some basic reforms could be established in churches, such as the marriage of clergy and reception of the sacrament in both kinds, or proceed to preach "a more radical gospel."[4]

Distinguishing Properly: The Church's Greatest Day

WHAT IS THIS DISTINCTION OF LAW AND GOSPEL and how does it work? Let me tell you a little story. The greatest day that the church ever knew was one of its earliest. It was hardly a generation old, a mere adolescent, when its great pillar Peter came for an ecumenical visit to Antioch with its new preacher Paul. There Peter ate hotdish with the Gentiles in the basement after service since the church was full of them, until "certain people came from James" and then Peter withdrew, "keeping himself separate for fear of the circumcision faction" (Galatians 2). Peter played the perfect church politician working like a bishop at making sure all sides had their say, fearing the consequences of disunity and seeking not to displease the other pillars of the church. So the grand old man made a little concession to the law by adding to the Gospel the prestigious tradition and divine command given to the Jews. Peter separated himself from the Gentile Christians so that he would remain clean, and the church back in Jerusalem would be pacified.

The day Paul learned of this he marched to Peter and "opposed him to his face" (Gal 2:11)—and what a church assembly it was! No vote was taken; only two attended but it was something to behold. Paul made a confession into the face of church authority by calling Peter out on the carpet, and Paul forced the equivocator into the true confession concerning how the church is one, holy, catholic and apostolic. In other words, Paul forced Peter to make the distinction between law and Gospel in a time of suffering and trial, and to quit mixing the two for the pacification of the church. Peter had made a small concession for the sake of church unity, and, thereby, cut off an undesirable part of the church for the sake of better part. After all, if you had to choose between Jews and Gentiles it was an easy decision to make. Yet Paul knew something bigger was at stake than agreement with Jerusalem. If Peter willingly added a bit of law to the mixture of Gospel he preached, then the Gospel itself was lost. Paul confronted Peter to his face with the proper distinction of law and gospel by which we have all we need for understanding the authority of Scripture, the authority of the church, the authority of the apostles, and what happens when church authority misunderstands itself and overthrows the Gospel for a law. Paul recognized that if you add just a little bit of arsenic to an otherwise delicious meal eating is just not the same anymore.

Martin Luther rehearsed this story for his own seminary students at the University of Wittenberg in his great lectures on Galatians, saying "This is a wonderful story to tell about very great men and pillars of the churches. Paul is the only one who has his eyes open wide and sees the sin of Peter . . ."[5] Paul has his eyes wide open. Peter has his eyes wide shut. The sin of Peter was to confuse law and gospel, and, thereby, lose the gospel:

> For, although they were preaching the Gospel, still by their pretense, which could not stand with the truth of the Gospel, they were establishing the Law. But the establishment of the Law is the abrogation of the Gospel. Therefore, whoever knows well how to distinguish the Gospel from the Law should give thanks to God and know that he is a real theologian.

The authority of Scripture, the authority of the church, and the authority of the apostolic proclamation depends on this distinction—it always has and it always will. Luther is not very hard on Peter in this instance, saying that he seems to have accepted Paul's condemnation graciously, since it was the pure gospel, and even though Peter could not seem to carry the tune very long, he knew Christ's voice when he heard it, and so must have said something like, "Oh, yes, Paul, I don't know what got into me, when I hear you say it, I know my Lord Christ is speaking to me, forgive me, let's go eat with Gentiles!"

Luther knew that the distinction of law and gospel has an aspect of science about it, in that one learns to identify keys in the grammar for distinguishing law and gospel such as when one is dealing with an imperative or an indicative. Yet one of Luther's own moments of enlightenment was that grammar is not the main thing. It is the function or effect or work done in the hearer's life that finally distinguishes law and gospel.

Moreover, the real test of distinguishing law and gospel occurs "in a time of temptation" such as Peter's, when he was sitting in the great new mission start of the Antioch church surrounded by foolish Gentiles when suddenly he got a visit from the Mother ship in Jerusalem telling him that he must mind his P's and Q's and obey the law's command that a Jew not eat with Gentiles. When the church council from Jerusalem is putting pressure on you, it is difficult to distinguish properly, nevertheless that is when distinguishing is crucial. How does one do this, especially when the political pressure is on?

The way to distinguish the one from the other is to locate the Gospel in heaven and the Law on earth, to call the righteousness of the Gospel heavenly and divine and the righteousness of the Law earthly and human, and to distinguish as sharply between the righteousness of the Gospel and that of the Law as God distinguishes between heaven and earth or between light and darkness or between day and night. Let the one be like the light and the day, and the other like the darkness and night. If we could only put an even greater distance between them![6]

So we learn to distinguish this way. When you are "busy on earth
. . . let the ass work, let him serve and carry the burden that has been laid
upon him, that is, let the body and its members be subject to the Law."
Luther took the old story of Abraham who had been commanded to sacrifice Isaac and noted how Abraham used the ass to haul the sticks for
the sacrifice until they reach the mountain, then they left the beast in the
valley below and ascended to the holy place. So Luther continued,

> But when you ascend into heaven, leave the ass, with his burdens on
> earth; for the conscience has no relation to the Law or to works or
> to earthly righteousness. Thus the ass remains in the valley; but the
> conscience ascends the mountain with Isaac, knowing absolutely
> nothing about the Law or its works but looking only to the forgive-
> ness of sins and the pure righteousness offered and given in Christ.[7]

In the political and social life, where hands and feet and the
"members" of the body are busy, the law is "strictly required," just as
Paul had observed in the seventh chapter of Romans. Yet in the conscience, in heaven, with the new creature made by Christ in baptism,
only the Gospel is heard with its strict freedom from the law in the form
of the forgiveness of sin. Luther concluded,

> Peter had confused this distinction between the Law and the Gospel,
> and thus he had persuaded the believers that they had to be justified
> by the Gospel and the Law together. This Paul refused to tolerate.
> Therefore, he rebuked Peter . . . There is a time to hear the Law and
> a time to despise the Law. There is a time to hear the Gospel and a
> time to know nothing about the Gospel. Let the Law go away now,
> and let the Gospel come; for this is the time to hear the Gospel, not
> the Law. But you have nothing good; in fact, you have sinned grave-
> ly. Granted. Nevertheless, "I have the forgiveness of sins through
> Christ on whose account all my sins are forgiven." But in a matter
> apart from conscience, when outward duties must be performed,
> then, whether you are a teacher, a pupil, etc., this is no time to lis-
> ten to the Gospel. You must listen to the Law and follow your voca-
> tion. Thus the Law remains in the valley with the ass, and the Gospel
> remains with Isaac on the mountain.[8]

Of course, people can fail at the distinction of the law and gospel, and use it badly. The devil works twenty-four hours a day to confuse the two, and it should not surprise us that this happens even in the churches. The greatest confusion of all comes when love and faith are lumped together, when in fact those two are "exact opposites."[9] Where love yields in the smallest trifles, faith never yields even to the strongest cosmic evil.

Peter likely thought he was doing the loving act both for the church in Jerusalem and Antioch. But this was no time for love, it was the time for faith alone! Sympathy is no excuse for attempting to discard the distinction and take up some other form of the authority of Scripture —like the bromide that Scripture's authority really resides in the community of the church at worship, or in the teaching authority of the church with its episcopacy and papacy, or that the authority resides in the immaculate conception of a Holy Book by the Holy Spirit—a book without flaw or historical error. Of course the book is thoroughly inspired and so written by the Holy Spirit, and of course Scripture's authority is exercised in the community of the church at worship, with or without the bishops. But the real issue of Scripture and its authority is the freeing reality that the word of Scripture, when preached purely, establishes two very different authorities in life that are marked by the biggest distinction known to humankind: life and death.

As long as people in the church insist on approaching Scripture without any sense about law and gospel, they will ruin preaching and the church created by the word. Confusers will come with one issue after another of what constitutes true justice and how the Bible either misses the point or can be used as a kind of manifesto for a righteous cause to liberate the oppressed. What else can you do when you function with only the authority of the law and by it seek to be made righteous? You have to adjust the law to your preferences for the best holy group you can assemble.

Group after group, person after person, comes knocking on the door of Scripture demanding to know what it wants, and demanding to be vindicated. Yet, when Scripture opens its door, lo and behold two things come flooding out: one is the law and the other the gospel. Both end up destroying all efforts to justify oneself, and only the gospel makes a brand new life by justification through Christ alone, faith alone, the word alone. This is why the gospel belongs in heaven, since it alone has a future. Down in the valley of the old world where the ass sits there is only the past and an uncertain present. The law only preserves—to some extent—the past which is even now coming to an end in Jesus Christ. That is why we need the gospel.

Two Kinds of Authority: Law and Gospel

THERE ARE TWO KINDS OF AUTHORITY, NOT ONE. Everyone who comes upon this truth is shocked and awed by it. Jesus, all the gospels say, amazed people with this announcement, "Now after John was arrested, Jesus came into Galilee, preaching the gospel of God" (Mark 1:14). Paul was undone by this second, new authority, coming to him as it did by ripping apart the heavens in the form of revelation that ended his old life and began the new:

> For I would have you know, brethren, that the gospel which was preached by me is not man's gospel. For I did not receive it from man, nor was I taught it, but it came through a revelation of Jesus Christ. For you have heard of my former life in Judaism, how I persecuted the church of God violently and tried to destroy it. (Galatians 1:11-13 RSV)

Even if we are not zealous for the first and old authority, as Paul was, we nevertheless find one old, well-known authority better than two since we can at least accustom ourselves to the law's predictable expectations. That God has two kinds of authority is unsettling, surprising and unavailable to our knowledge or experience except when normal authority is breached by a previously unknown authority that we do not really have a name for, except that we call it "new," or "Gospel."

Once the new authority breaks in upon us, the normal authority immediately becomes old. And what is most frightening about this is that both kinds of authority remain in their places and times, but we find our own selves transferred—violently—from one to the other. The law and the gospel are two worlds with death between them. Being transferred from one to the other means we die to the law and live only to the Gospel who is Jesus Christ. Nevertheless, once we have been translated from old to new authority, we describe this death to the old as "freedom"—true, evangelical freedom, "for freedom, Christ has set us free" (Galatians 5:1). Hence, the normal authority of the law that we experienced simply as demand is given its proper name and called "law."

The two kinds of authority are, therefore, properly named law and gospel.

Christians are the ones who describe these two authorities, neither of which the world adequately fathoms since it can only think of the law alone as authority and, therefore, law is its only possibility for a pro-

longed life. The world, not having the gospel, must place its hope in the law, karma, living a good life, contributing to society, etc., because there isn't any other place to put hope. On the other hand, Christians not only know of two kinds of authority, but they seek to keep these two utterly distinct. To law belongs obedience, to the gospel hope. Otherwise the second, eternal and heavenly authority is lost altogether. We make this distinction by using a peculiar, eschatological dialectic that teaches us why the law, which is God's greatest and most salutary gift to the world, nevertheless does not avail unto salvation—in fact the law actually hinders us there.

That means the Christian goal for doing theology is to identify these two kinds of authority and then keep them distinguished so that the second authority, along with the translation from one to the other is actually accomplished by preaching. Without preaching only the one authority of law exists, since no preacher is necessary for you to have God's divine law at work. God can work very well through gravity, parents and the public schools to execute authority by law. The gospel kind of authority, however, is revealed, announced, created and breaks into the old through the bestowal of Jesus Christ and this requires a preached promise given to particular people and particular places and times. When the promises are delivered well, they open an eternal future based entirely on Christ's giving or favor rather than our doing and earning.

Christian preachers must spend their time learning the science and art of distinguishing these two kinds of authority, law and gospel, so that every now and then they can help create the new authority and effect the transfer of people into it. To do this they must themselves be taken into the Gospel's authority and used for its purpose by the Holy Spirit so that preachers are not manipulators and controllers of the new authority, but its servants or slaves, which is simply another way of saying in the old language of authority that they are masters over the old by being free of it.

These preachers of the new authority are given their words, they do not generate them by themselves, and the words they are given come from previous preachers called Apostles, notably the Apostle Paul, though also Peter and the Jerusalem group when they are not confused about the Torah, who got their words from the first preacher of the Gospel, Jesus Christ himself. It is true Christ gave these also to the prophets of old and so the gospel was promised already to Adam and Eve and expected ever more immanently as the Scripture drives toward the coming of the Father's Son and Messiah. Yet Christ arrived in the flesh and was publicly announced by Him in the preaching of Jesus Christ, and what a stir he made whenever he preached it and wherever he went! As Luther once noted, this new authority, this new announcement of who holds the future should never have been written down, but because of sin, which stubbornly resists and hates the second and final authority, even this Gospel came to be written so that preachers following the Apostles would be given their words rather than take them or attempt to create them out of their own selves.

That means that in order to fight the temptation of the devil himself in the form of enthusiasm (drawing the words of preaching from within) we needed not only to have the promise of the gospel written so our preachers would have their proper words, but we needed the gospel itself to be given to us through hearing it preached for us. A written gospel remains the dead letter which actively kills (2 Cor 3) unless one thing is added in the form of a living, vocal preaching "for you." Even the written gospel in the condensed form of Paul's sermon kernel, "Jesus Christ was handed over for our trespasses and raised for our justification" (Romans 4:25) needs a living preacher announcing promise face to face with its intended sinners. Gospel authority is thus tied to the authority of written Scripture because of sin. Even dear old Peter needed a preacher that great and famous day when Paul made the true Church and united it in the Gospel alone. Peter needed Paul to preach the law and Gospel to him, and so Paul did, and so Peter heard it—again—and the Church was united.

First Authority: Law in the Form of Master and Slave

Now the default authority of life is the first authority, the voice of demand, or law which comes to us in its purest form on Moses' written tablets of stone. Most people don't get such tablets, they are thus mere Gentiles, but they, nevertheless, have the "code" or requirement in their consciences as Paul points out in Romans 1. The law's authority is everywhere present. It is there with or without a preacher, by God's own will and plan. It is as ever-present as gravity, and so is simply overlooked until one tries to act contrary to it. I could deny the law has any authority over me, but that would not let me leap off a tall building and fly. This authority is so dominant that it becomes synonymous with the word "authority," which is then experienced as the relation between a master and slave.

A master commands; a slave obeys. One person is in control the other is controlled. What would appear to be freedom and happiness in this singular arrangement is to become a master and not a slave. Sometimes we hear people say, "It's all right to be poor, but better to be rich." So this authority divides up all relations to people, creatures of the world, and Divinity itself into relations of dominance. It always asks, Who is on top and who is on the bottom? The problems with this authority start in relation to creation: What does it mean to have authority over all creatures like that given to Adam and Eve? The problem increases when considering relations to other people—what does it mean to have authority over another person such as a parent has over a child? The problem becomes acute when it comes to God: What does it mean to be controlled by God and yet to want nothing more than to be in control over God?

Authority really should mean to be authored, as in what it is like to be made a brilliant character in a book like Mark Twain's *Huckleberry Finn*. Huck was not there until penned in by Twain, and once written he has a type of presence that is nearly ubiquitous—if only fictional. Yet the problem when thinking of authority according to the first, legal sense, is that it drives toward one final goal: to become one's own author. That is what it means to be "free." So the fictional, written character seeks to have his own life like Pinocchio who gets tired of being a wooden puppet and wants to be a real boy. We seek to be our own autobiographer. Any other authority would seem to fall short of freedom since it demands that I serve the law of another instead my own inner law.

As long as the first, legal authority of life is the only one functioning it knows no end or limit. In that case it seeks infinity, limitlessness, and the only way it can become eternal is to curl up upon itself like a Scandinavian pastry under the assumption that if I am both my own master and my own slave, at least I will be gentler with myself than a foreign master would be. I cannot be a terror to myself can I?

Second and Final Authority:
Gospel in the Form of Forgiveness

EVEN WHEN A NEW, SECOND AUTHORITY breaks in by proclamation of Christ crucified, a revulsion emerges since this gospel authority makes me perfectly passive—doing nothing and being done unto. How else can this be understood than as the worst form of imposition by a harsh master controlling me against my will? For someone clinging to life in the form of autobiography, how could getting a new Author of life be anything other than the worst form of death? The Gospel's new authority is to be authored, rather than to be my own author. Isn't this death itself?

If two kinds of authority were not bad enough one of the worst realities is that Christians hold that these two authorities, law and gospel, overlap for a short time. This results in the rather absurd claim that I have two authors, two stories of my life being told at the same time—and the two contradict one another. Sometimes we call this the *simul justus et peccator*. One is the story of my own life that I am intent upon writing/living by myself. It is the story of how others attempt to dominate and control me, but how I, over time manage to throw off these false masters one after the other until I am my own master and write my own tale of victory over the dominators. Everyone is trying to control me, but in the end I win out over them all and control myself.

The other story has Christ as author or authorizer. He tells my story differently, as the story of his pursuit of me until he inevitably possesses me like a lost lamb who has wandered off from the ninety-nine. Strangely these two concurrent tales of my life overlap precisely at the point of Jesus Christ's own crucifixion. I personally tell the story of Christ in my life as the overcoming of a foreigner's attempt to grab and control me—one might say from the point of view of a lamb who has left the ninety-nine not because she is lost, but because she is finding her own self. Then when Christ tries to grab me, and the preacher tries to convert me, and the church tries to brainwash me, and the law tries to tell me what someone else's idea of perfection is, I resist and break free and start my own flock of exactly one with my own story of how I narrowly escaped the clutches of a Savior who wanted nothing but Himself and was ready to consign my life to oblivion. Ridding myself of Christ is then my moment of freedom. His death is my life. So the murder of Christ, if it enters my story at all, is told by me as a story of self-defense.

When Christ tells this story of me, and he gets to the part of his own death on the cross, he sees that even the very best thing in life, the authority of the law itself, is used against him in the vain attempt by sinners of trying to become their own author. Christ saw this story repeated so often that the inevitability of its end made him step out of a mere story and into history itself with his actual, bodily crucifixion. So we remember how Jesus told the story of the man who owned a vineyard and the workers in the vineyard were not tending it. The owner then sent representative after representative of his interests, each "master" killed by the servants in order to protect their freedom, until finally the son of the owner was sent, and he, of course, was killed in the same miserable repetition of sin's attempt to authorize itself according to the law.

To illustrate this conundrum of authority, Paul describes the situation of what it means to be translated away from one authority to the next, from the law to the gospel as if you were a little child in school. He says that prior to the Gospel's second authority arriving for you, you were a minor according to the law—bound to become an heir, but not yet able to live any different life from any other slave in this old world. That is the child of a wealthy man was treated like any other—until the date set by the father when the child should inherit the estate and come into his new authority—even over the teachers and disciplinarians of his youth:

> Now before faith came, we were imprisoned and guarded under the law until faith would be revealed. Therefore the law was our disciplinarian until Christ came, so that we might be justified by faith. . . . My point is this: heirs, as long as they are minors, are no better than slaves, though they are the owners of all the property; but they remain under guardians and trustees until the date set by the father. . . ." (Galatians 3 and 4 NRSV)

Christians, made so by the promise of Christ and thereby adopted by him, are heirs but as long as the law remains are treated like slaves.

Sinners seek to keep only one authority in life, which must then be the law. They know that authority; they know its rules and ways and though they chafe, they accept the process and dream that they can win at the game of master and slave if given enough time to fulfill the law by using their free will. To complete this task they cannot have others dominating, controlling and telling them what to do, including Christ with his funny ideas about love, peace, and forgiveness because those all end with Christ being the Lord of His own new kingdom and us being mere servants in it. Children who are heirs of a great kingdom would be foolish indeed to be made masters in the old world because then at most they become teachers, disciplinarians of others who know nothing of the freedom of the Gospel from the law itself. There is nothing better than to be a slave of the law in this old world as long as one has the promise of being an heir in the new kingdom since it is far greater than simply moving from slave to master. To be free of the law, rather than master under it, is the second form of authority—and when it is tasted in faith itself there is nothing sweeter, more real and deeply beloved than this: For neither circumcision nor uncircumcision is anything; but a new creation is everything (Galatians 6:15).

How Can You Turn Back?
Trying to Understand Scripture without Law and Gospel

NEVERTHELESS, PAUL CONTINUALLY CAME UPON PEOPLE like Peter who wanted to add the law to the gospel. The desire to be rid of the second authority of the gospel is so strong that one must call it the original sin itself, and it usually comes in the form of accepting the gospel, and then trying to improve on it with a little bit of law. The confusion of these two results then leads people to rid themselves of the distinction of law and gospel altogether, since it becomes a merely formal matter and is not believed to be written by the Holy Spirit into the Scripture and God's own way of working with sinners in the world. Refusing the distinction then appears to get rid of a Lord—even Christ—other than myself. It appears like some kind of freedom from a harsh master. It gets rid of a preacher whom I cannot help but think is one more control freak trying to dominate me by telling me her story rather than my own. It gets rid of Scripture as well, turning it into words of advice to people occupied with writing their own stories of triumph.

Just as we told the story of Peter and Paul, the whole history of the Christian church could be written as the attempt to reject the two distinct authorities by trying to return to the single authority of the law. To lay out that tale of how the church itself repeatedly rejects its own best light would require more than this essay can provide, but suffice it to say that by the time of Luther's entrance into the monastery and his taking up of Scripture as a teacher, the distinction of law and gospel needed "rediscovery." Better yet, it had to be revealed to Luther as it was revealed to Paul and as it is revealed to each person who has ears.

This distinction then became the bright light of the Reformation, and the second generation of evangelical preachers recognized it, even though the attempts to blow out the light were immediate among the Protestants. What is the threat of law and gospel? It is that if gospel authority is given freely to actual sinners then they have no motivation to improve, and, furthermore, their past efforts to be righteous according to the law will be counted as nothing. Worse yet, the church will not be united, but will fly apart hither and yon wherever preachers take it and appear among the most unsavory kinds of people like those Antiochenes who don't even know the most basic rules of religious life—that Jews do not eat with Gentiles. God's law could not have been wrong about that, could it? That at least must be eternal, right? Consequently, there is one historical wave of condemnation for this distinction of law and gospel after another, and one misuse after another of how to work with the authority of Scripture so that preaching both the law and the gospel is produced in the present.

Lutherans ruined their best light by making law and gospel dogmatic, as if it were a distinction of ideas. Then they made it experiential, as if it had nothing to do with the text and preaching and everything to do with the human heart. Then the very tools for distinguishing law and gospel were turned against the distinction and came to form what is presently called "historical-critical" method. This method thought it could actually overcome the forms of resistance to law and gospel that resulted in confessionalizing or denominational differences (all coming out of the original rejection of the Augsburg Confession by one "denominational" schismatic after another), which led to bloodshed all over Europe that eventually ended only by reducing law and gospel to a mere fallible "tradition" of certain wild-eyed hyper-Lutherans who could safely be caged by making theirs only one more method among others that could be discarded by a higher "objective" and "scientific" method that refused mere subjective points of view.

Here I am characterizing the attempt by the enlightenment to flatten out the various religions and their points of view precisely by getting rid of law and gospel and so getting rid of preachers themselves. Once you turn "preachers" into imparters of the one and only authority of the law they become easily dispensable, and so you bring "unity" and "peace" among the churches, the religions, and the whole earth by agreeing that there is only one authority, the law alone. Then there is, as Lessing saw, only waiting for the course of history to run and we shall see which group has the best, eternal law.

The promise of historical-critical method was to deal in facts of history that could be distinguished from the pious beliefs of the church —along with the recognition that the church housed many kinds of perspectives at any one time. That is, the church was really "the churches," and so you have not just one account of Jesus' life called a Gospel, but four, that each has a "point of view" along with the occasional observations of the maverick Paul. Matthew had a theology, Luke did, so did Mark and John, and Paul also with his negative references to the authority of law and his excessive remarks about a new, gospel authority.

The promise of historical-critical method as a theological enterprise was meant to get rid of preachers and restore unity to Europe and the church, but the attempt failed. Historians can't agree on much of anything as it turns out. When they do they are found to be using the same old authority of the law everyone else does—that is, they tell the story of the Bible and Christ in the way that gives them advantage over others, and what was supposed to be science that tells the truth about Jesus Christ as "the historical Jesus," and the truth about the church as people who somehow became convinced that Jesus miraculously rose from the dead, simply became one more form of autobiography and dominance. When this was finally realized by its greatest practitioners, we entered a post-liberal, post-historical age that most called "post-modern."

Now we deal with fragments of truths, which at most seek to point out the falsehood of dominant "master stories," and the end result for the churches and their preachers is that the story of Christ becomes the story of how each person seeks to throw off those who try to dominate them as slaves, and how each triumphs over such authority to become his or her own Lord.

First this comes out in the form of subgroups who believe they are marginalized, then these fracture and break until each person realizes that all other groups will marginalize them in their unique, particular, personal and private identities, and so the world really does become what the most negative thought it was all along—we are each fighting against each, each a master seeking to have slaves, and slaves seeking to rid themselves of their masters. Meanwhile, the Scripture becomes one more source of dominance that must be used differently by myself than those who preceded me in order to tell my own story of victory and mastery rather than to be dominated and used by others.

For now this means church groups are toying with the idea that there are two different, opposite and, nevertheless, true "interpretations" of Scripture when it comes to how the law applies to women, men, homosexuals, and various other group interests.

The odd person out in this process is Christ since he must become acted upon, rather than the one who acts upon us, otherwise he is experienced as a master, a harsh school teacher, who controls and limits rather than frees us. In other words, Christ simply becomes one more oppressive law-giver to me who is not telling me what I want to hear in order to be free. The problem with the ELCA presently is that the last dying embers of the old historical-critical method, a method begun on certain principles of the very Lutherans who taught us how to use law and gospel, are being trusted as the means to unity by means of getting rid of law and gospel.

The method has become the thing itself in which we put our hope. A method is just that, a method, and can never overcome the distinction of law and gospel or the actual preaching of the word, and chiefly it cannot take the place of Jesus Christ himself. The secret behind this moment when the method of critical examination of Scripture became the object of hope is that the method reveals natural law as a fraud. While natural law is routinely misconstrued and abused by people who wanted to dominate others, it is not true that law is whatever a particular community, nation or group wishes to make it. Law is never reduced to what is merely "posited," and so is effected by new "democratic" votes on what applies or does not apply. Working with law and gospel will never let law be treated so sanguinely as if it were our group puppet. The law remains a harsh disciplinarian in this old life until we are freed entirely and completely from it, and that awaits not an alteration in the law but its end in Christ himself and alone. Law cannot be made soft and amenable, even when it comes in the form of love.

The Word Remains Forever

DESPITE ALL EFFORTS TO THE CONTRARY the distinction of law and gospel continues to be made in the preaching office and so works in the real lives of people. This is not due to heroic efforts by churches, clergy, the royal priesthood or even the text of Scripture itself, but because the Holy Spirit will not have it any other way. The letter kills; the Spirit gives life. A church group or institution in this old world can, however, foster better preaching than we have right now. It does this by organizing its teaching institutions and its oversight of local preaching so that the proclamation of law and gospel is the highest art and science.

This is very hard, as teaching any art and science is hard. It is especially hard when we find ourselves as Peter did in some kind of churchly fight and the temptation of fostering unity by law comes bearing down upon us. Preaching can only proceed effectively when the two kinds of authority are identified and recognized as God's own double work with sinners, and this means that law and gospel remain God's own way of working rather than one more historical tradition invented by humans and used to oppress others. The distinction of law and gospel is truly the fount of diversity. It is the only teaching and art that recognizes more than one authority, and an actual end to the oppression of the harsh disciplinarian that we have come to see as our hope in life: the law itself.

This diversity comes, however, from the One God who works both kinds of authority, and so is the origin—or better yet the future of true unity. Foolish characterizations of law and gospel as not having meaning in the present, or otherwise not contributing any longer to discussions about authority of Scripture will fail in the end. So will churches that decide that various interpretations are possible while ignoring both the natural law of God planted in this old world and the new authority of the gospel alone as making us right with God by Christ's death on the cross.

It is hard for the sinner to admit there are two such authorities in life, and yet being transferred from the law to the gospel is not coming under another disciplinarian; it is to be adopted as God's own child by the Spirit of the Son who puts into our hearts the cry, "Abba, Father! —and lo we are no longer slaves, but heirs of the heavenly kingdom with the law behind us once and for all.

David N. Glesne is a native Minnesotan who received a B.A. from Concordia College, Moorhead, Minnesota, a M. Div. from Luther Seminary, St. Paul, Minnesota, and a D. Min. degree from Fuller Theological Seminary, Pasadena, California. He has been a pastor of churches in Illinois, California, and Minnesota. He currently serves as senior pastor of Redeemer Lutheran Church in Fridley, Minnesota. He also serves on the faculty of the Master's Institute, a graduate level seminary in the Minneapolis-St. Paul area. He is the author of *Understanding Homosexuality: Perspectives for the Local Church*, in which he assesses the biblical, theological, historical, social-scientific and pastoral issues surrounding the homosexuality debates. He and his wife, Mona, have four grown children.

For Glesne, the question, "What authority do the Scriptures have?" is much more than academic curiosity. As a pastor, on a daily basis he ministers in a congregational setting to the joys and sorrows of people in a variety of life's circumstances from birth to death. In these various situations the question becomes, "Is there a Word from God to speak into their lives or merely a human word?" When he speaks the words to one who is considering salvation, *"He who believes on the Son has everlasting life . . ."* is that a promise to which he can hold God? Or are these words written by humans who were using their own experiences to try to understand God's ways? When ministering to a woman on her death bed and speaking the promise, *"If you believe in the Son you will have eternal life"*, is that a word from God or words of humans groping upward? Is this God's Word whose authority is derived from the One who gives it or is it essentially a human word whose human interpretation becomes the final authoritative word?

For Glesne, the question of the Scriptures' authority is as practical as daily ministry. If the verbalized communication in the Scriptures is from God to human beings, then we have God speaking a life-giving Word into the human situation today.

That indeed is Good News! And that, Dave Glesne believes, is exactly what we have in the Scriptures.

ॐ 11 ॐ

Biblical Authority: Scripture's Claims for Itself

David N. Glesne

IN THIS WRITER'S MIND, the question of biblical revelation and inspiration is the theological watershed in the contemporary theological scene. At its root, it is the question of the authority of the Bible.

According to a recent poll by the Gallup organization, only a third of Americans believe the Bible is the actual Word of God and is to be taken at face value. In addition, one in five believes that the Bible is a book of ancient fables, legends, and history concocted by man. But are these beliefs about the Bible congruent with the Bible's claims for itself?

When commenting on or speaking about the Scriptures, one thing above all is crucial: the Scriptures must be allowed to speak for themselves. And that is more difficult than one might expect. The Bible essentially is a clean and simple book. But because it strikes so close to home and raises such basic human issues, we cannot be objective toward it. We read it through the glasses of our preconceived ideas. Therefore, as we come to the Scriptures, what we must do is the hardest of things —remove our glasses. However difficult, we must make the conscious attempt not to impose our own ideas, our own framework upon the Scriptures. We must let Scripture speak for itself and listen to it with openness. This is true of all of us. Whether we find ourselves on the more conservative or more liberal end of the theological spectrum, it is the same. All of us are heavily indoctrinated. It will be a struggle to set aside the glasses. But every time we come to the Scriptures, we need to make a conscious effort not to sift it through our own grid.

The central question we are asking is, "When the Scriptures are allowed to speak for themselves, what claims regarding authority do they make for themselves?" If we are truly going to go back to the Scriptures, then the Scriptures must be allowed to speak for themselves.

New Testament Claims for the Old Testament

WE WILL CONCENTRATE HERE ON the New Testament claims for the Old Testament. Within these New Testament claims, we will further narrow our focus to Christ himself and his presentation of the Old Testament as completely authoritative.[1]

In conversation with the Jewish leaders of that day in John 10, Jesus quotes from the Psalms and says, *"Is it not written in your law, 'I said, you are gods'?"* (v. 34)[2] Jesus constantly quotes from all parts of the Old Testament. *"It is written . . ."* is his constant usage from the time of his temptation in the wilderness until after his resurrection. Here it is striking that he calls the Psalms *"your law"* and treats it as having binding authority. If he had quoted from the Pentateuch, it would have been strong. But in speaking of the Psalms in this way, it is stronger still. "This is your law," says Jesus, and in so doing it is finished in his mind. For Jesus the discussion is over because in this setting he has quoted the authority of God.

More than this Jesus rebuked the Jews as foolish and slow of heart for not accepting all that the prophets had written. In Matthew 12:3, Jesus says to them, *"Have you not read what David did when he and his companions were hungry?"* This expression *"Have you not read . . . ?"* is the exact same mentality you find in Martin Luther and the Reformers who quoted Scripture and then understood the matter to be settled. You can discuss further, but the authority has been stated. This is the mentality of Jesus. One cannot with integrity take the mentality of modern negative biblical critics and transpose that mentality into the thinking of Jesus. Jesus said, *"Have you not read . . . ?"* One smashes many things, but it must be understood that one does violence in particular to Jesus' mentality toward Scripture when one does not take this posture that has been taken historically concerning the Scriptures.

Returning to John 10, we see Christ's whole attitude towards the Old Testament: *"If those to whom the word of God came were called 'gods' – and the scripture cannot be annulled . . ."* (v. 35) In other words, it is finished. "Has the scripture spoken? Well, then it is settled. The scripture cannot be wrong."

In his usage of the title *"the scripture,"* Jesus clearly recognizes and strongly underscores both the remarkable unity of the Old Testament and its uniqueness over all other writings. We think of the numerous cross references in the Old Testament, the perfect relationship of theme and historical fact, the unity preserved in the firm Jewish list of canonical books. Jesus' use of the definite article—THE Scriptures—is overwhelming in these situations. This usage shows there is a unity to the whole. It is not like an amoeba with just indefinite boundaries. There is a total unity and a clear uniqueness of content here and it cannot be wrong. This is Jesus' attitude. To Christ, the written Old Testament was self-evidently God's Word, and that is what gave them their total authority. As soon as we embrace another attitude, it is the mentality of Jesus toward the scriptures that is smashed.

Fulfillment of Prophecy

ON A NUMBER OF OCCASIONS our Lord emphatically stated that the scriptures must be fulfilled. This would be another way of saying it cannot be broken. We think of Daniel's view of the Book of Jeremiah. (Daniel

9:11-12) In the midst of the Babylonian Captivity, Daniel says that they (Israel) are in the situation they are in for the reason Jeremiah prophesied. They had not kept the law of God. Jesus takes the same view toward prophecy. "Has it been prophesied? Well, then it will happen, don't worry, it's final."

In Matthew 5:17-18 Jesus says, *"Do not think that I have come to abolish the law or the prophets; I have come not to abolish but to fulfill. For truly I tell you, until heaven and earth pass away, not one letter, not one stroke of a letter, will pass from the law until all is accomplished."* We notice how Jesus puts the law and the prophets together. Is there anything God has spoken in the law and the prophets? Did Jeremiah prophecy that the Jews would go back after seventy years? Well, they went back. Are there portions of scripture that are not yet fulfilled? "Don't worry," says Jesus, "they will be fulfilled." The scriptures cannot be broken or changed. The scriptures cannot be wrong.

In Luke 24:25-27 we are in a time after the resurrection: *"Then he said to them, 'Oh, how foolish you are, and how slow of heart to believe all that the prophets have declared! Was it not necessary that the Messiah should suffer these things and then enter into his glory?' Then beginning with Moses and all the prophets, he interpreted to them the things about himself in all the Scriptures."* This is very striking for anybody who gives any credence at all to the knowledge and authority of Christ. There is a total unity here in the whole of the Old Testament Scriptures concerning himself. "Why are you surprised? Didn't the prophets say this would happen?"

In Luke 24:44-46 Jesus said to them, *"'These are my words that I spoke to you while I was still with you—that everything written about me in the law of Moses, the prophets, and the psalms must be fulfilled.' Then he opened their minds to understand the scriptures, and he said to them, 'Thus it is written that the Messiah is to suffer and to rise from the dead on the third day. . . .'"* What is important to see here is that these are the three technical sections of the Old Testament Scriptures. When Jesus speaks of Moses, the prophets, and the psalms he is referring to exactly what the Jews referred to as THE Scriptures. Jesus is speaking of the total unity of the Old Testament. What could be stronger? This passage after the resurrection is just as tightly knit in its structure. It would be exactly the same if someone today said they believed the Scriptures and suddenly were surprised because Jesus came back tonight. Surely God would say, "Why are you surprised? Isn't it written in the prophecies? What did you expect? Isn't it settled?" That is exactly the same attitude as Jesus' attitude toward the Scriptures. He hearkens back and says, "When I was yet with you, didn't I say that all things must be fulfilled?" There is a total structure here.

In Matthew 22:36-40 some Pharisees come to Jesus and ask him: *"'Teacher, which commandment in the law is the greatest?' He said to him, 'You shall love the Lord your God with all your heart, and with all your soul, and with all your mind.' This is the greatest and first commandment. And a second is like it:'You shall love your neighbor as yourself.' On these two commandments hang all the law and the prophets."* The intriguing thing here is that the first part (v. 37) is a quotation from Deuteronomy 6:4 but the second part (v. 39) is Leviticus 19:18. Jesus reaches back and just puts them together. It is true they are both from the Pentateuch. But nevertheless they are both equal. Leviticus—Deuteronomy it does not make any difference. They are quoted as the law of God. This has great strength. It would be the same attitude as that of a person who believes the Bible today or the sixteenth-century Reformers who would reach where they will as they put it together properly in the context and in the historical-grammatical exegesis. You can just string it together because it is the same authority. It is the law of God. This is exactly the way Jesus uses it here.

Christ quoted all parts of the Scripture alike—the law, the prophets, the writings—as the Word of God. He didn't just quote from one section and leave out the others. He quoted from the three great sections as equally the Word of God. This means that points especially contested and attacked in modern times are accepted and given by Christ without question. Modern negative criticism has especially challenged the Mosaic authorship of the Pentateuch—including Leviticus, the creation, the giving of the Law on Mt. Sinai, the flood, the history of Abraham and God's

Covenant with him, the prophecy of Daniel, the historical books, Jonah spending three days in the great fish. In contrast, Jesus just quotes from them gently, as though he is saying, "Don't you remember yesterday? Don't you remember what happened when we were walking along the road and I stopped and picked a flower?" It is just this way. Jesus quotes from these books with complete quietness. "Don't you remember how yesterday we stopped to visit Mary and Martha?" In just the same way, "Don't you understand, 'It is written? That's the way it was because it is written'." In short, Christ accepted the whole Old Testament on the same basis as did the Jews of the time.

In Luke 16:29-31 Jesus is telling about the rich man and the beggar: *"Abraham replied, 'They have Moses and the prophets; they should listen to them.' He said, 'No, father Abraham; but if someone goes to them from the dead, they will repent.' He said to him, 'If they do not listen to Moses and the prophets, neither will they be convinced even if someone rises from the dead.'"* We note that Jesus puts Moses and the prophets together again as he does in other places. For Christ, the authority of the Old Testament is final. He is saying that if the rich man's brothers do not listen to Moses and the prophets, neither will they be persuaded if one rises from the dead. Notice that this was put in Moses' mouth but that Jesus takes the authority for it. It rests on his authority.

When one begins to put these many passages together, the fabric of the thing becomes overwhelmingly strong and certain. One just adds and adds and begins to think, "How could anyone take a different view?" Some people may of course throw the whole Bible out and that is a different thing. But that is not who I am thinking of here.

In John 5:39 Jesus says, *"You search the scriptures because you think that in them you have eternal life; and it is they that testify on my behalf."* Then he continues his thought in verses 46-47, *"If you believed Moses, you would believe me, for he wrote about me. But if you do not believe what he wrote, how will you believe what I say?"* Now Jesus is not saying that you would have believed on me. That is very different. He is saying that if you would have believed Moses, if you would have accepted the statement of Moses, you would have accepted my statement because Moses wrote of me. The Jews to whom he was speaking would have accepted Moses. But Jesus is equating his words with Moses' words and that would have shocked them.

In our generation it would be entirely reversed. People today say they accept Jesus' authority in some sense but Jesus equated his authority to Moses' authority. So in Christ's day this would have moved in one direction and in ours it moves in another. In Christ's day he would have said, "Does Moses have authority? Then mine is equal." In our day Jesus would just shout to the people of our generation, "You say you take my word as something? Then Moses' word is equal." Christ equates the Old Testament with his own teaching.

Historical Persons and Events

ALTHOUGH IT MAY NOT BE QUITE AS STRIKING, it is nevertheless intriguing how Christ deals with the historical details. As we take a quick run through some of these historical events as chronology would indicate, we find Jesus reaching all the way back to Abel and saying *"from the blood of Abel to the blood of Zechariah, who perished between the altar and the sanctuary."* (Luke 11:51) He is saying, "Don't you remember? Sure you weren't there, but isn't it written? Didn't Abel die? There is this historical detail of the blood of Abel.

In Luke 17:26-27 Jesus says, *"Just as it was in the days of Noah, so too it will be in the days of the Son of Man. They were eating and drinking, and marrying and being given in marriage, until the day Noah entered the ark, and the flood came and destroyed all of them."* Here is the detail of the flood. It is just stated in this sort of off-handed way. This is the way it is going to be when I come back. He is saying, "Do you remember what it was like in the days of Noah when the flood came?" in the same way he would say, "Do you remember what it was like yesterday?" He expects them to have the same certainty of history.

In John 8:56 Jesus mentions the Jews' ancestor Abraham. In Matthew 10:15 he is dealing with a little detail and mentions Sodom and Gomorrah as an historic situation. In Luke 17:28 he references the days of Lot. In Matthew 8:11 he speaks of Abraham and Isaac and Jacob. John 6:31 speaks of their ancestors eating the manna in the wilderness. In John 3:14 Jesus speaks of Moses lifting up the serpent in the wilderness just as the Son of Man will be lifted up. In Matthew 12:3 it is David. In Luke 4:25 he speaks of the many widows in Israel in the time of Elijah when the heaven was shut up three years and six months and there was a famine in the land. In Luke 4:27 Jesus speaks of the time of Elisha the prophet and Naaman the Syrian. It is the same with all these persons and these historic situations. "Do you remember Lot? Do you remember the famine in the land?" It's the very meekness and yet the certainty of it that is so strong. It shows his attitude toward the Scriptures.

We can say this is Jesus' methodology. Christ's methodology is completely contrary to the modern negative criticism of the Bible. The negative critics have one methodology. Jesus has a very different methodology. It is as though he is choosing these minute details just to give us the feel of the framework. Now, surely that is not the reason he is doing it. It is rather because each one leads on to what he wants to say and yet this is his methodology, his mentality. It makes a fabric which if you don't treat it honestly and simply overlook the methodology and mentality of Jesus, one does violence to the whole. Jesus just reaches back to whatever it is—Abel, the serpent in the wilderness, widows in the time of Elijah, Naaman the leper—and says "*it is written*" which speaks of an historic situation that you just use as an absolute base for talking on very gently. "Don't you remember?"

Christ himself presented the Old Testament as completely and totally authoritative, not just in matters of faith and morals but in the area of history as well. For Christ, the Scriptures cannot be broken because they have the authority of God behind them.

Summary Statements

WE HAVE LOOKED BRIEFLY AT CHRIST'S claims for the Old Testament. One could give several additional studies on this subject—the claims of the Old Testament for itself, the claims of the writers of the New Testament for the Old Testament—but there are two teaching statements in the New Testament that are widely used and well-known which summarize what the Scriptures teach about revelation and inspiration. They speak of the absolute reliability of the Scriptures and the confidence we can have in God's Word.

We consider these texts here as we close even though they are usually put first. The simple truth of the matter is, as wonderful as these two passages are, we don't need them. When one sees Christ's mentality towards the Old Testament it would be enough. If these two teaching statements could be destroyed, nothing would change. But we do have them and so we value them.

> **II Timothy 3:16-17:** *"All Scripture is inspired by God and is useful for teaching, for reproof, for correction, for training in righteousness, so that everyone who belongs to God may be proficient, equipped for every good work."*

This speaks of the *nature of Scripture* and the value of the Bible, namely, that its being profitable for teaching etc. is connected with its source, that is, that it is inspired by God. The operative words in this verse are *"inspired by God."* But the English word "inspired" can be misleading because it is capable of many different meanings. It is not used here in the sense of an 'inspired performance' as though the writers are really high—really inspired. It is not as though when I read the Bible, I get a lift. Now that ought to be true, but it is not the primary meaning. It is not an inspiring book in this sense.

Literally, the word is "God-breathed." Again when we say all Scripture is God-breathed, we don't mean that it was somehow there and then God breathed upon it or God breathed into it making it a Spirit-filled book. We could say this of a lot of good Christian books, that the author was really led of God in this writing and that God really breathed into the book. We mean something much stronger. When the Scripture asserts that it is "God-breathed" it means that it is the product of the creative breath of God.

All through the Scriptures the breath of God is a figure for God's creative agency. In the Old Testament God created man by forming him from the dust of the earth and then breathing into him the breath of life. It was a creative act. Or in Psalm 33:6, speaking of creation, we read, *"By the word of the Lord the heavens were made, and all their host by the breath of his mouth."* This is always the figure for God immediately and directly creating something. So when we say that all Scripture is "God-breathed" it is an assertion that the whole Scripture is a created product of the divine mind. The Scripture as a whole owes its existence to an activity of God. It is in the highest and truest sense—his creation. This is the strongest summary statement on the nature of the Bible.

As to the quality and *extent of that inspiration*, we have seen what Christ has said about this matter. Jesus you remember said, *"The Scripture cannot be broken. . . ."* His mentality, and what is being stated here, is that the Bible down to its smallest detail is reliable. In the context of these words in John 10, Jesus is arguing with the Pharisees who accuse him of blasphemy, and he says, "Wait a minute. Isn't there somewhere back in the Old Testament where the word G-o-d is applied to mere human beings? Therefore, why are you on my back for claiming to be God when I really am God?" Jesus' argument is a bit strange, but he argues from a point conceded by both sides, for both the Pharisees and Jesus would agree that the Scripture cannot be broken. The Scripture makes no mistakes and he applies this to the most incidental, minor, inconsequential phrase in the Old Testament, for it is just an assertion out of the middle of the Book of Psalms where G-o-d is applied to human rulers. The Scripture is inspired down to the smallest detail.

II Peter 1:20-21: *"First of all you must understand this, that no prophecy of scripture is a matter of one's own interpretation, because no prophecy ever came by human will, but men and women moved by the Holy Spirit spoke from God."*

This is the strongest summary statement we have on the ***mode of inspiration***, that is, exactly 'how' the Scripture was inspired. The Greek word translated here *"moved"* means "carried along" or "borne along". Men carried along by the Holy Spirit spoke from God. If you want to think of this visually, one could think of a little cart carrying somebody along. *"Men and women moved by the Holy Spirit spoke from God."* They were borne along by Him as they spoke. The passivity of the prophets is stressed here. They are not the movers but were moved. It didn't come by the will of man. They were borne along and spoke—in contrast to their own will. It isn't man groping upward. It is something different. It is a verbalized communication from God. What is being said is that the Holy Spirit so led the human authors, that when they wrote down what they wrote down, it was exactly what God wanted them to write down. They "spoke" as his mouthpieces as they were moved by the Holy Spirit. Without abrogating their unique personalities, vocabularies, writing conventions, etc.—which are amply evident in their writings—the human authors were carried along in their writing. A careful reading of the Old Testament reveals that this is precisely what occurred. What we see there could not be described better than the picture of them being carried along by the Holy Spirit. So the Old Testament Scriptures are a created product of the divine mind and completely human at the same time.

Now all too often, unhappily, people try to prove the Bible's inspiration only by quoting this as a proof text. When they do, it tends to stick out all by itself. But I am not approaching it this way. I am using it here as a sort of summary statement of all that Christ claims for the Old Testament and all that Scripture claims for itself.

It is nice that the proof text is there. But we don't need it. And if we use the proof text without feeling the force of how beautifully it captures what the whole of Scripture claims for itself, then people sort of shrug their shoulders and say, "Well, there are only these two verses." That just isn't true. There aren't just these two verses. It's the whole structure of what the Old Testament claims for itself and what Christ and the New Testament claims for the Old Testament. How strange then to accept parts of that Bible as significant or normative in our lives, if it is a book which claims such things for itself and they are not true.

When the Scriptures are allowed to speak for themselves, they claim for themselves to be God's revelation and completely authoritative, his written communication to us in ordinary human language.

Notes

[1] I am indebted for much of the material concerning Christ's claims to the L'Abri Fellowship lecture by Francis Schaeffer, "The Bible's Evaluation of Itself, New Testament—Part 6."

[2] All Scripture quotations are from the New Revised Standard Version.

James Arne Nestingen was first affiliated with Luther Seminary as an instructor from 1976-78. After serving two years as assistant to the pastor of St. Ansgar Lutheran Church in Toronto, Canada, he returned to Luther Seminary as assistant professor of church history in 1980. He was named professor of church history in 1992 and professor emeritus of church history in 2006.

A graduate of Concordia College, Moorhead, Minnesota, in 1967, Nestingen earned the master of divinity degree from Luther Seminary in 1971 and the master of theology degree in 1978. He received his doctorate in theology from St. Michael's College, University of Toronto, in 1984. Following his ordination in 1971, he served as pastor of Faith Lutheran Church in Coquille, Oregon, for three years before becoming curriculum editor at Augsburg Publishing House from 1974 to 1976.

Nestingen has written and spoken prolifically on Luther's catechisms and confessional Lutheran theology. In March 2001, he was one of the featured speakers at The Book of Concord Lectures held at Luther Seminary, which celebrated the latest translation of The Book of Concord and discussed its relevance for the twenty-first century.

Nestingen's books include: *Martin Luther: His Life and His Teachings* (2004, 1982) *Manger in the Mountains* (2000); *The Faith We Hold* (1983); *Roots of Our Faith* (1978); and *Free to Be* (with Gerhard Forde, 1975).

❧ 12 ❧

Scriptural Authority in the Lutheran Confessions

James Arne Nestingen

THE WORD ALONE" IS ONE of three exclusive sayings of the Lutheran reformers, with "grace alone" and "faith alone." As much effort as they put into clarifying grace and faith, however, the Lutheran confessions pay scant attention to the authority of the word. Through all of the early confessions—Luther's catechisms, the Augsburg Confession and Apology, the Smalcald Articles and the Treatise—it is assumed without ever really being defined. The issue really doesn't get taken up until "The Rule and Norm," the traditional name for what serves as an introduction to the Formula of Concord. But even there, the discussion doesn't focus so much on the origins of Scripture—there is no talk of inerrancy or infallibility, for example, and no theory of verbal inspiration—as much as it focuses on the function of the Bible in relation to traditions.

This strange silence has troubled later Lutherans. The Lutheran Church—Missouri Synod, in fact, has corrected the problem. In a church convention not so long past, Missourians officially adopted a supplemental statement spelling out a doctrine of authority now required by the church. Commenting on the Evangelical Lutheran Church in America's failure to provide further definition, Jacob A.O. Preus argued that the ELCA lives in fantasyland and that it wouldn't be long before virtually anything would go. Listening to discussions at ELCA assemblies, reading the reports afterwards, Preus sounds prophetic. Anything does go. The 2007 Chicago Assembly, in fact, claimed the authority to select which biblical law to enforce. Apparently God didn't get a vote—there must not be a quota category for divinity.

Given this situation, it seems worthwhile to make explicit what is implicit in the earlier Lutheran confessions, tracing out what they assume about the authority of Scripture. That summarized, the contribution of the Formula of Concord can be examined.

I

THE CONFESSION DISCUSSION of authority develops around the term word of God. The confessions use it in three senses, to speak of Christ, of Scripture and of preaching. But the critical point is a shift from what might be called a significative or referential understanding of authority to the performative.

First, last and always, the term word of God refers to Christ Jesus. John 1 and Hebrews 1 drive this reference: "in the beginning was the Word and the Word became flesh and dwelt among us" (John 1:1, 18); "in many and various ways God spoke through the men of old but now in these last days he has spoken to us by his son" (Hebrews 1:1,2). The term logos in John comes replete with all kinds of Greek philosophical overtones, enough to keep exegetes off the streets for a long time. But at bottom, the sense of both passages revolves around the English sense of the word "expression." People are said to express themselves in word, that is, put themselves out or make themselves available to their hearers. In the same way, Christ Jesus is God's self-expression, God becoming known in human terms.

Secondly, in the earlier Lutheran confessions the term word of God refers to the Scripture. Characteristically, the confessions do not speak of the authority of Scripture by describing its origin or qualities, but focus on its function or impact. The precedent comes from John 20:31, ". . . these things are written so that you may come to believe that Jesus is the Messiah, the Son of God, and through believing you may have life in his name," and from Romans 15:4, "Whatever was written in the former days was written for our instruction, so that by steadfastness and by the encouragement of scriptures we might have hope." Scripture is the word of God because it declares God's word, that is, it presents Christ Jesus in his person and works.

To be sure, the confessions recognize that the Scripture does other things as well. It declares the law as well as the gospel, requiring careful distinction so that both are proclaimed—considerations that continue throughout, from Luther's explanations of the commandments in the catechisms to Articles IV, V and VI of the Formula of Concord. The Scripture also provides the definitive resource for doctrine, a point particularly important to Melanchthon in the Apology and his students in the Formula.

But this said, the Lutheran confessions unabashedly set a strong priority on the gospel, clearly working with a canon within the canon. Like the church as a whole, they pay much closer attention to books like John, Romans and Galatians than to Jude or 2 Peter. These books exercise greater authority, showing up much more commonly in reference, because they preach Christ with such clarity and power. As Luther himself said in The Bondage of the Will, "Christ is the Lord of Scripture. Take Christ out and what do you have left?"

That, by the way, was Luther's problem with the Book of James. The whole letter makes only one reference to Christ and that formulaic. Observing this, Luther called it "a bell without a clapper"—Christ does not ring out of it. Still, in his translations, he did not take James out of the canon but kept testing it, wondering if he might hear something that he had previously missed.

The third use of the term "word of God" follows out of the first and second as the word expressed in Christ and declared in Scripture gets up on its hind legs and preaches. Scripture is the word of God because it preaches Christ Jesus; preaching becomes the word of God insofar as he is proclaimed.

To be sure, the law must have its place in proclamation. Preachers are called to this proclamation with the proviso that they know the difference: the law can never be more than pen-ultimate, the gospel alone is ultimate; the law addresses externals, the gospel takes the heart; the law addresses behavior, the gospel faith. The distinction made, Christ Jesus loans the preacher's mouth to Moses, the law speaker, but provisionally with the purpose of reclaiming it for his own work.

When in the Smalcald Articles Luther lists "the mutual conversation and consolation of the brothers and sisters" as one of the means of grace, it becomes clear that preaching is not simply limited to the pulpit. It happens wherever Christians speak the word to one another. As Gerhard Forde argued, the means of grace are confessionally interpreted not on the basis of paucity or shortage but by flood logic, sheer, wanton excess—the wedding at Cana, for example, with all of that wine spilling over or the feeding of the five thousand, with baskets of leftovers. When Christ Jesus goes to work, that is what happens: grace overflows.

Describing the word of God referentially, however, as important as the references are, serves only as a starting point for the critical point: God's word does what it says. As Luther wrote early in his vocation as a theologian, "The law says 'do this' and it is never done. The gospel says "believe in this" and it is done already.

It may be helpful at this point to make a distinction between the significative or referential use of language and the performative. Generally, in an argument going all the way back to Augustine, words are said to signify things. So upon reading or hearing a particular word, the hearer supplies the connection between what the word says and what it means, thereby understanding or interpreting. This description of the workings of language functions very well in describing the communication of information and the declaration of the law. But there is another use of language in which words overflow what they signify or actually accomplish what they declare.

Biblically as well as confessionally, this is the critical point. In Scripture, God creates by speaking—so Genesis 1, "God said . . . and it was so." By the same token the miracles of the Gospels with rare exception happen under the power of the divine word—"that you may know that the Son of God has authority on earth to forgive sins, I say to you, 'Rise, take up your pallet and walk." (Mark 2) So Jesus also says, "Whoever hears you hears me and whoever hears me hears the one who sent me." (Mark 9) God's self-expression in the word, because it is God's own word, bears all the power of God not only in Christ's speaking but in the witness of the community.

The classical statement of this point in the Lutheran Confessions takes place in Augustana V: "To obtain such faith (that is, the faith that justifies) God has instituted the means of grace, that is, provided the word and the sacraments. Through these as through means he works faith, when and where he pleases, in those who hear the gospel." Because the very power of God in Christ has been invested in the speaking of the word, "faith comes by hearing." (Romans 10) The word that created and in Christ's mouth, healed and freed, by the same power calls forth faith in its hearers.

The degenerate pietism that dogs Lutherans in the United States works from a different assumption. Blind to the transparent arrogance of such statements, it speaks of dead faith and dying congregations, promising to enliven them by enlisting the willpower of its adherents as though by some mystical transformation, old sinners will gather and will themselves into new being. The same piety goes on to speak of the Lutheran Confessions as a deposit out of the past that needs to be supplemented by the latest church growth techniques to become effective. In fact, once having kissed such blarney stones, the church just jabbers on and on, loquacious and simultaneously wordless, unable to tell the difference between the new birth and yet another News Years resolution.

God speaks in judgment and grace. The word of judgment condemns and puts to death the old sinner; the word of grace forgives sinners, raises the dead and so creates anew. The miracle of the gospel continues in

121

that God has made this word a human word, fit for the lips of sinners that in its speaking, literally does faith, hope and love to its hearers.

The confessional emphasis on the power of the word exposes a parallel, though the proportions are much more proximate, in human speech. As much as people use language significatively or referentially, a whole range of language depends on its power. The meaning of the four letter words that show up in profanity are buried so deep in their Anglo-Saxon origins that philologists can hardly find them. But it doesn't take long before even a child can figure out their function. Profanity has to be regulated because of its power. Similarly, words of love literally become "sweet nothings," hackneyed and cliché ridden at the level of meaning but overflowing with power as spoken by lover and beloved. Love literally gets made by such speech. If the words of sinners can gain such force, God's word has to be in a league by itself.

In the sixteenth century, Erasmus raised the objection now commonly made complaining of the ambiguity of Scripture. Luther replied in one of his most important works, *The Bondage of the Will*. While acknowledging the occasional uncertain biblical passage, he argued that the overwhelming clarity of the message of Scripture illuminates those verses that remain obscure. This clarity makes Scripture sufficient to itself. It requires no additional authority—be it biblical scholar, church assembly or pope—to certify its meaning.

II.

SOME FORTY YEARS, MORE THAN A GENERATION, elapsed between the time of the earlier confessions—up to and including the Treatise on the Power and Primacy of the Pope—and the final drafting the Formula of Concord. The intervening years had brought some important changes. In the middle 1530s, Roman Catholicism still set the table in the ecumenical discussion; in the middle 1570s, Lutherans had legally separated from Catholicism only to be challenged by a new opponent, the Calvinists. In the middle 1530s, Luther and Melanchthon still led the Lutheran reform; in the mid-seventies, another generation had taken over.

Given these changes, the Formula of Concord faced some pressures unknown to the earlier confessors. For one thing, the Calvinists had effectively filled in the blanks, developing a doctrine of verbal inspiration to buttress the biblical priority. For another, for all of its biblical orientation, Lutheranism had clearly become a tradition. The authors of the Formula looked to Luther's Small Catechism as "the laymen's Bible," invoking it with reverence, and looking back on the earlier reformation, announced their loyalty: "we are minded to manufacture nothing new." Understandable and laudable as it may have been, this loyalty provoked a question of its standing in relationship to the biblical word.

Given this situation, the Formula sets out to establish the biblical priority and then puts tradition in its place. Of the Scripture, it says: "We believe, teach, and confess that the only rule and guiding principle according to which all teachings and teachers are to be evaluated and judged are the prophetic and apostolic writings of the Old and New Testament alone . . ." (Kolb and Wengert, 486.1) This places other sources, such as the ecumenical creeds and the prior confessions, at a secondary level. So ". . . Holy Scripture alone remains the only judge, rule and guiding principle, according to which, as the only touchstone, all teachings should and must be recognized and judged. . . ." Authoritative texts outside the Scripture ". . . are only witnesses and explanations of the faith, which show how Holy Scripture has at various times been understood and interpreted in the church of God. . . ." (487.8)

The traditional way of describing the two levels of authority set by the Formula uses the Latin terms, *norma Normans, norma normata*. The Scripture, in the participial construction, provides the norm that norms. Other statements, including the creeds and the confessions themselves, are norms only in so far as they have previously been normed by the Scripture.

The Formula of Concord makes a very important contribution in this distribution of authority. The slogans word alone and its variant, *sola*

Scriptura or Scripture alone, have commonly been misinterpreted as anti-thetical to tradition. In fact, the human community cannot exist without traditions. Rather, as Gerhard Ebeling argues in the title essay of his collection of confessional essays, The Word of God and Tradition, instead of attempting to eliminate it, the Formula subjects all tradition to critical test—its facilitation of the proclamation of Christ Jesus.

While the Formula of Concord's treatment of Scripture completes the confessional discussion, it did not settle the question even for the next generation. Even though it didn't produce a doctrine of inspiration in the confessions, even a cursory reading of his commentaries shows that Luther assumed the Spirit's inspiration of the text. Given that fact and as well as the Calvinist critique, the orthodox theologians of the seventeenth century went the next step, insisting on the Holy Spirit's inspiration of the full text of Scripture, additionally making it a fixture of the Lutheran argument. The Lutheran Church-Missouri Synod can therefore claim ample precedent for setting an extra-biblical, extra-confessional standard.

Should the ELCA do the same? Clearly, Jack Preus' derisive comment about fantasyland deserves some further consideration. Even in the late 1980s, it was hard to imagine the deconstruction of the biblical text that has become so much a part of the discussion of biblical, sexual standards. Ambiguity has become a hermeneutical principle so that whenever the Scripture challenges the mores of the upper middle class—which provides most of the students at seminaries and with rare exception, all of the faculty—someone is sure to pop up with claims to multiple possibilities of interpretation and the consequent assurance that the text has lost its standing. Openness has its own naïve way of imposing closure. Under such terms, no conversation seems likely.

There is, however, the assurance of Scripture itself along with Article V concerning the power of the word. The ambiguity argument rests on the assumption that the word functions only at a significative level, that meaning is what you make it. The Lutheran witness rests on the assumption that the risen Christ has broken loose by his Spirit in the word, that even now he is seeking and saving the lost. If such a promise no longer captures the heart of the ELCA, there are still enough sinners around to let it rip and have some fun.

Jeffray Greene is an ELCA pastor, ordained in 1989. He has served parishes in Phoenix and Tucson, Arizona, La Habra, California, and is currently serving American Lutheran Church in Rantoul, Illinois, as the senior pastor. He holds degrees in History, Geography, a Master of Divinity, and a Ph.D. in Church Administration. His dissertation was on the historic development of the constitutions of the Lutheran Churches in the United States. He has served on many boards and commissions, and is currently serving as the editor for FOCL Point, a quarterly newsletter based in Northern California that is concerned with upholding a Confessional consistency in the Lutheran Church. He has been active on the national scene, working with many groups and organizations, offering his expertise in constitutions.

Married to his wife Lorene for twenty-two years, they are the parents of three energetic children—Rosalynne, Dane and Alisa. Together, the family maintains an active church and social life, as well as personal activities. Pastor Greene says it takes time to grow the Gospel in someone's heart, so he enjoys framing, concrete work and fixing almost anything while he waits. He's an avid reader who loves movies, enjoys learning, and sharing what he has learned with others.

Raised on the Central Coast of California, and now serving in the Heartland, has given interesting insights to some of the issues that are facing the church in our time. Above all the knowledge, degrees and

experience, he relies on the overwhelming supremacy of the grace of Jesus Christ and the promises of God to work all things for glory. It is on the authority of Christ, the Word Incarnate that his hope, work and passion are lived out in daily life.

What Belongs and
What Does Not?

Jeffray Greene

THE ELCA, IN ITS STATEMENT of faith, declares that Scripture is the source and norm for faith and life in this church. We have spent a great amount of time questioning Scripture's source with a critical method of study, and are currently locked in a debate over its ability as a means for declaring how it can be used as a norm for faith and life.

We argue about what belongs and what does not. We argue about whether or not God has spoken with certain words, or whether they are merely transmitted concepts locked in a particular time and for a particular situation. If we do not understand what we mean with this constitutional and historic declaration of Scripture as the source and norm for our faith, we can by no means come to a consensus of how to use Scripture with authority, even though our statement of faith declares that this is our intent: that we consistently and commonly agree upon an understanding of how to live a life of faith.

A group of pharisees came to Jesus and asked Him by what authority He was doing the things He did. Jesus said to them, "I will ask you a question; answer me, and I will tell you by what authority I do these things. Was the baptism of John from heaven or from men?

Answer me." And they argued with one another, "If we say, 'From heaven,' he will say, 'Why then did you not believe him?' But shall we say, 'From men?'"—they were afraid of the people, for all held that John was a real prophet. So they answered Jesus, "We do not know." And Jesus said to them, "Neither will I tell you by what authority I do these things." (Mark 11:29-33 NSV)

Those who confronted Jesus wanted to stop Him, but fear of God and fear of the people kept them from accomplishing what they desired. They wanted to be rid of this confrontation of the Word. "From where does the power come which causes the things you are doing to be done," they asked? It is always a legitimate question to ask anyone who is wielding power by what authority do they do these things?

Scripture tells us very important things in this discussion that can help us move to the ultimate source of authority, which is God. In the beginning, God created all things. There is a revelation of Scripture which proclaims that everything that exists comes from God. God is the One by whom all things have their being. The source of all power emanates from God. A concept introduced in Scripture is that this power of creation comes through the Word. Was the baptism done by John a creative act of God? The people believed it was.

"In the beginning was the Word, and the Word was with God, and the Word was God. He was in the world, and the world was made through him, yet the world knew him not." (John 1:1, 10) Words have power, and the Word of God is the power of God revealed. In the state of sin, we are unable to comprehend the Word.

The basis of authority for the church must always be taken from within its historic context. The Ecumenical Councils that produced the Creeds which the ELCA upholds in its Confession of faith, are drawn from the continuity of the struggle to uphold a faithful witness to the revelation of God's power by the authority granted to the church to be an incarnation of God's Word with a consistent and truthful proclamation. The tensions and conflicts that have emanated from an ongoing struggle over God's proclamation as the source and norm for faith and life continue into our present age, and we must not look in an isolated way at these struggles, but see them in light of the tensions and conflicts of ages past. We need to recognize and affirm the decisions made by those who have passed along the faith to us in order that we may pass it along to future generations. If we are to carry the baton of God's authority and power—it must be His; for if it does not come from God, it is illusory, and nothing more than our imaginations captivated by sin. And God's people will bear out His truth over time.

Before we dive into a discussion of authority and power, however, we need to understand what we mean by the use of the word, "Word." If we are to discern what we mean by the declaration of God, which we call the "Word," we should come to a common understanding of what is meant, beginning our focus on the words "authority" and "power," culminating in a discussion of the word, "Word."

In the development of language, there is history, culture, and human experience which cause words to come to a place where they have specific meanings within specific contexts. The truth is always present in the true Word, for God is unchanging, but conveying the truth becomes clouded by ever-changing meanings and contexts of words and their uses. A battle over fundamentalism in the church has raged for centuries based on looking merely at the words presented without seeking understanding from context and historical understanding of the words as spoken in time and place. If we follow the trail of these words, we can further elaborate our discussion and bring about greater understanding.

The word for authority comes from the Latin *auctoritatem* (nom. *auctoritas*), which means "invention, advice, opinion, influence, or command." It is further derived from *auctor,* or "author," but from which we also derive the word, "actor." We see from Scripture that God is both the inventor of creation as well as the author of history, and seen centered in the Word, the main actor of history, which is why we declare in our statement of faith that God both inspired Scripture and was in the midst of creation through the Incarnation of the Word. God's declaration seeks to influence humanity with advice and command, both of which are in abundance in this device we call the Word; what we mean when we say, "Scripture." The Incarnation, who is Jesus Christ, also gave command and advice concurrent with the Word we call Scripture. It is for this reason that we can say that canonical Scripture records and announces God's revelation, centering in Jesus Christ, and is the authoritative source and norm for faith and life.

The second word introduced in this discussion is the word "power," derived from the Latin, *potens,* from which we also derive the word, "potential." Humanity's potential comes from God alone. This particular word also derives meaning in our context through the Greek word *kyros*, which we translate as "Lord"; also meaning power and/or authority. During our corporate worship, we sing or say a *Kyrie*, calling on the power of God among us, who is the Lord, to act upon us for the Creator's sake. There is a double-entendre here which is both title, acknowledgment of whom we are addressing, as well as a power or action that will be effected amongst the gathered by His presence. It is both noun, in the Greek sense, and verb in the Hebrew sense. It is the Lord of all creation, from whom all authority and power comes, requested to be in our midst with grace and mercy acting upon His people to perform His will. It is for this reason that the message of the Gospel, which is the Incarnation of God through the Word, is declared to be the power of God to create and sustain the church for God's mission in the world.

From Middle English, the Greek word *kyros* comes down to us as *chirche*. Notice that this word is the same as the Modern German word for church. Therefore, we see authority and power emanating through the church, but its source always remains as coming from God. The *chirche*, the church, is not an authority unto itself, but a physical declaration of God's authority lived out through the living body of Christ which is called the church. In order to be a true declaration filled with God's power, sinfulness must be displaced with God's truth revealed. The church does hold authority in the right proclamation of God's Word, and understanding "right" proclamation has also been a source of contention for the church. These struggles have emanated from seeking to understand what the truthful proclamation of God's Word is. In no small part, this is an essential ingredient that brought about the Reformation.

As the church has struggled through the ages to hold fast to a right proclamation of God's Word, the church has debated what this right proclamation looks like and how it is effected. The intent of the right proclamation of God's Word was a point argued and decided upon with this church's "Galesburg Rule," born over a controversy of who should or should not be allowed at the Lord's table, and who should or should not preside at the table, and how a right proclamation of the Word of God was to be upheld and protected.

The "Galesburg Rule" resulted from a Nineteenth Century concern for upholding truth in the midst of contemporary struggles and pressures to modify the understood order of things. In his comments concerning the issuance of this rule by the General Council in 1877, Charles Porterfield Krauth said, "If the present division of Christendom can be justified, if the so-called denominationalism is to stand before the judgement bar of God, it must be able to show a ground of supreme necessity for its existence. Unless a denomination has a divine warrant for its separate existence, it is simply a sect. If it claims no divine warrant, but alleges mere human convenience or preference for its existence, it is a self-convicted sect." If the authority by which we do things is not from God, then we are, in the words of Krauth, a self-convicted sect and not in compliance with the Word, His bride, the church, or the truth that God has eternally declared. We therefore would have no authority nor power to do the things we do. It is for this very reason that we do well to ask the question, "By what authority do we do these things?"

All power and authority come from God. And God has revealed Himself through the Word. Note that the word, *Word*," is intentionally capitalized throughout this essay. This is intentional because there is a double-entendre in the use of this particular set of letters, meaning both what God has declared, and the Incarnation of God's power and authority in time and space in the person of Jesus Christ. It is a formal granting of respect to the One through whom all things have their being.

God has revealed Himself through the Incarnation, that is, by becoming flesh and dwelling among us. This is a declaration of God's power in the flesh. Two forms should be understood about God's revelation. One, through the life, death, resurrection and ascension of the power of God, the Word, Jesus Christ; and two, in the revelation of Scripture, given to the church, as it becomes incarnate through God's power and authority revealed—a revelation of His power on earth in contemporary time and space. God's advice, instruction and command are given through the declared Word, inspired by the Holy Spirit, notably present through the Sacraments, with the mixing of the creation and God's Word, to incarnate the image of Christ in the individual who believes and has been given the power to become a child of God.

In a very Hebrew fashion, this is an example of both/and logic upon which Hebrew understanding is built. When the word, "Word," is used, it connotes both God's revelation through Scripture of the Incarnation and its ongoing revelation through the proclamation of the "Word" in and for the church. Because God declares that He is unchanging, the Word proclaimed purely must be unchanging. Changes in words used are only to regain understanding from the continuous perversion in sinful humanity's proclivity to moderate a word's original meaning. But because sinful humanity is given the potential (note that this is also derived from the same Latin word for "power") to proclaim the Word, sinful humanity can equally choose, in rebellion, to misuse the Word for their own ends and proclaim a false word which has neither power nor authority.

We see this in the reality of words that ever-migrate from their original meaning, often to a perversity of their original intent in communication. This makes it a difficult process in hermeneutics because we must constantly seek for a pure proclamation, to bring truthful understanding of what God has declared and is declaring in contemporary situations. It is in this process used by sinful people that the church finds itself constantly at odds over particular understandings of what God means, in contrast with specific declarations that have been handed down to us over the ages.

We need to further understand that there is a seamless intertwining of power, Word, church and authority, all of which derive their origin from God, and are given for His purpose. When it comes to questioning whether or not something is truly of God, we do well to use the wisdom of Gamaliel and recognize that if it is of God, it will flourish, but if it is not, it will meet its own demise. For authority and power to be truly authority and power, they must come from God.

Time is the element which sets all things on their true and correct course. History teaches us through the wisdom of the early church Fathers to pay attention to particularities that were argued over and resolved long ago. The church has made declaration of what is the true Word through Scripture, passing to us canon, the creeds and the faith understood; passed on by those with whom we declare fellowship when we proclaim we believe in the communion of saints.

The church has also told us what is true Word in the understandings of the proclamations that have been handed down to us over the ages. This is why we further declare the understanding of our faith in terms of what the creeds tell us and as they have been passed down through the ages. The unique understanding of God the Word declared, and co-equal and of One being with the Father and the Holy Spirit in Trinity in eternity.

Credo in Deum Patrem omnipotentem; Creatorem coeli et terrae. God Omnipotent, Almighty, Father Son and Holy Spirit, Creator of the earth. We have a definitive declaration in the creeds of our faith, passed along through the great ecumenical councils, as one that is Trinitarian in creation, Scriptural in proclamation, understanding the Word as co-creator of all things, clearly specified in the *filioque* (Latin, *the son*) of the Nicene Creed. Introducing a heresy of thinking that one can come to God apart from God as a faithful Christian witness is silliness in light of what we declare to be true. If one wants to meet God, one must meet God. To say that another can stand in God's place and be seen as the same is axiomatic and not the truth. Our Confession of faith declares that the Word centers in life, mission, ministry, death, resurrection of God the Word, the fulness of God's revelation, Jesus Christ. There is no other way to meet God.

If we are to use what Scripture teaches us from the life and ministry of Jesus, we must also incorporate an understanding of the means by which this understanding has come to us. If we hold the revelation of the Incarnation as being truly a revelation of God's power for creation, then we do well to understand the means by which He has delivered His authority into our hands. Simply put, God has delivered His power through the Word to the church, which is the incarnation of His power on earth continuing, centering on the life, death and resurrection of the Incarnate Word, Jesus Christ. That does not mean that a particular sect or denomination holds the power of God, but that God's power is revealed through the One Holy catholic church, which is also an incarnation of the Word. Wherever the truth of God is delivered and received, there is the church. Wherever the truth of God is not delivered, there is a sectarian rebellion against the truth.

Indeed, throughout the ages, the Word has been misused for humanity's own purpose, but in order to be consistent with God's intended proclamation, we need to understand the purpose of what God has declared. We declare that the Word Incarnate suffered, died, was resurrected and ascended, using the words of the Creeds, which the church catholic has given us from ages past.

This is God's message to a rebellious people: that He will cause the same process to be experienced for those who come to Him through His Word—to die, be resurrected and ascend to God's presence and purpose. The Law kills, but the Word resurrects. We cannot, nor should not, if we are to be faithful to what we declare as being the truth, separate judgement and mercy, word and deed, law and Gospel.

Therefore, the purpose of God's declaration is made each time we gather for corporate worship, when we confess and receive absolution, stating our need and God's action that causes us to die to self and be resurrected for God's purpose of living in accordance with His Word. We proclaim judgement and claim mercy. We seek empowerment to make God's Word active in us. It is only in this first step that we begin the journey of living a life of faith and coming to that place where the

Incarnation becomes knowable. "If we say we have no sin, we deceive ourselves and the truth is not in us," is the beginning of declaring the truth that resurrects us from death to life.

Without reiterating the catechesis in full, we should agree that the catholic faith teaches us that the summation of the Law, which Jesus gave with, "Love the Lord your God with all your heart and soul and mind; and love your neighbor as yourself." The Law broken declares the penalty of death. The Gospel proclaims forgiveness in repentance to those who, by the power of the Holy Spirit, seek God's Word as the final Word for faith and life; that the Word took upon Himself the penalty of our lawlessness. Law and Gospel are directives which set our purpose to be about bringing life in a place of death when we say we abide in the Word of God. A simple catechetical conclusion should cause us to ask the question, "Will what I am contemplating bring life or death?" Does this authority I claim promote life, or death? If it promotes life, it may be from God. If it is God's will, the power is from Him. If it promotes death, it cannot be from God. God is the author of life. Sin is the author of death. Death is the recompense of sin, which is why Scripture declares, "the sting of the Law is death;" sin produces death. It is not that the Law kills, but that the breaking of the Law brings death. God simply declares the means by which life exists, and that is living in His will; living according to His purpose, and coming to Him through His declared means, which is the Word. It is the only way to life from the death created by sin. This is why Jesus said, "I am the way, the truth and the life; no one comes to the Father but through me." (John 14:6)

Contemporary exegesis seeks to understand Scripture in light of its context, intended meaning, and applicable use. It is not simply a matter of arguing over whether or not one particular set of words is valid, but whether or not the words used are in accordance with God's intended purpose of bringing life to a place filled with death.

Luther did not see value in the Epistle of James, declaring it as an Epistle of straw. Yet, he was unwilling to argue that it be excluded from the writ handed down by the early church, because he recognized the power and authority that handed down this particular writ. Luther respected the authority and power of the church catholic, even though he found aspects of what was practiced in the name of the church troubling and problematic within its contemporary context. We do well to learn from his example to not make light of what has been given us. Indeed, it may seem that one portion of what we've been handed is not particularly useful and even problematic in a contemporary context, but if we are to remain constant and truthful to the continuity of the faith delivered, we do not have permission, nor the power, to dismiss outright what has been handed down. For if it is of God, then it comes with His authority and power. It meets us in our sin for the purpose of confronting that sin, killing it in order to bring life. It is in understanding the power of Scripture to kill sin that we discover what we mean in our statement of faith when we say that Scripture is the "norm" for faith and life. It creates not only the standard by which life in faith is to be lived, but also the advice and commands understood within the original meaning of authority by which a life of faith is lived.

When sinful humanity confronts the Word in order to dismiss the Word's purpose to bring life, the answer of the Word seems unclear. "Neither will I tell you by what authority I do these things." But when the Incarnation is experienced, it becomes very clear that the full power and authority of God is revealed. "By their fruits, you will know them," Jesus taught His followers.

It doesn't matter if someone seems to have power or authority, for if it is not of God, it is neither power, nor authority in the true sense. What matters is that the power and authority of God is revealed through His Word. Because of the unchanging character of God, we do well to seek to move beyond our sinful selves and be recipients of God's authority and power through His Word incarnated in our midst.

If it is of God, it will bring life. If it is not of God, it will lead to death. God gave strict warning and command to those who would come in His Name that they neither add to, nor take away from His Word revealed. We do well to take to heart what God has declared and walk in grace toward the light of the revealed Word, who is Christ, known through the Word of God inspired. So it is always appropriate to ask, "By what authority do you do these things?" We might also ask, "For what purpose do you use this authority?" That is, to ask Luther's catechetical question, "What does this mean?"

Those who wield authority as from God, do well to make sure it is from God, recognizing the Word's admonition of judgement for those who wield power in God's name. A Lutheran understanding, the hermeneutic of the Word, always holds a tension between two evident and present points. It is not law or Gospel, it is both. It is not Scripture or Christ, it is Word and Word. It is not wielding power and authority over those who are to submit, but submitting to the Word in the power and authority of God. It is always time to die to the self, that the Word might resurrect God's purpose to His authority and power in a sinful world. May the Word Incarnate reveal His Word in us, that we walk in the true authority and power of the Living God, thereby being equipped by the power of His Holy Spirit to give an account of the hope that is within us.

Frederick W. Baltz is Pastor of St. Matthew Lutheran Church in Galena, Illinois, where he also directs Bible Alive, a unique Bible learning center complete with a planetarium. He is married to Cindia, and they have four children. Dr. Baltz has written confirmation curriculum and several books including: *As of First Importance: A Theology and Practice of Evangelism for Mainline Churches*; *Lazarus and the Fourth Gospel Community* which identifies the enigmatic "Disciple Whom Jesus Loved"; and a historical novel, *Herod*. With his son Warren, a computer illustrator, he has developed a video: "Herod's Temple, the Temple Jesus Knew" available through Vision Video.

Dr. Baltz graduated from Dana College in Blair, Nebraska. He has an M.Div. degree from Wartburg Seminary, an S.T.M. degree also from Wartburg Seminary and a D.Min. from the University of Dubuque Theological Seminary. His primary areas of writing and study are the New Testament and the ministry of evangelism.

Among other activities he serves as Vice Chair of the Board of Directors of the WordAlone Network, and President of the Board of Education for Galena Unit District 120 in Illinois.

❧ 14 ☙

Scripture Authorizes Women

Frederick W. Baltz

FOR NEARLY FORTY YEARS THE MAJORITY of Lutherans in the United States have ordained women to the ministry of Word and Sacrament. In 1970 decisions were reached by conventions of The Lutheran Church in America (LCA) and The American Lutheran Church (ALC) to change the previous policies of the respective bodies. Lutheran state churches in Europe had already begun ordaining women years before this, but in North America no such change could take place without the affirmative votes of a majority of representatives from the churches gathered in their respective conventions.

A survey of the process leading to these votes is enlightening and instructive for all concerned with the question of whether Scripture is truly considered the final authority among ELCA Lutherans today. A review of the events of that time will show that the decision to ordain women to the ministry was not made primarily on the basis of Scripture, but rather to keep pace with secular, societal changes. The decision to ordain women was the right decision, but a decision not reached with the Scriptures as the primary voice. A flawed method with its underlying assumptions was carried forward and remains in use. The potential consequences of that method now threaten to lead to decisions that are neither correct, nor scriptural.

It is sometimes said that the church has decided rightly in the past to go against the teaching of Scripture on matters including slavery, the ordination of women, and divorce. This generalization has no basis in fact, but falsely presupposes that the Scriptures really do support the institution of slavery, prohibit the full inclusion of women in the church, and consign all troubled marriages to unceasing misery and even at times violence. This serious misunderstanding of the Scriptures, I submit, is a direct result of the flawed method described above.

The Biblical Texts

THE STUDENT OF SCRIPTURE WHO PURSUES the general question of what leadership role rightly belongs to women in the church encounters texts that seem to be in conflict. The fact is this: those specific texts that seem to prohibit women from any role that would require authority over men, therefore precluding the later concept of ordination, constitute a minority over against a majority of texts that require women's full inclusion in leadership.

Texts interpreted as against the ordination of women . . .

THE FOLLOWING TEXTS ARE CITED BY THOSE who believe women should not hold positions in church leadership that make them equal to men. To these we might also add statements like Ephesians 5:22 and 1 Peter 3:1, which state that women should be subordinate to men, or subject to men. While not directly addressing the authority question as far as leadership is concerned, the latter do reflect a culture in which male leadership is considered normative.

1 Corinthians 14:33b-35 . . ."*As in all the churches of the saints, women should be silent in the churches. For they are not permitted to speak, but should be subordinate as the law also says. If there is anything they desire to know, let them ask their husbands at home. For it is shameful for a woman to speak in church.*"

1 Timothy 2:11-12 (RSV) . . . "*Let a woman learn in silence with full submission.I permit no woman to teach or to have authority over a man; she is to keep silent.*"

In the case of the 1 Corinthians passage scholars have long noted that the oldest manuscripts give these words in two different places, and that in neither setting do they relate directly to the subject being discussed by Paul. This raises the question of whether they were ever part of Paul's Corinthian correspondence, a question made more cogent by the widely-held opinion that 1 and 2 Corinthians is really not a straightforward set of two letters, but rather includes at least part of a third letter within the second. In other words, we already have reason to suspect that the Corinthian correspondence is not just as Paul wrote it. Thus, many who have devoted their lives to the in-depth study of Paul and his writings believe 1 Corinthians 14:33b-35 is an interpolation into Paul's actual letter, made by someone who did not share Paul's views on the extent to which women should participate in leadership. Scholars reach this conclusion precisely because of what Paul himself says about women elsewhere. If these words are not an interpolation, they may have been written due to practices among the followers of the Eleusian mystery religion or the Delphi cult. Both these religions existed in the region of Corinth. There is reason to believe that women practiced ecstatic speech in these religions, and Paul may have meant to draw a line of demarcation between that behavior and Christian worship. That would explain, at least to some extent, the apparent conflict between the directive in 1 Corinthians against women speaking in church and the clear openness to women's full participation elsewhere.

In the 1 Timothy passage, it should be noted, Paul writes, "I permit . . ." While male-led home and marriage was indeed the norm for

Jews through centuries before and after Paul, his words here bring to mind what he writes in 1 Corinthians 7:12: "To the rest I say—I and not the Lord . . ." Paul can distinguish his opinion, which he might strongly urge a church to accept, while still not claiming to speak for the Lord. It is what Paul says in favor of women at other places that requires us to consider that possibility here. We shall not even open the subject of whether Paul is really the author, or whether someone has written the letter in his name. The letter has been accepted as part of the canon of the New Testament. However, for some this will be an additional issue. In summary, Paul's, "I permit no . . ." may mean "I Paul, but not the Lord, permit no..." Even that is hard to understand from Paul who is so affirming of women's ministry, as we shall see.

Texts used in support of the ordination of women . . .

ALL MUST ADMIT THAT WOMEN'S CONTRIBUTION in the early churches was major indeed, as the greetings at the ends of Paul's letters demonstrate (C.f. Romans 16; Philippians 4:2; 1 Thessalonians 5:26; 1 Timothy 5:3-16; 2 Timothy 4:19-21.). But does any of this require their having "authority over men?" The answer is: without question.

> Acts 2:16-18 (RSV) . . . *"No, this is what was spoken through the prophet Joel: 'In the last days it will be, God declares, that I will pour out my Spirit upon all flesh, and your sons and your daughters shall prophesy, and your young men shall see visions, and your old men shall dream dreams. Even upon my servants, both men and women, in those days I will pour out my Spirit; and they shall prophesy.'"*

The setting here is Jerusalem on the day of Pentecost immediately following the crucifixion and resurrection of Jesus Christ. The 120 waiting believers are all together in one place when the Spirit falls upon them. They are presumably in or near the Temple, because a crowd of Jews and proselytes from all over the world hears the supernatural wind and converges where the 120 are. It is noteworthy that the major entrance to the Temple was through two sets of gates on the southern wall, the double and triple gate. These were known as the Huldah gates, in memory of a little-known prophetess from centuries before. Our Old Testament provides stories of remarkable women whom God appointed to positions of leadership, women like Miriam and the Judge Deborah. In Deborah's case her status as a woman contributed to her victory over Sisera. The Scriptures used by Peter and the other Apostles already made provision for women under some circumstances to be bearers of the Spirit and exercise authority over men.

Not only does the Joel prophecy, related by Peter as now fulfilled, say of women that they will receive God's Spirit as men will. It specifically states that they will prophesy. That requires speaking the Word of the Lord in public. It would be preposterous to think that women's prophecy could only happen before other women, and that if a man should appear she would have to stop!

The Pentecost episode presents paradigms for believers. Certainly the most important is 2:37, 38, which gives the pattern for receiving salvation itself. Equally, we must understand the incorporated words of Joel as paradigmatic: the role of women was to be equal in function and importance to that of men from the first. We must also point out that Luke presents us with other women who have borne the Spirit and taught men: the prophetess Anna and the daughters of Philip the evangelist.

1 Corinthians 11:4-5 (RSV) . . . *"Any man who prays or prophesies with his head covered dishonors his head, but any woman who prays or prophesies with her head unveiled dishonors her head."*

Here is another case of women exercising the spiritual gift of prophecy. It is assumed to be happening at Corinth, assumed this time by Paul himself. But isn't this the Paul who said women must keep silent? Indeed, there are statements from Paul that make it impossible for some serious scholars to believe he truly wrote the passage cited above, 1 Corinthians 14:33b-35!

> Galatians 3:28 (RSV) . . . *"There is neither Jew nor Greek, there is neither slave nor free, there is neither male nor female; for you are all one in Christ Jesus."*

In Paul's world there were profound differences between Jew and Greek, slave and free, male and female. His point was that for those in Christ this has changed. Within the company of believers the outsider's status and value systems were not to be permitted to stand. To assert as some do that these words of Paul refer to the principal of equality, but stop short of equality in paths of serving, is to create a dichotomy in the text. To those who would hold that view we would simply ask: What would this equality have meant in the community if there were no real signs of it?

> Romans 16:7 (RSV) . . . *"Greet Andronicus and Junia, my relatives who were in prison with me; they are prominent among the apostles, and they were in Christ before I was."*

Not until recent years has the importance of this sentence come to light. It is not fair to expect that Lutherans in the late 1960's should have included it in their deliberations. We include it here because it is part of Scripture's witness to the equal role of women in the early church, and for Paul as well.

It is now recognized that Junia is a woman's name. Here we have Paul saying of a woman that she was not only an apostle, but an apostle before he was! Given a date for Paul's call to apostleship between eighteen months and three years after Jesus' death and resurrection, Junia must have been an eyewitness to Jesus from Judea, Samaria, or Galilee. Ben Witherington III presents the fascinating possibility that she was actually Joanna, the wife of Herod's chief steward Chuza, whom Luke says followed Jesus along with Mary Magdalene and helped fund the cost of the Kingdom campaign.

And that brings us to other Scripture references we have not yet cited, because they do not specifically relate to what women were or were not doing in the early church. Before the early church there were Mary Magdalene and other women who became the first witnesses to the Resurrection itself. It was the report of women to men that in God's design first brought the Gospel to men, and thus to the world.

> 1 Corinthians 9:20-22 (RSV) . . . *"To the Jews I became a Jew in order to win Jews. To those under the law I became as one under the law (though I myself am not under the law) so that I might win those under the law. To those outside the law I became as one outside the law (though I am not free from God's law but am under Christ's law) so that I might win those outside the law. To the weak I became weak, so that I might win the weak. I have become all things to all people, that I might by all means save some."*

Here was Paul at his apostolic finest! He articulated the principle for mission which he had followed himself. Educated in Jewish tradition and well-versed in Hellenistic culture as well, he met the people he hoped to be saved on their own ground, in their own setting, speaking their own language, aware of their own customs, having read their own authors. For them to be saved was not to make them replace their culture with a new one, though radical changes were probably necessary in their own. Paul knew that culture should not be ignored in the evangelistic work to which he had been called.

So he accommodated his listeners in all possible ways as long as they remained within the bounds of the ethical and moral. To be true to this mission principle the church must call women to the preaching of the Gospel as well as men in a society where women have access to countless other avenues for determining what they will do with their lives. To do otherwise jeopardizes the message. Paul's words to the Romans (2:24) about sinful conduct on the part of Jews resulting in the blaspheming of God's name by Gentiles has a corollary here. Paul's mission principle makes us ask: What will the world think if we do not give equality to women in the church?

The Texts and a Lutheran Context

IN THE LATE 1960'S DISCUSSIONS on inter-Lutheran cooperation continued. From 1932 to 1962 the Lutheran Church-Missouri Synod (LCMS) had relaxed some of its doctrinal rigidity and became the leader in seeking closer relations with other Lutherans! In the 1950's the Missouri Synod had been charged with "unionism" for this by the Wisconsin Evangelical Lutheran Synod and the Evangelical Lutheran Synod. Missouri Synod-Joint Lutheran Committee (ALC predecessors) discussions led to "pulpit and altar fellowship" between the Lutheran Church-Missouri Synod and the new American Lutheran Church in 1964. Invited to participate in negotiations, the also-new LCA declined, citing the Seventh Article of the Augsburg Confession. A "Joint Statement and Declaration" adopted by the LCMS in 1967 and the ALC in 1968 meant doctrinal agreement had been reached by the two church bodies. The LCA continued to assert from a distance that Augsburg VII was the proper framework for inter-Lutheran discussion and cooperation, rather than attempts to forge agreements that did not rise to the importance of the pure teaching of the Gospel and the right administration of the Sacraments.

With the election of Jacob A.O. Preus, Jr., in 1969 as president of the Lutheran Church-Missouri Synod radical decisions and actions reversed the direction of LCMS. The 1973 convention has been called the second battle of New Orleans. The winning faction insisted that only those who believed in the complete inerrancy of the Bible could hold any teaching position in the church.

It was just prior to this that the American Lutheran Church had studied the issue of women's ordination. The idea was certainly considered unbiblical by LCMS, and by some within the ALC. This would have been the kairos time for thorough biblical study on this issue for all in the church. This would have been the kairos time to declare that the ordination of women is not simply biblically permissible, but a biblically required idea which the church must accept if it considers the Scriptures to be the written Word of God.

What Actually Happened

ACCORDING TO SOCIOLOGIST MARK CHAVES, *(Ordaining Women: Culture and Conflict in Religious Organizations)* the decision to ordain women has never really been a decision based on the Scriptures, but based on other considerations instead. This is true not only for Lutherans, but for basically all American churches.

"From this perspective, rules about women's ordination largely serve as symbolic display to the outside world, and they point to (or away from) a broader liberal agenda associated with modernity and religious accommodation to the spirit of the age." (Chaves, p. 192)

The ordination of women has always been an issue strongly identified with liberalism. The new leadership of LCMS in 1969 was concerned for several reasons that the path toward greater cooperation with the ALC would result in a liberal church, and so it resisted with church politics at its bloodiest. It was the matter of women's ordination more than any other that severed the so-called pulpit and altar fellowship with the ALC. In 1971 the LCMS asked the ALC to reconsider its action to admit women to the ordained ministry. The ALC reaffirmed its decision in 1972. In 1981 the LCMS' state of fellowship with the ALC, which had been under protest since 1977, came to its formal end.

So, in the history of that time the LCMS claimed to speak for the Bible, and the ALC was seen as speaking for equality and modernity with only a secondary appeal to the Bible as not actually barring the ordination of women. The tragedy as far as this observer is concerned is that the ALC did not insist that its position was in fact the Scriptural one, not conceding on this point through failure to insist on what the Scriptures actually say. If one had asked an LCMS member about women's ordination then, the answer would have been: the Bible forbids it. If one had asked an ALC member the same question, the answer would have been: we believe we should now allow it. The ALC member's answer should have been: We have carefully read the Bible, and the Bible requires it.

But this was not the response of the ALC, or the LCA, either. The LCA printed report for its 1970 convention is quite interesting, given Mark Chaves' conclusion. While a very small amount of space is given to the Scriptures in both LCA documents and ALC documents, the LCA's official report entitled "The Role of Women in the Life of the Church" begins by saying that it is "imperative to make three basic statements (LCA Fifth Meeting, p. 441). The first statement—really a paragraph—speaks of "the effects and implications for women of the worldwide revolution in the economic, political, and social structures of secular society . . ." The second statement begins: "It is already too late for the church to exercise its genius for the role of pioneer, but not too late to provide creative responses . . ." (p. 441) The third statement begins by saying that the liberation movement for women must be considered by the church in light of "the church's teaching on creation, redemption, baptism, rite as over against sacrament, the concept of vocation, the freedom of the Christian, sacredness of individuality, ecumenism, and a new and dynamic concept of the ministries of the church." (p. 441) Nowhere in this list did the Scriptures appear independently as God's Word to which the church must listen. Nowhere was Scripture named in the three imperative basic statements about the ordination of women.

Thus, the predecessor bodies of the ELCA established the practice of making decisions on the basis of what modernity expects, rather than on the basis of the Bible itself, though all branches of the Lutheran family would maintain in their constitutions that the Scriptures were their final authority. In time it became possible to assume that the Bible would often stand in the way of progress, and people who quoted the Bible were not to be trusted as leaders.

It has been through the effective surrender of the Bible in this way that the Bible has actually lost the trust of church members. The "Enthusiasts" of Luther's time claimed direct revelation from God over against the Bible. We have their equivalent today. The following statement was made by an ordained pastor on the floor of a synod assembly in 2005 with respect to the sexuality study under discussion in the church at that time: "Don't listen to the Bible; listen to your heart!" A pastor with the Enthusiasts' view of Scripture can complete the candidacy process in the ELCA and go unchallenged in his or her synod today. One suspects that this pastor and many others are closer in their thinking to Henry David Thoreau than to the Apostle Paul or Martin Luther.

This worldview holds that the spirit of the times *(Zeitgeist)* will always be in agreement with the Holy Spirit, and no other source or norm need be appealed to than conscience. A large, or at least influential, part of the ELCA now seems to hold this worldview that assumes we are moving beyond the Bible to some better way of knowing God's will. The Scriptures have even come to be seen as the weapon of conservatives against what is good and just.

Yet it was the Scriptures that called for gender equality in the church long before it became secular reality through the two women's movements of the twentieth century. It was Scripture where one found Paul calling on Philemon to consider freeing his slave Onesimus, more than a thousand years before anyone in the world first considered the concept of human rights. It was Scripture where one found Jesus uttering a standard for marriage which, if respected fully and with proper understanding, still proves to be superior for spouses and their children to the often-harmful, lesser standard of the secular world.

"There has been a virtual silencing of the Bible in many churches today," says Karl Donfried *(Who Owns the Bible? Toward the Recovery of a Christian Hermeneutic,* New York: Crossroad, 2006. p. 3.) This sad state needs to be reformed. Those who understand what has happened, and how it happened, must make their voices heard.

Notes

Chaves, Mark, *Ordaining Women: Culture and Conflict in Religious Organizations,* Cambridge: Harvard University Press, 1997.

Donfried, Karl, *Who Owns the Bible? Toward the Recovery of a Christian Hermeneutic,* New York: Crossroad, 2006.

Nelson, E. Clifford, ed., *The Lutherans in North America*, Philadelphia: Fortress Press, 1975.

Mickelson, Arnold R., *1972 Reports and Actions*, Sixth General Convention of The American Lutheran Church.

Minutes of the Fifth Biennial Convention of the Lutheran Church in America, Board of Publication of the Lutheran Church in America, 1970.

Witherington, Ben III, *What Have They Done With Jesus? Beyond Strange Theories and Bad History—Why We Can Trust the Bible,* Harper: San Francisco, 2006.

Mark C. Mattes chairs the Departments of Philosophy and Religion at Grand View College in Des Moines, Iowa. Prior to this call, he served parishes in Gardner, Illinois and Antigo, Wisconsin. He holds the Ph.D. from The University of Chicago, the M.Div. from Luther Seminary, and he earned his BA from St. Olaf College, where he was also elected to Phi Beta Kappa. He has authored *The Role of Justification in Contemporary Theology*, has co-authored *Imaging the Journey*, has co-translated *Theology the Lutheran Way* by Oswald Bayer, has co-edited the collected papers of Gerhard Forde, *A More Radical Gospel* and *The Preached God*, and has co-edited *The Grand View College Reader*, has additionally authored numerous essays and reviews for peer-reviewed journals. He serves on the Board of Theta Alpha Kappa, the national honor society for Theology/ Religious Studies and helps edit articles for *Lutheran Quarterly* and *Logia: A Journal of Lutheran Theology*.

152

ঙ 15 ন

Authority Over What?

Mark C. Mattes

T HE WORD "AUTHORITY" IS NOT HIGHLY regarded today. If there is an authority over some aspect of our lives, or even our lives themselves, then the notion that we are the captains of our own fate is challenged. Appealing to an authority to defend a claim is bound to provoke our mechanisms for self-defense. The danger is that the authority just might be right.

What is overlooked in the word "authority" is the small word embedded in it: author. An author is a writer, a creator. What transpires in the exercise of authority when it is done for communal health is the authoring, scripting, or sculpting of life.

Evangelical-Lutherans confess that the Bible is the inspired Word of God, the source of truth in all matters of faith and life. We claim the scriptures as our authority. But it is such, not in the sense that it is something we own or possess but in that this very text is the instrument by which the Spirit authors our lives. As such, the roles in interpretation are reversed. It is primarily the Bible which is interpreting us and not we the Bible. The Bible's interpretation of us is very clear: we are sinners, who refuse to trust God and are justly condemned for the violence in the world to which we have contributed, and we, through faith in Christ, are righteous ones, are also those in whom God is creating "clean hearts" and a "right spirit."

Over the last several decades, there has been a tendency to separate "Word" from Bible. In this view, the word, properly, is Jesus Christ himself. And, Jesus Christ gives himself for our well-being in the church's preaching and in the means of grace. Hence, it is common to appeal to Luther's metaphor that the Bible is the "manger" which conveys Christ. Christ, not the Bible, is the true author of our lives. So, a three-fold distinction about the word is made: the word is (1) Christ himself, (2) the preached word, and (3) the written word—the Bible.

Undoubtedly, the concept of word can be helpfully analyzed in such a threefold way. Often, however, the distinction comes to be used against itself; one aspect of the word is pitted against the others. When this occurs those wishing to protect Christ from the Bible need to be challenged. They seek to preserve the purity of Christian truth from perceived elements of the Bible which, to an "enlightened" mind, come across as crude, far-fetched, or oppressive. But we should beware of this tendency. It has a Manichean strain to it. That is, it tends to separate truth from how that truth is conveyed. Content and style, however, are not so clearly demarcated. The scriptures do not so easily separate themselves from Christ!

If the core of our teaching is Christ crucified—foolishness to the Greeks—then we should be skeptical of any alien agenda seeking to establish truth, a standard to determine what's acceptable and what's not, apart from scripture. The Bible and its truth all come of one piece. If parts of scripture come across, for contemporary people, as less than desirable, this is no different than those undesirable traits that a lover might find in a beloved (and vice versa). Those traits are merely a perception. And, when it comes to the relationship of love, it is the whole which is far greater than the parts. God's word is deeply enfleshed, not only in the man Jesus Christ, but also in the sacred scriptures. The scriptures are indeed words of people but, as the canon or rule of faith, they are the inspired word of God.

The Bible is the book of a specific people, God's old covenant people and the earliest followers of the risen Jesus Christ. As the book of a people, it is composed of a variety of literature: history, poetry, wisdom sayings, prophecies, gospels, letters devised with rhetorical power, and apocalyptic visions of the end. It contains books that celebrate romance (Song of Solomon) and books that challenge our fundamental assumptions of life's meaning (Ecclesiastes). In the scriptures, we have an interpretation of human experience, conveyed over the course of thousands of years, and which has likewise invoked extensive commentary, both Jewish and Christian, over the last two millennia. In the scriptures, humans are brought into the narrative of God's redemption and discover that their lives are an adventure well worth living when guided by the Spirit.

When Martin Luther's barber, Peter, asked him for insight on understanding scripture, Luther urged that scripture be taken in a fourfold aspect, as a school book, a song book, a penitential book, and a prayer book. In this way, the Bible addresses us with four crucial questions: (1) What am I taught about God? (2) For what should I give God thanks? (3) What sins are uncovered that I should confess? and (4) For what does this text teach me to pray?[1]

Again, in this way of entering scripture, it is not we who approach the scriptures to dissect them with a particular method whereby we would get to the truth. All too often, the underlying goal of our methods seeks to neutralize the power of the scriptures. And most modern methods of scripture, as configured by the biases of the Enlightenment, seek exactly to limit the hold of scripture on our lives. The Enlightenment venerates autonomy—the exercise of one's will to choose moral principles based on universal human reason—as the criteria for genuine human freedom. A follower of the Enlightenment, our third President, Thomas Jefferson, in the White House no less, took scissors to the New Testament, deleting all those passages that no "rational man" could believe.[2] Naturally, stories of Jesus' miracles were deleted, since they challenge the laws of physics, while most of Jesus' ethics were retained.

Post-modernity continues this pattern set by modernity with the caveat that those principles by which one defines oneself need not be universal: one creates the rules as one goes along. Thus, autonomy has given way to *autopoeisis*—one is one's own maker. In this regard, postmodernity is apt no longer to see knowledge as power but power as knowledge. Thereby, the scriptures can be unmasked as the self-justification of the winners in a power struggle.

Both modernity and postmodernity are inclined to liberate humanity from tradition, which is seen as inherently oppressive or stifling the individual's self-expressive creativity. There is a high cost, however, for our individualism in America today. More lawyers live in our nation than in any other country. Lacking the social cohesion which a common tradition provides (even if that tradition is constituted in a debate over the good, as Alisdair MacIntyre reminds us),[3] we flee to lawyers to rectify the injustices we inflict on each other. Similarly, as isolated individuals, we must struggle with our pain alone, bereft of the support offered in either the wisdom of the past or a community bonded around a common life. Many Americans are depressed, and our quest for either autonomy or self-creation is not able to free us—and perhaps even contributes to this crises.

In response to these concerns, we can first of all see that the Christian challenges the views of freedom presented by modernity and postmodernity. The quest for freedom, forged independently of human nature as it actually is and as it is defined in scripture, will fail. Humans, at the core, are not the isolated individuals that modernity makes of them. We are, only as we are, in relation to others—ultimately, and most definitively, to God as Other.

Likewise, in response to the critique that the Bible is simply the written artifact of the winners in the power struggles within ancient Israel, we agree that many books of the Bible were written, indeed forged, in the furnaces of power struggles—specifically between that of Yahweh and Baal. That said, the scriptures blow to smithereens all attempts at acquisitive power for self-justification. Power used to abuse one's neighbor can, ultimately, never be justified from scripture, because we are to love our neighbors as ourselves. Before the scriptures, we learn a vital truth: we are not in charge of our own lives. Humans do not own themselves, as the Enlightenment philosophers taught, but are owned by God. In this light, no "scientific" method used to interpret scripture is to be used uncritically, since these methods share fundamental assumptions of the Enlightenment that simply are false. Such methods, used without critical care, can serve as defense mechanisms before the God who challenges all our self-justifications.

All things in the world, as creation, address us about our relationship to God. In the changing autumn leaves, in the fresh blades of spring grass, in mountain and ocean grandeur, in the flight of the butterfly and bumblebee, we sense something of God's awesome power, wisdom, majesty, beauty, and holiness. Creation is also, however, the theatre of earthquakes, tsunamis, tornados, and storms. In creation, we encounter God as masked (*larva dei*), since we are everywhere surrounded by and engulfed in God, in both the greatest things (the unimaginable vastness of galaxies) and the least things (subatomic particles and the empty space which contain them and by which they are contained). In nature, however, we never have certainty or clarity about our relationship to God: God is not only giving but also threatening. It is only in Jesus Christ where we can find certainty and clarity with respect to God. As German theologian Oswald Bayer points out, it is the office of Jesus Christ to make God known with certainty.[4] For that reason, preaching attuned to scripture will always aim to properly distinguish (though not separate) God's requirements from his promise, law from gospel.

One learns of Jesus Christ in the preached word which conveys Christ's very life. However, that preached word is intertwined with the written words of scripture. It draws its life from the scriptures, heard in the context of worship or contemplative study, and return us back to the scriptures. There is a kind of *communicatio idiomatum* (communication of attributes), one might say, between the preached word and the written word. Luther confirms this view when he writes,

> When you open the book containing the gospels and read or hear
> how Christ comes here or there, or how someone is brought to
> Him, you should therein perceive the sermon or the gospel through
> which He is coming to you, or you are being brought to Him. For
> the preaching of the gospel is nothing else than Christ coming to us,
> or we being brought to Him . . . if you believe that He benefits and
> helps you, then you really have it. Then Christ is yours, presented to
> you as a gift.[5]

If we are to take the scriptures seriously in their function to
"exegete" or interpret our lives, we need to let them become a dear
friend. We need to spend time with the scriptures, and thoroughly ingest
them, and keep them at the forefront of all that we say and do. The scriptures thereby translate us outside of ourselves and into the promise of
God, so that the promise becomes definitive of our lives. As it opens us
to God's promise, scripture saves us from our own defensive tendencies
to protect ourselves from others and from even challenges in life itself.
Through the scriptures we are granted and can claim freedom. Hence,
Luther notes, "This is the reason why our theology is certain: it snatch-
es us away from ourselves and places us outside ourselves, so that we do
not depend on our own strength, conscience, experience, person, or
works, but depend on that which is outside ourselves, that is, on the
promise and truth of God, which cannot deceive."[6]

Through the scriptures God makes us to be people of faith. On
the basis of his interpretation of Psalm 119, Luther conceived three rules
for the study of scriptures: prayer (*oratio*), meditation (*meditatio*), and
spiritual attack or trial (*tentatio*).[7] In other words, we read the Bible
prayerfully, meditate on it in faith, and claim it in the face of all that
threatens us with death. And, in this life, such threats are unavoidable.

Many Americans do not especially care to read, despite the
appeal of upscale, mass-marketing bookstores or the availability of public libraries. This is where Christians must be quite counter-cultural. We
must read and encourage our children and youth to read the scriptures.
In our time, we need to recover that scenario, after the Reformation,

described by the Roman Catholic critic of Luther, Cochlaeus. Of the transformative social power of Luther's translation of the new testament, Cochlaeus wrote, "Luther's New Testament, through its printing, was disseminated to such an amazing extent that even cobblers and women and other simple people, if they had ever learned German at all and in so far as they were Lutherans, read it with greatest desire as the well of all truth. They carried the translation with themselves on their bosoms in order to impress it on their memory by means of frequent reading."[8] Yes, it is exactly this frequent reading which we need to encourage today.

Again, through these scriptures—the core of which is to convey Christ's promise—our lives are granted perspective and given a context so that life is seen as a gift and not a result of a haphazard toss of the dice. We are given certainty that in Christ we have received a "right spirit" with God, and we are given direction, guidance, and counsel for our lives in those various relations in which we live. Through their own internal discussion amongst themselves, as guided by the Holy Spirit, the authors of the scriptures provide us both with a necessary and sufficient body of teaching, saving truth, and a generous guide for a healthy and productive life. The scriptures do not answer all questions that we might generate, but they do provide specific answers to the questions: (1) What am I to do with my life? and (2) How am I to be saved? The church's confession of faith, public teaching, and overall perspective are to be thoroughly grounded in, guided and judged by the Bible.

The Bible as authority is sole authority, *sola scriptura*. It is not enframed by other authorities but maintains its own integrity in the face of all other contenders. This polemical doctrine was raised against the view of the Roman Catholic Church, which taught that it is the Roman episcopal hierarchy, embodied chiefly in the papal office, which is the proper interpreter of the scriptures. Against this view, the *Formula of Concord* teaches that "the only rule and norm according to which all teachings, together with all teachers, should be evaluated and judged are the prophetic and apostolic Scriptures of the Old and New Testament alone."[9]

However, the misuse of scripture in the Roman Catholic tradition can be echoed elsewhere, and just as loudly in non-Catholic circles. All too often, the Bible becomes an idol of our own skewed views of salvation. For instance, the Bible might be perceived primarily as a chart which outlines the end times. Thereby, we can clearly perceive those devils amongst us who will lead us to the apocalypse and we can also affirm our escape of divine judgment in the rapture. With this Gnostic approach to the "Bible" we can walk by sight, since we have knowledge otherwise hidden with respect to the end times, and not faith. True: Christ will indeed return to judge the living and the dead, but we are not privy to the details.

Or, the Bible might offer the blueprint for a Christian America. All America needs to do is follow the rules presented in the Bible and she will be blessed. To disdain those rules will bring a curse among us, who should be God's chosen people. What Christians must seek to do is Christianize our godless culture and purify it with upright living. Again, this "Bible" disdains the election of all who put their faith in the crucified and replaces it with a twisted, nationalistic theology of glory, as if America alone had a highly favored status with God.

Or, the Bible might be seen as God's word because of its liberating potential—God sides up with the poor and oppressed or socially marginalized against the bourgeois. We are clued in about who the villains and who the good are and thus with whom we are to side. Now, we must be clear: our hearts go out to those whose lives are distorted by injustices and we must seek to challenge a system willing to feed off victims for the well-being of those victims. However, even the Bible is not affirmed because of a vision of an egalitarian utopianism. It is affirmed because it is true conveys God's judgment on all and proffer of mercy to all. At an important level, the Bible equalizes both oppressor and oppressed before the cross.

When it is not used as an idol mirroring one's own power and self-righteousness, the Bible becomes a vehicle in which the horizons of our experience are opened in new ways. For instance, reading Genesis, we discern God's purpose not only in the patriarch Joseph's life, even though God is not a direct actor in that narrative, but in the course of our own lives, when God's direct engagement with us is not apparent. We likewise recognize that in the history of Israel, with its cycles of calling, rebellion, judgment, and renewal we can discern God's work in our own lives and even secular history. We must also claim those scriptural promises of a new heaven and a new earth. And, we discern Jesus Christ as the center of history even though secular society affords him no such status. Because the texts of scripture interpret our contexts, our contexts are given meaning, meaningfulness, and truth. There is no figure eight here, shuttling between text and context. The world is oriented to scripture, not scripture to the world. Apart from the texts of scripture, we can only be enmeshed in the nightmare of a nihilism that no human philosophy can overcome and indeed only contributes to.

At the heart of the authority of Scripture—God's work in the Bible to author our lives—are those "two chief works," (1) to afflict the self-righteous and (2) to comfort those terrorized by God's holy law. "Into these two works all Scripture has been distributed. . . . One part is the Law. . . . The other part is the Gospel."[10] These two ways are the chief ways that God exegetes us.

But they are not the only ways. Digested through frequent reading, the scriptures also renew our affections. Having the Psalter memorized from his years in the monastery, Luther expressed how the Psalter provides a mirror for the human soul. He writes,

> Where does one find finer words of joy than in the psalms of praise and thanksgiving? There you look into the hearts of all the saints, as into fair and pleasant gardens, yes, as into heaven itself. There you see what fine and pleasant flowers of the heart spring up from all sorts of fair and happy thoughts toward God, because of his blessings. On the other hand, where do you find deeper, more sorrowful, more pitiful words of sadness than in the psalms of lamentation? There again you look into the hearts of all the saints, as into death, yes, as into hell itself. How gloomy and dark it is there, with all kinds of troubled forebodings about the wrath of God! . . . when

161

they speak of fear and hope, they use such words that no painter could so depict for you fear or hope, and no Cicero or other orator so portray them.[11]

Our affections, our greatest joys and our deepest depressions, are comprehended and given meaning in light of the Psalter. Thereby our lives make sense.

When our lives are not configured by the scriptures, we can expect that that vacuum will be overrun by our culture, which is all too often both narcissistic and nihilistic. What, then, would the lives of our congregations and church look like if we took the authority of scripture seriously—permitted scripture to author our lives? Of course, we would expect pastors to preach on scripture regularly. We would anticipate that laity would clamor for regular Bible study. More importantly, we would discern that we are supported by God's power which authorizes our ministry both on Sunday morning and in daily life. We would not be as shy in our outreach. And, we would test our assumptions about life and the world, and how we conduct ourselves in daily and family affairs, in light of the scriptures. Most importantly, we would recognize that as authored, the center of our lives is outside of ourselves in God. Once the ultimate is properly ordered—once we recognize that our justification before the ultimate judge is solely in that's judge's hands as argued by our advocate Jesus Christ—the penultimate can fall into its proper place. Justified by grace through faith, we will not make penultimate things to be ultimate or the ultimate to be penultimate. As then free, we can love the Lord our God with all our minds and hearts and our neighbors as ourselves.

Supported by scripture, we share in the experience of God's people diachronistically, across the ages, and synchronistically, throughout the world. In contrast to that black hole of nihilism, ominously growing at the core of our culture, we can, through the scriptures, experience life abundantly (John 10:10). Because of the scriptures, we know that God understands us. As understood by God, we are not alone in life with all those tasks which beset us. Not ultimately alone, we are supported by

God's power, a source of light and life at all times and in all places. The scriptures ever point to Christ and Christ will be magnified as we live from them.

Notes

1. Martin Luther, "A Simple Way to Pray" (1535) in *Luther's Works* (Saint Louis and Philadelphia: Concordia and Fortress, 1958-86 (hereafter LW) 43:209. For a helpful introduction for laity to the authority of scripture, I have found John Pless, *Handling the Word of Truth: Law and Gospel in the Church Today* (St. Louis: Concordia, 2004) to be beneficial. For a discussion of the concept of authority in contemporary society, see Eugene Kennedy and Sara C. Charles, *Authority: The Most Misunderstood Idea in America* (New York: Free Press, 1997).

2. Thomas Jefferson, *The Jefferson Bible: The Life and Morals of Jesus of Nazareth* (Boston: Beacon Press, 1989).

3. Alasdair MacIntyre, *After Virtue: A Study in Moral Theory* (Notre Dame, Indiana: University of Notre Dame Press, 1984), 222.

4. Oswald Bayer, *Theology the Lutheran Way*, translated Jeffrey Silcock and Mark Mattes (Grand Rapids, MI: Eerdmans, 2007), 103.

5. Martin Luther, "A Brief Instruction on What to Look for and Expect in the Gospels" (1521) in LW 35:121.

6. Martin Luther, "Lectures on Galatians" (1519) in LW 27:387.

7. Martin Luther, "Preface to the Wittenberg Edition of Luther's German Writings" (1539) in LW 34:285.

8. As quoted in Oswald Bayer, "Luther as an interpreter of holy scripture," trans. Mark C. Mattes (Cambridge: Cambridge University Press, 2003.

9. Epitome, Summary 1 in *The Book of Concord: The Confessions of the Evangelical Lutheran Church*, ed. Robert Kolb and Timothy J. Wengert (Minneapolis: Fortress, 2000) (hereafter BC), 486.

10. Apology XII:53 in BC, 196.

11. Martin Luther, "Preface to the Psalter" (1545) in LW 35:255-256.

Charles Lindquist and his family have served with the World Mission Prayer League since 1976, in Ecuador and in the Prayer League's Home Office in Minneapolis. In Ecuador, Chuck served as Director of the Lutheran Center for Theological Education (CLET) as well as Coordinator for a regional consortium of Lutheran Bible Schools in the Andes. In 1986 Chuck became the Prayer League's Personnel Secretary in Minneapolis, and in 1997 he was installed as General Director. Chuck is a pastor of the Evangelical Lutheran Church in America. He has attended Augsburg College (BA 1974), Luther Seminary (MDiv 1979), and Fuller Seminary (MTh 1991).

Chuck and Cindy Lindquist have three children, Ruth, Nathan and Joel—and a son-in-law and daughter-in-law. In February 2007 they were made grandparents, as well. The entire family lives in the Twin Cities.

The World Mission Prayer League is a Lutheran missionary society, fielding some 120 missionaries in seventeen countries around the world. For more information see <http://wmpl.org>.

෩ 16 ෨

By What Authority? The World Mission of the Church

Charles Lindquist

Martin Luther, commenting on Luke 24:46-47: "(Jesus) says, this preaching will start in Jerusalem and thereafter resound in the whole world, i.e., the preaching that Christ had to die and rise from the dead. In whose name? in his name and no other shall repentance and the forgiveness of sins be preached. Consequently, repentance and the forgiveness of sins are not valid in St. Peter's or St. Paul's name. Even less valid are they in my own name so that I should become a monk, do this or some other work in order that I might thereby earn the forgiveness of sins. In his name one shall preach forgiveness, that he has acquired this by his suffering and his resurrection, that whoever wants the forgiveness of sins shall believe that Christ has suffered for him and rose again from the dead. This shall be the right preaching. . . ." (cited in Öberg 2007:150)

BY WHAT AUTHORITY? WE ASK IN THIS VOLUME. As it touches the world mission of the church, it is a question that concerns the fundamental *"Why?"* of Christian missions rather than the "What?" or the "How?" And the question lies at the very heart of our faith, if we will ask it honestly.

By what authority do we announce the Good News among people and cultures quite content, it would seem, with their own spiritual traditions? By what authority do we suppose to speak for God? By what authority do we understand that the human race stands in need of God, in any case? What makes our "Good News" *good*—and good for the entire world? By what authority?

The question reminds me of a discussion by James Scherer, appearing in *Gospel, Church and Kingdom* (Minneapolis: Augsburg 1987). It rings quite as true today, I think, as it did at that time.

"The Christian missionary movement today is in a state of *crisis* because the larger community of faith of which it is a part is also in a prolonged state of crisis," Scherer explains. "Gone for the most part are the simple faith, confidence, and activism" of previous generations of missionary practitioners. "Global mission has now become a problematic task, fraught with fundamental theological problems about which Christians increasingly disagree—both as to *what* it is and *whether* it should be done at all" (*Ibid*: 21, 22).

On the one hand, Scherer goes on to describe the collapse of "the old missionary order." The "colonial framework" under which the gospel was proclaimed in much of the world has collapsed—and good riddance! What is more, "Christendom"—Scherer means the Christian West—is no longer as Christian as once it seemed. Indeed, the West itself has become a mission field. The axis of global Christianity—not only in numbers, but also in vision, leadership, and missionary initiative—has shifted from traditional latitudes in the north and west, to the global south, a shift that has accelerated dramatically in the last two decades (Jenkins, 2002).

All of themselves, radical changes such as these might leave Western Christians asking whether cross-cultural missions remain appropriate at all. But there is something deeper at work, in Scherer's estimation. It is "the *crisis of faith*, spirit, and theological conviction in the Western world." "The fundamental question . . . is really whether people still *believe* that Christian faith is so vital that it must be shared with others" (*Ibid*: 33, 34). By what authority?

The issue is profoundly significant, if we are honest with ourselves. "Either it is a missionary church, or it is not the church of Jesus Christ," Scherer goes on to say. "The crisis of Western Christianity, insofar as it raises questions about the validity of mission activity and evangelism, is a crisis which touches the very foundation of Christian faith and the life of the church." Scherer makes the issue absolutely crucial: "In the West, for the time being, questions about the foundation and goal of mission must take precedence over all other issues" (*Ibid*: 34). "For if one can validly raise the question, Why missions? it will soon be impossible to avoid answering the question, Why the church? Why even the gospel? Why bother to believe in Jesus Christ?" (*Ibid*: 36).

Professor Scherer didn't know about September 11, the "war on terror," or the further erosion of Western influence, prestige, and persuasive advantage that complicate the practice of Christian missions today, especially from the West. Yet the questions he raises remain relevant—exactly right, in fact. Developments in church and society in recent years have made Scherer's questions, if anything, yet more acute. *Why missions? By what authority?*

Getting It Wrong

UNFORTUNATELY, OFTEN ENOUGH, we have gotten the issue wrong through the years.

We have sometimes conflated our authority with the institutions of *the church*. We have supposed that the church authorizes the mission of God in the world. Perhaps we have gotten the idea by observing pastors and bishops consecrating missionaries, from time to time, apparently authorizing or legitimizing their service.

Much mischief has come from this idea. At very worst, the institutions of the church may get the idea that it falls to them to limit and define the mission of God in the world. All kinds of churchly schemes may follow, from right-leaning crusading to left-leaning liberations. It may even occur to the church to "unauthorize" the practice of Christian missions, if it presumes to have authorized the effort in the first place. I have heard one church leader pronounce recently that the "age of Christian missions is over."

It is not the church, however, that sends its people into mission. The church itself is sent. The church does not own the mission of God, to authorize or perhaps "unauthorize" its exercise. The church is itself owned by God's mission in the world.

We have sometimes conflated our authority with the institutions of "*the crown*." In previous centuries, it was not uncommon for Christian monarchs to authorize Christian missionary efforts directly, even funding some enterprise entirely. We no longer have Christian monarchs, or not many. Yet even today, "faith-based initiatives" bring government funding and legitimacy into church or mission efforts—and not only in America. The Department for International Development introduces British funding in overseas Christian projects. The Norwegian Agency for Development Cooperation seems to prefer international Christian projects for international Norwegian aid. So with the Finnish International Development Agency, and so on.

There is nothing wrong with this inherently. Yet mischief may ensue here, as well. A few years ago I visited a large international project, built in partnership with several international missions, that corresponded to nothing so clearly as the need for a European government to invest a considerable amount of money in a considerable international project. Today the entire project is abandoned and crumbling.

Large-scale, international "faith-based initiatives" represent an alternative power and authority—and the subtle danger of confusing our sense of legitimacy and allegiance. If a European monarch has underwritten your service entirely, some hundreds of years ago, *who* precisely do you represent? By what authority do you serve? And what if United States Agency for International Development has underwritten your missionary project?

Perhaps worst of all, we have sometimes found our authority, simply, *within ourselves*—based in our own motivating compassion, or compelling convictions, or even the sway of our guilt.

Sometimes we have confused our authority with an overwhelming experience of simple personal compassion. It is not difficult, certainly, to feel moved by the images of poverty, illness, violence and oppression that characterize so much of the world that surrounds us. Yet mission fueled by hot compassion can become, strangely, mission about me and my needs. *My* guilt needs to be assuaged; *my* compassion needs satisfaction—whatever the mission of God or needs on the ground may otherwise reveal.

This is where the so-called "white man's burden" came from—a burden to share one's own culture, language, technical expertise, and religion with those who do not enjoy their benefits. It is an urgent, guilt-ridden burden, and it does not pause for long to appreciate the culture, language, technical expertise, etc., of the "targets" of one's largesse. At its worst, it becomes an effort to make the world over in one's own image.

The very terminology involved here—"mission," "sending," and so on—lends itself to misunderstandings such as these. In his monumental *"Transforming Mission"* (Orbis 1992), David Bosch points out: "The term 'mission' presupposes a sender, a person or persons sent by the sender, those to whom the one is sent, and an assignment. The entire terminology thus presumes that the one who sends has the *authority* to do so." Bosch explains that most missionary efforts have argued through the years that their real "sender" was God. "In practice, however, the authority was understood to be vested in the church or in a mission society, or even in a Christian potentate" (1-2).

Getting It Right

AS IT IS, THERE IS BUT ONE SOURCE and one Authority at the root of Christian missions. And it is not church, not crown, and not found in the vagaries of the human heart.

Consider an early episode from the life of the apostles immediately following the Ascension of the Resurrected Lord. The disciples have been busy in the mission of God. A crippled beggar is healed (Acts 3:1ff.). The gospel is announced (3:11ff.). Thousands are coming to faith in Jesus Christ (4:4). But the commotion has annoyed the leaders of the synagogue, and Peter and John are brought before the Council. "By what power, or by what name did you do this?" they are asked (4:7-10). It is a question about authority.

Their response is instructive, and utterly simple. Peter and John point to the name of Jesus Christ of Nazareth (4:10). Jesus is glorified by "the God of Abraham, the God of Isaac, and the God of Jacob" (3:13). Jesus has become the "Holy and Righteous One," the "Author of life" (3:14,15). It is "his name itself" that has healed the crippled beggar (3:16). Jesus has become the crucial center of salvation history, from "what was foretold through all the prophets" (3:18) to the coming of Messiah at the very end of times (3:20-21). Jesus has become the fulfillment of the promise to Abraham, "And in your descendents all the families of the earth shall be blessed" (3:25; ref. Genesis 12:1-3). Lesslie Newbigin observes, "(Peter and John) can only refer to 'the name of Jesus,' and by that name they refer to an ultimate authority and to their own final commitment to that authority" (Newbigin 1978:16).

This is the way that believing Christians have tended to respond, if they are honest. By what authority are the people of God engaged in the mission of God? Not certainly by their own "power or piety" (Acts 3:12)—but simply "by faith in his name" (3:16). It was Jesus who gave his life and rose again. It was he who met the disciples on the Mountain of Ascension. It was he who proclaimed: "All authority in heaven and on earth has been given me. Go therefore and make disciples of all nations" (Matthew 28:18-20). It is a simple, straightforward command, after all —a clear and great commission.

Yet in Acts 4, the disciples did not appeal to the Great Commission, per se. In the words once again of Lesslie Newbigin, they pointed their interlocutors to "the total fact of Jesus" – not simply a pronouncement on the Mountain of Ascension. "The Christian missionary has nothing to do but to bring men (sic) face to face with Jesus Christ, the total fact of Jesus" (Newbigin 1961:57). Newbigin means a Trinitarian Jesus, the Eternal Son of the Eternal Father, Creator, Judge, and Savior, as we find him in the Scriptures. He means the crux and center of God's redemptive plan for the world. He means the fulfillment of all of God's promises and the clear bright hope of heaven.

I remember a little book by Max Warren titled, "*I Believe in the Great Commission*" (Grand Rapids: Eerdmans 1976). The book's argument may be summarized very simply: *The Great Commission is Jesus himself*. The "commission" is more than a few brief words at the end of Matthew, clear and compelling as they are. *Jesus himself is the Great*

Commission. Knowing him is coming under his mission to the world. Christian faith is also Christian purpose. By grace through faith in Jesus Christ, we come into relationship with the Almighty King—and a King who rules, who acts, who graciously deploys all things in his redemptive plan for the entire world.

We are made ambassadors, as the Apostle Paul explains (2 Corinthians 5:14-21). We are brought into service of a King and a

Kingdom. We are speaking, after all, of the mission of God – the *missio Dei* – not the project of some human agency, church, crown, or effort of compassion. "So if anyone is in Christ, there is a new creation: everything old has passed away; see, everything has become new!" (5:17 NRSV). And Paul goes on: "All this is from God, who reconciled us to himself through Christ, and has given us the ministry of reconciliation; that is, in Christ God was reconciling the world to himself, not counting their trespasses against them, and entrusting the message of reconciliation to us" (5:18-19 NRSV). God in Christ reconciles the world to himself; God in Christ makes us reconcilers in the bargain. They are two sides of the same coin; you cannot take in one without the other. The same movement of grace that reconciles Paul, makes Paul an ambassador to the world. "So we are ambassadors for Christ, since God is making his appeal through us . . ." (5:20 NRSV).

"*Everything* has become new." It is not as if believers are presented with a menu of appropriate Christian activities and may select an item or two that pleases them. Coming into the faith is not like coming to church on "Rally Day"—where you might wander from booth to booth, consider your disposable resources and schedule, and "sign up" for a bit of Christian mission. Coming into the faith is coming into relationship with the "total fact" of Jesus. It is coming into the orbit of the One who fulfills the promise to Abraham. It is coming to be known by the Author and Source of God's astounding grace. And in him, believers are swept up and into the story of God's redemptive plan for all the earth.

Missionary authority is a derivative authority, and it derives from a story. *The* story, in fact. It is the story of the *missio Dei*, the story of God's own mission of love and redemption for the entire universe of his creation. It is the story, precisely, about Jesus. We discover that God is doing something utterly extraordinary in the life, death, and resurrection of Jesus Christ. Something final; something unique. Something authoritative in an absolute sort of way—because it is authored by the Creator himself. Once again, David Bosch: "Mission has its origin in the heart of

God. God is a fountain of sending love. This is the deepest source of mission. It is impossible to penetrate deeper still; there is mission because God loves people" (*op.cit.*:392).

And God writes his people into the story of his redeeming love. "The faith that is through Jesus"—not only heals the cripple (Acts 3:16) —but makes Peter and John and Paul what they are. God the Father sends God the Son; the Father and the Son together send the Paraclete, the Holy Spirit; and Father, Son and Holy Spirit *send the church* into the world. This, indeed, has become a fundamental part of our identity in Christ. We are the called ones (Matthew 4:21; cf. Hebrews 9:15). We are the sent ones (John 20:21). Yet it is not as if we have come to possess some special "power or piety" to legitimate the practice of Christian missions. To the contrary, the authoritative story of God possesses us.

This is why many theologians and missiologists find it impossible to separate the church from its mission in the world. This is why Scherer finds a dangerous "crisis of faith" in a church that has forgotten its mission. "The church exists by mission, as a fire exists by burning," said Emil Brunner famously. Where there is no mission, there can be no church. Not because the church must "perform mission" as a condition or requirement in order to become or remain the church. Much to the contrary, it is because the church is missionary by its very nature. If we have come to participate in its life, we have come necessarily to participate in its mission in the world. "It has become impossible to talk about the church without at the same time talking about mission" (Bosch 1992:372).

A Few Implications

OUR DISCUSSION CONCERNING AUTHORITY may have seemed a bit theoretical. Let me suggest a few practical implications, too.

We must observe, first of all, that the authoritative story of Christian missions—the *missio Dei* that operates in and through and beyond the missionary practice of the church through the ages—is *not about us*. It is not about church, or crown, or personal compassion. It is entirely about God, from first to last, and God's own redemptive plan in Jesus Christ of Nazareth. The insight represents a kind of "Copernican revolution" in perspective. The traditional "centers" of our missionary practice and thinking no longer hold.

The church is no longer the center. The story of God's redemptive love is *not about the church*. The story is not about a denomination, either —as if advancing the reach of Lutheranism equals growth in the Kingdom of God. It is not about the well-being of my particular congregation—as if involvements and activities that motivate us, in particular, or fit our schedules or needs or dispositions, equal the gracious program of God for the world.

We must be alert to the broad agenda of the mission of God in the world. Participation may lead us into creative partnerships in international and interdenominational teams. We must anticipate holistic participation, too—healing the cripple, as Peter and John did, as well as announcing the good news about Jesus.

The ordained are no longer the center. David Bosch explains: "An unmistakable shift is taking place. Laypersons are no longer just the scouts who, returning from the 'outside world' with eyewitness accounts and perhaps some bunches of grapes, report to the 'operational basis'; they *are* the operational basis from which the *missio Dei* proceeds. It is in fact not *they* who have to 'accompany' those who hold 'special offices' in the *latter's* mission in the world. Rather, it is the *office bearers* who have to accompany the laity, the people of God" (Bosch, 472).

The West is no longer the center. And not only in terms of demography—viz., the simple fact that church and mission are populated today by majorities of non-Western peoples. The West is no longer the center in terms of leadership, vision, or goal, either. In an important way, it never was.

The early church, of course, was dominated by Africans and Middle Easterners. It is again today—and by Asians and Latin Americans, as well.

Now we can meet our sisters and brothers in the faith, from Asia, Africa, Latin America—as well as from Memphis and Minneapolis—as co-participants in the story of God's love for the nations. Now we can see the story develop in quite its own way around the world. In the words of Philip Jenkins, we live in the day of *"The Next Christendom"* (Orbis 2002).

"Success" is no longer the center. Or maybe better said, "success" is no longer easy to discern. "The faith that is through Jesus" (Acts 3:16) has made us appear in the story of God's redemptive plan for the world; but we are not exactly writing it. Can we discern how things should work, when they work out well? Can we predict how the story should go from moment to moment? Can we recognize "success" in our own particular roles and ministries? What will it consist of? Numbers, statistical trends, and so on?

Human conceptions of "success" have never been the center of God's mission. The story of God's mission is a story that stands under the cross. "The *missio Dei* purifies the church," says David Bosch. He means that the *missio Dei* disabuses us of the supposition that *our* programs, *our* activities, *our* "successes," *our* numbers and analyses, are directly synonymous with the mission of God in the world. "The *missio Dei* . . . sets (the church) under the cross—the only place where it is ever safe. The cross is the place of humiliation and judgment, but also the place of refreshment and new birth" (Bosch, 519).

Finally, let me say that *guilt* is no longer the center, either. Nor is compassion. Nor is good will.

Christians, missionaries and caregivers of all kinds are susceptible to "compassion fatigue." (I have just now done an Internet search; Google turns up 191,000 references.) The phenomenon has become a part of the *American Heritage Dictionary*: "*(n.)* A jaded attitude on the part of a contributor toward appeals for donations or charitable aid." But what is really at work, I think, is "guilt fatigue." We make a "burden" our authority. We make guilt our motivator; my own Scandinavian Lutheran heritage is particularly adept at it. But it is poor authority and poor motivation for missions.

Jesus himself is the authority and motivation for missions; not guilt, not a harangue, not even heartfelt compassion. The insight should affect workshops and preaching on "Mission Sundays" throughout the church. The biblical route to mobilization is in and through the person of Jesus Christ. We do not need another harangue. We do not need pronouncements or guilt trips. Missionaries are made by encounter with Jesus Christ; missionary enthusiasts should simply preach him.

Conclusion

In conclusion, let us return to the question made to the disciples long ago: "By what authority do you do these things?" We might as well ask, "By what authority do you believe at all?" We have seen that there is but one answer. We believe; we are redeemed; we are commissioned —*in Jesus*.

If you have come to believe—if God has worked this miracle in your heart, by the power of his grace-filled word—then you have become part of something much bigger and more adventurous than you might have imagined. It cannot, in fact, be otherwise.

You have come to Jesus. And Jesus has made you a part of the mission of God.

References

Bosch, David J., *Transforming Mission*. Maryknoll, New York: Orbis, 1992.

Jenkins, Philip, *The Next Christendom: The Coming of Global Christianity*. New York: Oxford University Press, 2002.

Newbigin, J.E. Lesslie, *A Faith for this One World?* New York: Harper & Brothers, 1961.

The Open Secret: An Introduction to the Theology of Mission. Grand Rapids: William B. Eerdmans, 1978.

Öberg, Ingemar; Dean M. Apel (trans.), *Luther and Missions*. St. Louis: Concordia, 2007.

Scherer, James A., *Gospel, Church and Kingdom*. Minneapolis: Augsburg Publishing House, 1987.

Warren, Max, *I Believe in the Great Commission*. Grand Rapids: William B. Eerdmans, 1976.

V.F. (Bud) Thompson received a BA from Lutheran College in Decorah, Iowa (1969), a MDiv from Luther Seminary in St. Paul, Minnesota (1973), and a ThM from Princeton Seminary in 1977. For over thirty years he served the church as parish pastor. Currently he lives in Spokane, Washington, and teaches New Testament at Gonzaga University, continuing to serve, as well, as the managing editor of *Lutheran Quarterly*, a position he has happily held since 1987 when the new series of *Lutheran Quarterly* was put into publication.

In recent years theological discourse has grown increasingly sensitive to the way in which point of view is influenced not only by confessional identity, but as well by prior experience, standing in the community, vested interests, along with other factors that determine the stance from which one engages in the conversation.

While my contribution to the present volume is shaped by many influences none is more significant than that of over thirty years of pastoral service to congregations of the church. I can only say, on that basis, the actuality of congregational life reveals that no one person or office exercises sole authority for the church—not bishops, church-wide bureaucrats, pastors, parents, seminary faculties, or renewal movements within the church.

Rather authority resides in the process of deliberation in which all the above mentioned partners have a voice. Pastors are frequently in the position of managing the congregational discussion—both formal and informal—about how faith finds its way in some situation or another. Exercising the administrative responsibilities is a complex enterprise comprised of many components.

To me the single most important component is often the most neglected, namely, education in the biblical and confessional tradition of the church. And as Luther never tired of pointing out, education in the faith is a long and arduous road we travel together. But there is no other road if we are to be consequential for the gospel, if we are to guard against the temptation to exploit the biblical and historic tradition in the interest of establishing without further discussion a particular point of view as though it is the only faithful point of view.

None of us is above that, of course—not bishops, pastors, seminary faculties, parents, or renewing movements in the church. That's why we need to attend to the cultivation of an educated church, and never relax our grip on the plow. As Melanchthon observed, "Apart from the

continuing work of cultivating an educated membership, the church becomes a very smelly enterprise."

So there it is, at the outset, the point of view, the prejudice, of my little reflection about authority in the church. Authority anchored in the priesthood of believers becomes a foul smelling affair apart from the continuing and rigorous education of the saints.

ன 17 ௸

Something You Should Know
V.F. (Bud) Thompson

HEN I WAS A YOUNG PASTOR to the church I was introduced to the question, "By What Authority?" by a member of the congregation I was serving at the time. Greeting me at the door after my first attempt to lead the congregation in worship, the member invited me for a visit in the coming week. During the course of the visit my new friend announced, "There is something you should know: Your name may be on the office door, but it does not mean that automatically you will be in fact my pastor."

At the time, being somewhat theologically remedial, by no fault of my teachers, I may not have had sufficient savvy to understand the announcement in theological perspective, but the message was somehow nonetheless, quite clear to me. My friend was making the same sort of distinction which other members of the congregation would occasionally make by greeting the preacher at the door and commenting on the sermon, "Well, that's fine, pastor, but it is just your opinion."

Such observations were of course troubling. By way of response I defensively declared, "Not just my opinion, by God, but the WORD OF LORD!" To which the congregation replied, "Perhaps, but also just as likely, just your opinion writ large to appear as the WORD OF LORD."

179

In retrospect, after over thirty years of parish service under my belt and that many years to stew in and over the theology of Luther and those who stand in that confession of faith, I think I understand somewhat better the question of authority, which is of course absolutely crucial to faithful and effective ministry.

We Lutherans distinguish two authorities, which we articulate in a variety of ways: law and gospel, promise and command, legal authority and evangelical authority. However, the distinction is named, the point is to recognize, as my friend those many years ago sought to help me understand, the nature of the two authorities: law and gospel. As he invoked the distinction, I think I now understand, he was not making an observation about the legal authority of the pastor. Rather, he was making an observation about the limit of legal authority, inviting the new pastor to appreciate the difference between authority based in and upon the law, on the one hand, and authority which arises from delivering the gospel in a way that creates and sustains faith, on the other hand.

At the time I could have, under the pressure of my friend's disconcerting announcement, insisted that by God and the call extended to me by the church I had been duly installed as his pastor and he had better respect the fact of it! But it would have been pointless, wasted breath, and only showing that I didn't understand a distinction as basic to the Lutheran confession as the catechism itself. My friend did not lack for intelligence, nor for knowledge of the confession to which he belonged by faith. He was well aware of the distinction between law and gospel. He was merely extending the invitation for the new pastor to appreciate that effective ministry would rise and fall on the actual speaking and hearing of the life-giving word of the gospel, and the law, no matter how loudly or insistently proclaimed could not substitute.

The law, rightly proclaimed might well serve to keep order and provide protection in a community of sinners, but only the gospel promises to create, where the Holy Spirit wills, the community of saints.

As a young pastor to the church I continued to learn the distinction between the two authorities from Reidar Daehlin, the bishop of the old Rocky Mountain District of the American Lutheran Church. The Rocky Mountain District had rules to govern the service of its pastors. For example, pastors were expected to attend the annual gatherings of the district—the annual convention of congregational delegates and the annual pastors' conference. Pastors who failed to attend could expect a personal visit from the bishop to explain their absence and to receive a reprimand for failing the communion of faith. The rules and their enforcement were not one hundred percent effective, but effective enough to preserve that aspect of the district's life. In fact most pastors willingly abided by the rules of attendance because the vitality of the district's life together in Christ was so inviting.

Our bishop also exercised an authority, which reached out to redeem sinners, to create, as he had in the title of a little but powerful book, *The Family of the Forgiven*. The life of the church in Montana fell and rose on the evangelical witness of bishop and preachers, lay and ordained, creating the desire to belong to that family and its work and life together, forgiven sinners freeloading on the grace of the Lord, as Oliver Jones, thirty-five years preacher to the miners in Butte, used to put it.

While the two authorities—law and gospel—serve the same end, the end of the old and the beginning of life as the new creation in Christ, the crucial insight for the church's ministry is to recognize that the administration of law and gospel requires discernment. Discernment which understands the nature and limits of the law and the promise of the gospel, and the difference between the two.

Mentoring Voice of Scripture and Confession

To understand the distinction between law and gospel is one thing, and to live the distinction in the rough and tumble of our life together is quite another thing. Going to school in the distinction is a schooling from which we never graduate. To imagine that we have mas-

tered the distinction and now go on to something else has proven disas-
trous for the individual and corporate life of faith.

In this essay I am not able to explore the full complexity of making and living the distinction between promise and command, but we
can set down at two crucial points. Consider first the promise of Jesus in
John 14: "The Advocate, the Holy Spirit, whom the Father will send in
my name, will teach you everything, and remind you of all that I have
said to you." Apart from this promise the question "By What
Authority?" would be a complete despair. The promise is our sole confidence.

But first, a word about the other authority in the life of faith, the
legal authority of dogma: Twenty years ago Joe Burgess gave a lecture
in which he argued against the contention that Lutherans are in a mess
because the tradition is without a recognizable teaching authority.
Burgess admitted that if one is looking for a teaching authority that functions in a hierarchal fashion as in the Catholic tradition it would appear
that Lutherans have no teaching authority. However one would be
remiss to conclude on that basis that Lutherans have no teaching authority to instruct the contemporary church in the historic essentials of faith.

According to Lutheran tradition, those in positions of responsibility for the well being of their neighbor—parent, pastor, seminary faculty, catechist, and so on—exercise together through instruction, nurture, discussion, and debate discernment and guidance regarding how
faith on the basis of the classic confession of the tradition continues to
make its way in the world.

These two voices promise to lead us faithfully into the question.
Apart from the promise of Jesus it is impossible to imagine how
Lutherans might justifiably hold out hope for ever arriving at mutual
submission to theological truth. The danger of theological deliberation
scarcely needs to be belabored. Theological discourse can lead to disunity and discord, and frequently has, just as likely as not. One need only
think of the major issues of the past couple of decades, from sexuality to
church order to relations with other non-Lutheran churches, all attest to

the truth of it. It is not surprising. Individual parties within the communion come to the table with strong convictions, political prowess, and theological facility. We have learned to be suspicious of one another, which is completely understandable. We have vested interests to protect.

There is nothing to be gained by making believe to enter into theological deliberation with a blank slate, with no convictions, no hunches about what constitutes the truth of the matter, and no vested interests to protect. My own experience has been that those who lobby loudest for open-mindedness and tolerance have about as much struggle with closed-mindedness and intolerance as anyone else.

In the quest for unity and concord our tendency in recent years has been to proceed by narrowing the field of discourse by eliminating those of different outlook. We seek to discredit, discount, and dismiss those who hold perceptions and convictions different and incompatible with our own. Consider for example in this regard the slogans by which we characterize one another: "We operate with the plain truth of scripture. They distort the plain truth." "We are traditionalist. They are revisionist." "We are evangelical. They are legalistic."

And if name calling doesn't do the trick we seek to politically outmaneuver the opposition. Nothing against political engagement, the Lord can of course use political maneuvering to govern the affairs of his church just as well as theological discourse. But political maneuvering in interest of having our way without having to bother engaging those who are different is plain and simple a denial of baptism and the One who constitutes his church through this means. When we seek to use brute political maneuvering to establish our authority over our neighbor in faith we should not be surprised to get from our Lord what the sons of Zebedee got that day when they lobbied the Lord for positions of political authority in his kingdom: "You know that among the Gentiles those whom they recognize as their rulers lord it over them, and their great ones are tyrants over them. But it is not so among you; but whoever wishes to become great among you must be your servant, and whoever wishes to be first among you must be slave of all. For the Son of Man came not to be served but to serve, and to give his life a ransom for many" (Mk 10:42-45 NRSV).

The Lord's sermon provides a radical reorientation to the question of authority. Instead of merely being opposed to incompatible differences we are given to be for precisely those who hold them. The most loving approach to those with incompatible differences is to engage them in honest and rigorous debate, trusting the Lord to use this means to lead us to truth.

Absolution—The Alpha and Omega

IN OTHER WORDS, FOR THOSE OF US who enter theological deliberation with vested interests and limited point of view, which it is hard to imagine that there are any exceptions, the beginning and the end of theological deliberation is the absolution of our Lord. In the promise of the absolution we are free to call a thing what it is. In the absolution of the Lord we have one another in a way that otherwise we should never have one another, the great company of theological beggars freeloading on the grace of our Lord. We may never be able to rise above the deadly duo - vested interests and limited point of view - but we may trust that our Lord will use them to create a communion of believers free in the truth of his absolution. That's the Authority to which every knee in heaven and earth is destined to bow in obeisance, praise and adoration. It is also the freedom to sin boldly in service of the neighbor.

When we come together at the table of theological discourse we may offer our point of view, attempting to make persuasive argument for its adoption by the communion of our neighbors in faith. This I think is what has been missing in our life together. We tend to treat the truth of faith as a decree which is transparently and readily recognizable by any reasonable person. When our assertions are not met with the affirmation that we willingly give them we tend then to separate into smaller sectarian groups within the communion, for example, denominational Lutherans and evangelical catholics, which it does not require deep imagination to imagine who invented those party designations.

Trusting the Spirit and the operating with a Lutheran understanding of teaching authority in the church suggests a better way, the way of honoring the communion into which we have been baptized and the Lord by and in whose authority our adoption has taken place, the way of patient persuasion, seeking to make arguments for the adoption of our point of view by the entire communion and honoring those with different and opposing points of view until the communion freely confesses, "Yes, this is the truth of the Lord by which faith makes its way into the future."

To my imagination the final word on the question of authority belongs to the Third Article of the Apostles' Creed, as Luther explains, "I believe that I cannot by my own understanding or effort believe in Jesus Christ my Lord, or come to him. But the Holy Spirit has called me through the gospel, enlightened me with his gifts, and sanctified and kept me in true faith. In the same way he calls, gathers, enlightens, and sanctifies the whole Christian church on earth, and keeps it united with Jesus Christ in the one true faith. In this Christian church day after day he fully forgives my sins and the sins of all believers. On the last day he will raise me and all the dead and give me and all believers in Christ eternal life. This is most certainly true."

I met Jesus in 1948 at age twenty and I was hooked. My family had some opinions about those who believed in Jesus. Followers of Jesus were considered to be either intellectually challenged and not smart enough to see that this whole thing about Jesus was just a big hoax, or of weak character and not strong enough to deal with life's realities without a religious crutch.

Throughout my life, from the days I did intensive New Testament studies under Ernst Fuchs, to the "God Is Dead" controversy of the mid-sixties, to the present rise of Revisionist Theology, I had to deal with theologies that did not match my experience with Jesus.

I studied theology at the universities of Hamburg, and Tuebingen in Germany, and at the Lutheran College and Seminary in Saskatoon. Ordained in 1953. I served as a Lutheran pastor in Winnipeg, MB, Calgary, AB, Vancouver, BC, and Edmonton, AB. I served as Conference President of Manitoba (ULCA), and Dean of Southern Alberta, and Dean of Northern Alberta (LCA) I did graduate studies at seminaries at Chicago and Vancouver (STM 1969). My doctoral work focused on managing change in normative and voluntary organizations, (McCormick, Chicago, D. Min.,1974)

I worked with the ELCIC as well as several synods as a management consultant in strategic planning and conflict management. I also taught courses and worked as a consultant in organization effectiveness with the oil industry (Syncrude, Canada Ltd) and the Government of Alberta. My recent books include "Thinking in the Presence of God" (2004), "Mostly True Stories About Mostly Good People" (2005), and "Is It Now OK to Sin?" (2007). I am married since 1955 to Hanna, a fellow

Lutheran pastor. We have three children and ten grandchildren and live on an acreage near Sherwood Park, AB.

Contact Lothar Schwabe at: lotharschwabe@shaw.ca

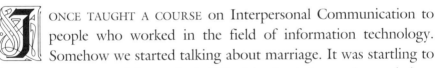

❧ 18 ☙

Technology, Thinking, and Theology

Lothar Schwabe

Technology Influences How We Use Our Brain

I ONCE TAUGHT A COURSE on Interpersonal Communication to people who worked in the field of information technology. Somehow we started talking about marriage. It was startling to hear how many participants had difficulties in their marriage relationships or had even experienced divorce. Even though this was only a small sample and based on anecdotal evidence, it nonetheless made me wonder. Was there a connection between the type of work they did and their relationships to their spouses?

Does technology influence behavior? Does our interaction with the technology we use influence the way we think and subsequently behave? Can people develop a case of technitis which inhibits their capacity to relate?

It has been noted that children who spend much time at computer games and less time at play with other children are impeded in the development of their social skills.

An intensive interaction with a technology that requires exclusively left-brainish, logical, and sequential thinking patterns can lead to a

187

predominant use of left-brainish thinking in areas of life that require a different approach.

If we work in such a technological environment that predominantly uses left-brainish thinking patterns then we can be influenced to process all of life's experiences accordingly. All social relationships may then be subjected to analytical scrutiny. Some married couples adjust to a relationship in which everything has to be "worked out" through reasoning. Others get tired of endless arguing. A healthy relationship uses both right-brainish thinking (the heart) as well as left-brainish thinking (the head) in an interactive way.

There are cultures that have maintained an appreciation of a right-brainish relationship orientation. Our western culture has had a strong preference for left-brainish rational and linear thinking since humanism became the accepted philosophy. The impact of technologies that require a high degree of logical thinking has only amplified the problem of a neglect of relational skills.

Tragically, a society that has lost its capacity to process relationships on the right side of the brain and uses the left side of the brain for what it is not designed to be used, experiences a relational meltdown.

We must admit that the best of left-brainish thinking has not prevented our world from plunging into an environmental disaster. Reason has not prevented our society from plunging into a host of social problems.

Drug education courses in our schools have not solved that huge social problem. If reason alone is such a reliable instrument then why do we still have sexually transmitted diseases? Not every lawyer is more law abiding than other people just because of their knowledge of the law. It cannot be said that all health professionals lead a healthy lifestyle because they have the knowledge to make the right lifestyle decisions. Nor are priests and ministers prevented from committing acts that clearly go against what they know to be wrong.

It takes more than reasoning and logical arguments to produce desirable behaviors.

We have good reasons to be critical of a culture that declares values to be a personal option and that dismisses the validity of faith in God who prescribes values through the Ten Commandments.

God has given us the capacity to act in a rational way through the use of the left hemisphere of the brain. God has also given us the capacity to have faith and to love, feel, trust, and to relate to others through the use of the right hemisphere of the brain.

There is no compelling reason to declare the supremacy of the left side of the brain over the right side of the brain. Each hemisphere has its own valid functions to perform. It is only when both are fully utilized that a healthy balance through the appropriate use of both hemispheres is achieved.

Revisionist Theology Is Applying a Methodolgy That Does Not Suit the Bible

WHAT HAPPENS WHEN THEOLOGICAL STUDIES become infected with technitis? What happens when theologians, in the pursuit of scientific objectivity, process all theology only through left-brainish thinking? What happens when theologians forget that God gave us the use of the right side of the brain to have faith and to relate and instead predominantly use their reasoning capacity to establish the teachings of the church?

The sincerity, integrity, and intellectual honesty of theologians for whom the historical critical method is the only way to read Scriptures are not in question. There is something charming and very attractive about academics who subject themselves to the vigorous application of a scientific method.

In question is the suitability of a scientific method for the subject of the Bible. We do not use a sieve to fetch water from the ocean. What we get is gravel and sand, anything but water. The Bible is a book of faith for people of faith.

Jesus affirmed the authority of Scripture and freely quoted Scriptures. He taught Scriptures as the final authority, "Have you not read . . ."(Matthew 19:4) and, "They have Moses and the prophets; they should listen to them."(Luke 16:28)

Authors of the New Testament affirm the authority of Scriptures. In 1 Corinthians 14:21 Paul quotes Isaiah 28:11. Matthew quotes Scriptures in Matthew 1:21-23, 2:14-15. Acts 4: 24-25 states that is was the Holy Spirit who inspired David to write the words of Psalm 2:1-2.

The writers of Scriptures were guided by the Holy Spirit to write Scriptures for people who understand the message with the aid of the Holy Spirit. It is the Holy Spirit who calls and enlightens. A scientific method is incapable of capturing the Holy Spirit. The historical critical method cannot capture revealed theology.

We must remind ourselves that the wonderful gift to be rational must be balanced by the gift to have faith and read Scriptures through the eyes of faith. Unfortunately, some of our current theologians have swallowed the historical critical method hook, line, and sinker. There are valuable insights to be gained through historical biblical criticism. But it is heretical to insist that divine truth is limited by what human reason can comprehend. The full understanding of the message of Scriptures cannot be assembled by reason alone.

It is illogical to speak of an all powerful God and then reduce what God can do to fit our mental capacity.

It is plainly wrong to assume that God, the Father Almighty, creator of heaven and earth, cannot do miracles. Any God that can be dissected by a scientific method is too small. Virgin birth is something that any scientific approach to Scriptures must reject. Yet, for God, who designed DNA, virgin birth is a very minor task. The truly spiritual dimensions of Scriptures that are demonstrated and experienced in the lives of Christians are an unsuitable subject for the historical critical method. The products of a left-brainish scientific investigation feed the mind but not the soul. Scientific methods do well in investigating subjects of a three dimensional world only.

As Eta Linnemann observed, the historical critical method is an ideology as much as it is a method. It is an ideology based on a choice that replaces "Faith alone 'with' Reason Alone." Eta Linnemann studied New Testament under Bultmann and Fuchs in Germany, did her doctorate and her post doctorate in New Testament, taught New Testament at the University of Marburg, was admitted to the elite Society for New Testament Studies, and published Revisionist Theology until she had a conversion experience. That changed her whole outlook on the nature of Scriptures. She published "Historical Criticism of the Bible, Methodology or Ideology?" in 1990. Her brief journey of faith, Confessions of a Former Bultmannian can be accessed through Google.

In "Historical Criticism of the Bible, Methodology or Ideology?" Linnemann draws on her own experience as a professor in Germany who applied historical criticism to the Bible and taught such at the University of Marburg:

The fundamental presupposition of university theology in its entirety, as it is presently espoused in our universities, is the conviction that the final authority regarding what is true is the trained, professionally informed, regimented critical intellect. That is, Holy Scripture is subordinated to reason. Reason decides what in the Scriptures is true and real. Reason decides what is certain, probable, or improbable in the Bible and what did not, does not, and never will occur. The critical intellect decides whether God is to be viewed as someone who acts and speaks or whether "God" is actually simply human ideas and concepts about a hypothetical divine being.

Here reason makes use of the possibilities of knowing that are inherent to it. Critical intellect cannot conceive of a truly unique event; it must therefore assert as a fundamental presupposition the basic uniformity of all that happens and ever has happened. Critical intellect acquires knowledge only through comparison and differentiation. Where, therefore, it seeks knowledge, it must first lay out levels of comparison. Revelation is inconceivable to critical intellect; its standard is what is common to all human experience at all times."
Pages 107-108

Under the Guise of Scientific Objectivity, Revisionist Theology Has Led Christians Away from Traditional Christian Theology

REVISIONIST THEOLOGIANS HAVE TO REPENT of their attitude that puts down Christians who dare to believe with their heart (right side of the brain) as well as with their left side of the brain, who refuse to accept a theology that is based on reason alone. There are aspects of the divinity of Jesus that are accessible to us only through the Holy Spirit. The Holy Spirit still reveals to us what the left side of the brain cannot comprehend.

It is unfair to proclaim that there are only two theological alternatives, the theology of the Jesus Seminar theologians and the theology of Biblicists who insist on the literal interpretation of Scriptures. Luther did not fit into either of these categories. Luther looked at Scriptures critically, hence his assessment of the book of James as the "Epistle of straw." But he also looked at Scriptures through the eyes of faith. The Lutheran approach to Scriptures is a holistic approach using both hemispheres of the brain in an interactive way. There is something about our faith that "passes all human understanding." A holistic approach to Scriptures prevents theologians from the extremes like the Revisionist Theology and also from a literalist interpretation of Scriptures such as the creation story.

We fall in love in the right side of the brain and then try to articulate our feelings by using the left side of the brain. Equally, we believe and relate to our Lord Jesus in the right side of the brain and then articulate that faith using the left side of the brain. In the process of that articulation, such as stated in our ecumenical creeds, we make statements that go beyond what pure reason can comprehend.

Under the cloak of scientific neutrality and objectivity Revisionist Theology subordinates faith under the lordship of reason. There is an ideological leap between the use of historical criticism as a hermeneutical tool and Revisionist Theology. A denial that Jesus died for our sins and a denial of his resurrection has made that ideological leap.

Such ideological leap has occurred in the theology of Marcus Borg. According to his autobiography, *Me and Jesus*, "The gospel of John is highly symbolic and essentially not historical. . . . Most (perhaps all) of the 'exalted titles' by which Jesus is known in the Christian tradition do not go back to Jesus himself. He did not speak of or think of himself as 'the Son of God,' or as 'one with the Father,' or as 'the light of the world,' or as 'the way, the truth, and the life,' or as 'the savior of the world. . . . It follows that Jesus' message was not about himself or the importance of believing in him. . . . I do not believe that Christianity is the only way to salvation, or that the Bible is the revealed will of God, or that Jesus was the unique Son of God. Rather, I now see that the Christian tradition—including its claims about Jesus—is not something to be believed, but something to be lived in.'"

Revisionist theologians, too, talk about faith. But it is a faith that is radically subjected to left-brainish reason. Revisionist theologians also pray, reflect, meditate, listen to the Spirit, and attempt to live out their faith in the world. They use the same terms as confessional Lutherans. Yet they arrive at a faith that is far removed from the faith of Martin Luther.

R. Bultmann admitted that "presuppositionless exegesis" is impossible. The arrogance of Revisionist theologians is exposed in their claim that anything that offends reason and logic must be false. There is no logical reason to love someone. Nor can reason access God. Goethe's line in Dr. Faustus "You are equal to the Spirit whom you understand (Du gleichst dem Geist den Du begreifts)" stipulates that a God who is comprehended by human reason cannot be greater than a human mind. God cannot be accessed by human reason. Any effort to prove the existence of God (Gottes Beweise) must fail. It is rational to admit that reason has its limits.

The historical critical method is a good method for historical research. But it does not fit the subject of the Bible as the exclusive tool to understanding Scriptures. It is as suitable to deal with the subject of faith as it would be to deal with the subject of love. It is an inadequate tool to exclusively understand the message of Scriptures.

There are helpful applications of the historical critical method in dealing with Scriptures. It would also be helpful if those who apply the use of the historical critical method would admit the limitations of that method rather than making it the only way to understand Scriptures.

If the only tool you have is a hammer, then everything gets treated like a nail.

It is the Holy Spirit who "has called me through the Gospel, enlightened me with his gifts, and sanctified me in the true faith" (Luther).

The historical critical method crosses the line from being a method to becoming an ideology by making the assumption that anything that cannot be processed on the left side of the brain could not have happened. A sieve is not designed to fetch water. It is the wrong tool. Making the assumption that anything a sieve cannot fetch does not exist would be an ideological assumption.

Academically it is not very glamorous to tell "the old, old story." To advance in academia one must come up with a new angle or make a new discovery, one must push the envelope. But it is a totally different thing when the basic Gospel is changed.

It is a basic change in the Gospel when

• the doctrine of substitutional atonement that Jesus died for our sins is denied.

• it is proclaimed that Jesus did not really rise from the dead and that the resurrection only happened in the minds of the believers.

• it is proclaimed that Jesus was such a good person that people actually believed that he was the Son of God and that in fact Jesus never made that claim.

Those changes attack the very core of the Christian faith.

Admittedly, it does not make any scientific sense that Jesus is the incarnate God who died for our sins and rose from the dead. It did not even make sense in the days of the first Christian church. (1 Corinthians 15: 12-19)

Lutheran theology has therefore upheld that a full understanding of Scriptures can only be achieved with the aid of the Holy Spirit. The Bible is a book of faith. It is through faith that we "understand" God as we by faith "stand under" God. Revisionist Theology based on historical critical exegesis as proclaimed by Borg, Spong, and Crossan in the "Living the Questions" DVD series, ignores the validity of the faith that Lutherans have been taught and have heard preached for generations. It ignores "the peace that passes all understanding."

It is a tragedy that some theological and ecclesiastical Lutherans have succumbed to Revisionist Theology. In doing so Lutheran roots have been abandoned. For those of us who have been in the Lutheran ministry for a long time, it is legitimately left-brainish to ask, "If Revisionist theologians are right, did we preach a false Gospel?" But it is also legitimate to ask, "Is there the emergence of a false Gospel in our days that Scriptures warn us against?"

"For the time is coming when people will not endure sound teaching, but having itchy ears they will accumulate for themselves teachers to suit their own likings and will turn away from listening to the truth and wander into myths." (2. Timothy 4: 3-5 RSV)

The uncomfortable truth is that either Christians have been preaching and teaching myths for well over a thousand years or that we are now in one of those periods in church history when, well intended as they are, some theologians and pastors have developed a case of itchy ears. (Or is it too left-brainish to ask such a question?)

As Lutherans we have a theology that is not limited by reason. Let us hope that some of those who have been influenced by Revisionist Theology will rediscover the joy of being Lutherans who use both hemispheres of the God-given capacity of their brain.

The challenge is to rediscover the theology of Paul and Augustine and Luther and Bonhoeffer which was not infected by technitis.

Hans Schwarz is a pastor of the Evangelical Lutheran Church of America, Professor Emeritus of Protestant Theology (Systematic Theology and Contemporary Theological Issues) of the University of Regensburg in Germany, and visiting professor at the Lutheran Theological Southern Seminary in Columbia, South Carolina, teaching there every other year since 1984. He was born in 1939 in Schwabach, Bavaria, received his theological education at the universities of Erlangen and Göttingen and obtained his doctorate in Systematic Theology *summa cum laude* at Erlangen University in 1963. He was professor at Trinity Lutheran Seminary in Columbus, Ohio (1967-1981), before accepting a call to Regensburg University (1981) where he still continues to teach.

Under his guidance more than thirty theologians from four continents received their doctorate in theology. While lecturing in more than twenty countries, he has presented more than 400 lectures and numerous sermons. He is active in his local congregation in Regensburg, having served for twenty-some years on the church council. He has written more than twenty books, his most recent ones being *Theology in a Global Context: The Last Two Hundred Years*

(Eerdmans, 2005), and *Creation* (Eerdmans, 2002). He has received two honorary doctorates, one from an Orthodox theological faculty (Oradea 2004) and another one from a Reformed faculty (Debrecen 2006).

Norms for Life and Living

Hans Schwarz

ACCORDING TO THEIR OWN SELF-UNDERSTANDING Lutherans did not promulgate any new doctrines. They believe in the triune God, they believe in Jesus Christ as their only savior, and accept the doctrinal decisions of the undivided church, such as the decisions of the councils of Nicaea and Chalcedon. They also regard the prophetic and apostolic writings of the Old and New Testament as sole rule and norm according to which all teachers and all teaching should be judged as they claim in the *Formula of Concord*. In this way we as Lutherans should have it easier to arrive at a consensus than other denominations that are less encumbered by history and confessions.

When we look at doctrinal statements then this assumption seems to be valid since doctrinal dissension is relatively rare at least in the ELCA. But this "peaceful doctrinal existence" may be deceiving. It could also stem from the notion that doctrine takes second place to day to day existential issues. When we look at our sister denomination, the Lutheran Church—Missouri Synod we realize that there is much less peace regarding doctrine. The LCMS is much more plagued with doctrinal controversies than the ELCA. But the ELCA is not free either from its own share of problems which often stem from day to day existential issues. While many of us desire a clear word from "a place on high" once such a word is forthcoming and does not coincide with what we expected we question whether he or she had the authority to tell us what to do or in which direction we should think. We are confronted here with center of the Reformation insight that we have no other authority above us but Christ himself. All other voices have only guiding but not prescriptive value. Martin Luther rightly cautioned:

> When you wish to say on your deathbed: the pope has said this, the councils have decided that, the holy fathers . . . have determined this, the devil will immediately bore a hole and break in asking, "What if it is not true? Could it not be that they have erred? "So you are pushed right back down. So you must know without doubt that you can say, "This is the Word of God and here I stand."[1]

But how can we discern what the Word of God is in a given situation? As Lutherans we remember that Luther claimed that in Jesus Christ God has shown us his heart, meaning God has indicated what God has in store for us and how we should respond. The ethicist James A. Gustafson rightly claimed: "Christ as Lord, as Master, for Christians often does, can, and ought to give them a particular perspective on life, a particular posture toward life."[2] Since Christ is not tangibly accessible, we are pointed to Scripture to discern the mind of Christ. But turning to Scripture does not resolve ambiguity, since Scripture can be approached in different ways.

There is firstly the *literal approach* in which the New Testament is understood as a divinely revealed document which reveals certain moral precepts. Since the ELCA "accepts the canonical Scriptures of the Old and the New Testaments as the inspired Word of God and the authoritative source and norm of its proclamation, faith, and life,"[3] one could interpret the New Testament as the quintessential law book which tells us what to do. Yet such a literalist view is too simplistic. As we can see from sectarian groups of Christianity, literalists are usually selective in what is to be adhered to literally.

More promising would be the *mainstream approach*. It is popular with many Christians and does not seek the moral precepts of the New Testament, but rather asks: "What would Jesus do?" Jesus is perceived there as the example to follow and who inspires us to Christ-like conduct. There the condemning character often associated with the legalistic interpretation is averted while urgency of the New Testament teachings is maintained. Still, both the legalist and the mainstream assume that one can lift certain rules from the New Testament text and apply it to the contemporary scene.

This is different from the *spiritualist approach*. There we encounter an interesting mixture of loyalty to Scripture and a relativizing of its message. For instance, at the beginning of the twentieth century the German theologian Adolf von Harnack praised Jesus' proclamation of "*the infinite value of the human soul*."[4] At the same time he claimed that Jesus' view of the kingdom of God conflicted with the kingdom of the devil, which resulted in a supreme battle at the end of time, "was an idea which Jesus simply shared with his contemporaries."[5] One looks for eternal or all-encompassing principles and treats others as of less importance. Jesus is then understood to stand for liberation, love, or hope; Scripture in general for promise and fulfilment, law and gospel. While these themes are foreign neither to Jesus nor the New Testament, such generalizations tend to obliterate other equally important themes. They also ignore that God's self-disclosure occurred in history, namely Scripture as the reflection upon this self-disclosure, is itself a historical document. The "themes" of subsequent history must always be measured against Scripture's history. Absolutizing such themes means perverting them since they pretend to express all of Scripture instead of just one aspect.

Once the historical question is raised, one can no longer confine oneself to the mere meaning of the words, but must consider yet a fourth approach, the *intentional approach*. This hermeneutic asks about the text in its original and subsequent contexts. This intentional approach is illustrated by Martin Luther in his explanation of the fifth commandment. The legalist and the fundamentalist might interpret "Thou shalt not kill" to mean that one should not bring a person by force from life to death, while the spiritualist might discern that perhaps not all force was executed wilfully. But the intention of this commandment, explained in the Sermon on the Mount and reiterated by Luther, does not just focus on violence. Luther states in the Small Catechism: "We should so fear and love God, as not to do our neighbor any bodily harm or injury, but rather assist and comfort him in danger and want."[6] From this one example, one sees the intentional approach is much more comprehensive than a literalist or a spiritualist interpretation.

The intentional approach can be ambiguous. For instance Jesus praises the attentive Mary for listening to him, while he scolds the busy Martha for working (Lk. 10:42). Paul, however, confronted with sloth and misunderstood eschatological expectations declares: "Anyone unwilling to work should not eat" (2 Thess. 3:10 NRSV). An intentional approach gives rise to situational and contextual ethics. But if we do not claim that our present context is normative for us, what situation or context is; that of Jesus, or of the Evangelists, or of Paul? Moreover, can we still unearth with sufficient clarity the intention of the scriptural norms on either one of these levels? Again Martin Luther was convinced of the clarity of Scripture against the scepticism of the humanist Erasmus of Rotterdam. Scripture is clear and understandable and it is the final authority. Luther states: "Scripture, therefore, is its own light. It is good, then, when Scripture interprets itself."[7] Yet can we still affirm this claim given our modern exegetical insights? Especially with the so-called third wave of the life of Jesus research (Marcus Borg) there is a renewed interest by laity and New Testament scholars in the Jesus of history and also in Jesus' continuity or discontinuity with both his religious and secular environment.

As a member of the Jewish community, Jesus derived many of his ethical norms from the Old Testament. He affirmed the apodictic law (Mk. 10:17-19), recognized the cultic law (Mk. 1:44), and could even acknowledge the whole tradition (Mt. 7:12). Yet in proclaiming the will of God as if he stood in God's place, he distinguished between God's will and the tradition (Mk. 7:11). In summing up the moral norms in the

Great Commandment to love God and the neighbor (Mk. 12:28-31) Jesus drew on the Old Testament (Lev. 19:18 and Dtn. 6:5), but tied these precepts to his person and destiny. Love is not to be understood as an ideal to be aspired or as a universal law of conduct. As unconditionally as the love of God encounters us in Jesus, our love is also to be extended toward our neighbors and even our enemies. James Childs rightly states: "Experiencing gospel grace by the trust of faith, energized by the Spirit, enables us to reach out in love to others as God has reached out in love to us."[8]

All the norms contained in Jesus' proclamation are not to be taken in isolation, contrary to what, for instance, the Hindu Ghandi did, when he lifted some of our precepts from the Sermon on the Mount and applied them to the struggle for India's independence from Great Britain's colonial rule. No, these precepts receive their source of information, their content, and their direction from our encounter with Jesus. If God is the kind of God who is disclosed in the life and destiny of Jesus, there are only two choices open to us: either to reject God and therewith our source and goal of life, or to respond to God with total dedication. This means Jesus' norms of conduct are intended for his followers as a response to his life and destiny. They are not intended to be universal rules. Therefore the laws of the land may either be wider or more restrictive than these rules of Christ-like conduct.

Since Jesus is no longer physically present to give us guidance in our lives, we have no other means to approach him but through Scripture with the aid of the Holy Spirit. This also helps us to see how his commands were received by the early Christian community. While they felt as do we that Christ is present through his Spirit promised to his followers (Acts 1:2), they also found it necessary, in attempting to live in conformity with his will, to introduce norms in his name (Mt. 18:15ff.). Especially in the writings of the Apostle Paul, the urgency to emulate Christ is maintained. In a *christological way* Paul emphasizes that Christians are new beings. Through Christ there is a new creation and a new humanity. This newness is not something automatically given but is to be realized and can be realized through salvation accomplished in Jesus Christ. Therefore Paul urges the Christians to fulfil the norms of Christ, to become Christ-like, because Christians are saved through Christ. The fact that Christians are new beings in Christ enables and encourages them to fulfil Christ's imperatives, but does not abolish them.

In a *sacramental way* Paul arrives at the same sequence of promise and command. Since through baptism Christians die and rise with Christ, becoming children of God, they are no longer under the dominion of sin (Rom. 6:4.11-12.14). Christians are now freed from the enslavement to sin and are able to follow the precepts of Christ. Martin Luther actualises this baptismal imagery when he states in his *Small Catechism* "that the old creature in us with all sins and evil desires is to be drowned and die through daily contrition and repentance, and on the other hand that daily a new person is to come forth and rise up to live before God in righteousness and purity forever."[9] Luther as well as Paul realized that even Christians revert to their old being and therefore need daily repentance and daily renewal.

Paul could also in a *pneumatological way* encourage the Christians to bring forth the fruits of the Spirit (Gal. 5:22). The law of the Spirit under which Christians live is exclusive of the law of sin under which they formerly lived (Rom. 8:2). Now they can live and walk by the Spirit (Gal. 5:25). Since Christ has died and was risen "for us" we are encouraged to a life-style of response to this gracious action. This means that we as Christians are exhorted to a different, Christ-like life.

But how can we obtain more specific pointers of what this entails? Though the Bible is the ultimate authority for our life and living, it is no directory which would cover every detail of our lives. Yet some guidelines are clear and must be followed if we want to name ourselves after Christ: The world has its own rules and cannot set the agenda for the Christian community. The approach reflected in Josh. 25:15: "But as for me and my household, we will serve the Lord," is analogous to that of the Christian community. But Christians do not live in splendid isolation. While endeavouring to avoid the sins of the world, they are free to learn from the virtues of the world. They can accept any custom which does not conflict with the gospel (1 Cor. 11:2-16); they can pursue that which is considered true, just, and honorable (Phil. 4:8); they can appeal to conscience (Rom. 2:15), and can even refer to the teachings of nature (1 Cor. 11:14). The criterion for that which can be learned from the world insists that it does not compromise Christ and the radicalism of God's will. This claim does not mean an ossification of laws. One needs only to note interpretative changes of certain precepts of the Old Testament covenant community by Jesus, and then again by Paul, and the evangelists, e.g., divorce, or the role of women. However, there are other precepts which remain virtually unchanged, such as faithfulness to one's spouse, or injunctions against homosexuality. Perhaps we can learn from Luther's insistence on infant baptism over against those who opted for believer's baptism. Luther maintained that any changes should only be made if there is a clear mandate from Scripture. If we want to remain faithful to the Bible as our sole rule and norm for life and living, we must discern the constants as well as the variables and not exchange one for the other.

Christ-like conduct requires us to have compassion for both faithful and sinners, but it requires us to discern between faithful living and sin, to espouse the former and to reject the latter. While we welcome everybody into our midst, especially those for whom Jesus cared, namely the poor, despised, and the outcast of society, we dare not bless or condone that which the Bible in all its witness to God's saving action disproves. This does not mean that we are righteous and the others are sinners. While we still live on this side of heaven, we also have a broken existence, being both sinners and saints, and are in need of God's forgiveness. Therefore those of us, be it laity or clergy, who in utmost sincerity attempt to discern God's will in a given situation may come down on different sides of the same issue. Only in heaven will all conflicts be resolved. Being both saints and sinners, however, is no licence for sinning but mandates to consider the other position not a priori heretical or unethical.

Notes

[1]Martin Luther in a sermon on Mt. 7:15ff., *Predigten des Jahres 1522*, in *WA* 10 III, 259.13-18.

[2]James Gustafson, *Christ and the Moral Life* (New York: Harper & Row, 1968), p. 242.

[3]ELCA, *Confession of Faith*.

[4]Adolf von Harnack, *What Is Christianity?* trans. Thomas B. Saunders (Philadelphia: Fortress, 1986), p. 51.

[5]Harnack, *What Is Christianity?* p. 54.

[6]Martin Luther, *Small Catechism* (Rock Island, Illinois: Augustana Book Concern, 1922), p. 7.

[7]Martin Luther in a sermon from July 25, 1522, *Predigten des Jahres 1522,* in *WA* 10,III,238, pp. 10-11.

[8]James Childs, *Faith, Formation, and Decision* (Minneapolis: Fortress, 1992), p. 75.

[9]Martin Luther, *Small Catechism*, p. 360.

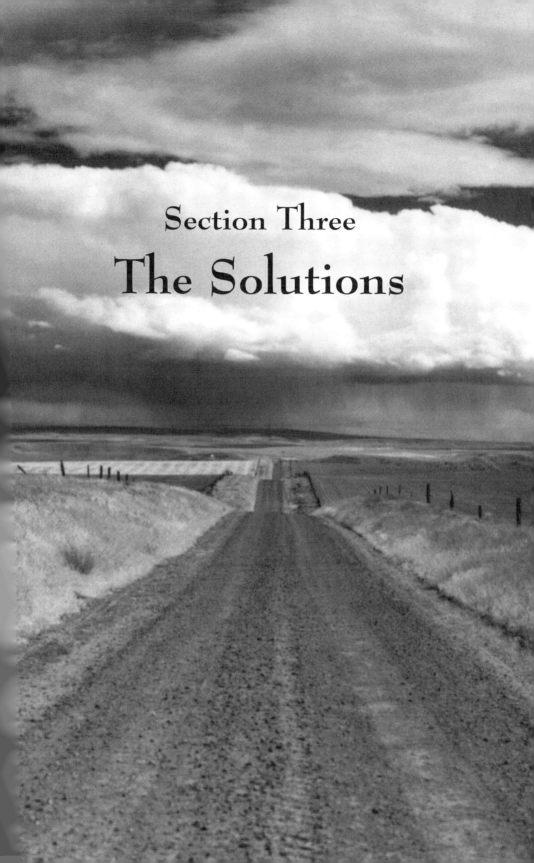

Section Three
The Solutions

Mark Chavez was born in Denver, Colorado, and was raised in Colorado and California. He is married to Jocelyn M. Bateman of Philadelphia, Pennsylvania. They have six children.

He is a graduate of the U.S. Air Force Academy and Queen's College, Oxford University, United Kingdom.

He served as a commissioned officer in the U.S. Air Force from 1976 to 1983, primarily in the Directorate of Soviet Affairs, Air Force Intelligence Service, Bolling Air Force Base, Washington, D.C. He served on a briefing team that traveled to Air Force installations worldwide and presented briefings on the Soviet Union's economy, political system, foreign policy and armed forces.

Mark resigned his commission in the Air Force in 1983 to attend Luther Northwestern Theological Seminary in St. Paul, Minnesota. He served his internship at First Lutheran Church, Miles City, Montana, in 1985-1986.

Pastor Harold S. Goers ordained him at St. Matthew Evangelical Lutheran Church, Washington, D.C., in 1987. He served as Pastor at: Peace Lutheran Church, Glen Burnie, Maryland, from 1987 to 1999; and Zion Evangelical Lutheran Church, East Petersburg, Pennsylvania from 1999 to 2000. He is currently under call to Faith Lutheran Church, Hutchinson, Minnesota, which deployed him to serve the WordAlone Network, an evangelical renewing and confessing movement within the Evangelical Lutheran Church in America.

After joining the e-mail discussion list in the spring of 1997, Mark became involved in the WordAlone movement. He attended the first WordAlone meeting in February 1999 and served as a regional leader for WordAlone in Maryland and Pennsylvania. Since August 2000 he has served as director of the WordAlone Network—for six years in New Brighton,

Minnesota, and since fall 2006 in Landisville, Pennsylvania. Since the formation of Lutheran CORE, the coalition for reform, in fall 2005, he has also served as director of Lutheran CORE.

❧ 20 ❧

Do People Fear the Living God?

Mark C. Chavez

It is a fearful thing to fall into the hands of the living God.
Hebrews 10:31 (ESV)

THE QUESTION THE JERUSALEM TEMPLE authorities asked Jesus—
"By what authority are you doing these things, and who gave
you this authority?"—makes sense only in a world in which people generally have respect for authority. The question challenges and
confronts only if people are usually careful not to act without proper
authority. If people generally agree that it would be wrong for someone
to take matters into his hands with no authority to do so, the question
is serious and demands a response.

The presupposition behind the temple authorities question is
that someone who acts without proper authority might have some guilt
or even fear for doing so. Behind the question is the assumption that
people ought ultimately to fear God.

Do those presuppositions hold true for people in North America
in the twenty-first century? What about people in Protestant mainline
churches and other churches? What if people aren't cautious at all about

taking matters into their own hands? What if people are not at all fearful about acting without authority?

What if people do not fear the ultimate authority, the Author of Life, the almighty God and creator of all that exists? The apostle Paul reminds us that "there is no authority except from God, and those that exist have been instituted by God." (Romans 13:1b ESV)

On the eve of World War II, Ole Hallesby, a Norwegian Lutheran pastor wrote these words in a meditation on Luke 12:5 ("But I will warn you whom to fear: fear him who, after he has killed, has authority to cast into hell. Yes, I tell you, fear him!"):

> The disciples needed an admonition to fear God. We need it too. Yes, I often ask myself: Is there anything our generation needs more urgently than to really fear God? There is fear enough otherwise in our day and age. We fear illness. . . . We fear poverty. . . . We fear people. . . . Yes, there is enough fear. Jesus tells us that this fear which stunts the growth of a person's character and contaminates the soul is all due to the fact that we do not fear the *only* one whom we *should* fear, namely, the living God. (*God's Word for Today*, translated by Clarence J. Carlson, Augsburg Fortress, 1994, original edition, 1937)

Hallesby's observation seventy years ago in Norway could just as well been written about twenty-first century North Americans. In general, there appears to be much more fear of earthly matters than divine. Judging by the regular pronouncements of some church leaders, we ought to be more afraid of global warming, AIDS, and wars than the living God.

Ironically, leaders of Protestant mainline denominations, including leaders in the Evangelical Lutheran Church in America (ELCA), who are so fearful of earthly dangers, have the temerity to do whatever they want with the Word of God. In many ways, church leaders, and by that I mean specifically clergy and theologians, take matters into their own hands and make themselves the authorities over God's Word. It is not unusual to find church leaders and churches fashioning the god they want or think they need. The biblical word for this activity is idolatry.

It would be easy to focus on the most blatant idolatry found in North America: the Jesus Seminar in which "scholars" periodically vote to decide what they think Jesus truly said and didn't say; Ebenezer Lutheran Church in San Francisco, Calif., an ELCA church whose web site (www.herchurch.org) publicly professes the congregation's god to be a pagan goddess; or the radical feminist re-imagining conferences that have explicitly rejected the need for a male savior who died on a cross. Temerity abounds in all these projects.

However, I want to focus on two other indications that Christian churches make themselves the authorities over the ultimate Authority. One is the implicit, if not explicit assumption, that humans determine what God says. The second, more subtle and perhaps more pervasive, is a weakness of the ecumenical Revised Common Lectionary, the assigned Scripture readings for worship in liturgical churches. Some of those readings intentionally avoid discomforting Scripture passages that might cause sinners to squirm or perhaps even be a little fearful of the living God who reveals Himself in the Bible.

Human Institutions Given Authority over the Word of God

FIRST, I CITE THE ELCA'S CURRENT PROCESS leading to a social statement on sexuality and the particular questions of whether or not to bless same-sex unions and ordain practicing homosexuals. The current process began in 2001 and ELCA leaders have described the process as one of discerning what God might be saying about homosexual behavior and relationships. Leaders of international Lutheran churches who are companion churches with ELCA synods were told right after the 2007 churchwide assembly that in this process the ELCA is seeking "to discern God's will for this church." (August 15, 2007 letter from Presiding Bishop Mark Hanson and Reverend Rafael Malpica Padilla, Global Mission executive director).

The ELCA Conference of Bishops issued a pastoral statement in March 2007 on the ELCA study of sexuality leading to an upcoming proposed social statement on sexuality. This was the final paragraph in the bishops' statement:

> We trust the Holy Spirit to guide us and have confidence in the constitutional process that orders our conversation as we engage together in moral deliberation at Synod Assemblies and the Church-wide Assembly.
> The Conference of Bishops of the Evangelical Lutheran Church in America commits itself to faithful leadership as, together, we seek the mind of Christ on these matters.

When the bishops used language like "engage together in moral deliberation" and "seek the mind of Christ on these matters" they simply repeated the language used by the ELCA churchwide organization and many ELCA leaders since the formation of the denomination in 1988. The underlying assumption is that by engaging in studies, debating the issues at assemblies and then voting on those issues, the ELCA is doing "moral deliberation" and discovering the "mind of Christ on these matters."

For example, The ELCA Church Council said in its preface to its recommendations on the sexuality studies to the 2005 churchwide assembly:

> From the outset the (sexuality) task force attempted to make clear that the study process was indeed a study, not a poll or a survey. The experience was to be a time of learning and discerning that would: . . . Help the church to discern what is a faithful response to the question of blessing same-sex unions and admitting people in such committed unions into the rostered ministries of the ELCA.

The "discerning" process will eventually end in a vote by a churchwide assembly or the church council. That vote will decide what the ELCA is hearing from God regarding homosexual behavior and relationships. The bishops expressed their "confidence in the constitutional process" that leads to that decision.

Suppose an ELCA churchwide assembly, the "highest legislative authority" (ELCA Constitution 12.11), "discerns" that God is now saying to the ELCA that homosexual behavior is not sin. By what authority would the assembly and the ELCA make that decision? Are ELCA leaders so unafraid of the living God as to believe that an assembly vote can actually tell God and ELCA members what He is saying? Do ELCA bishops (and other leaders) really have that much trust and "confidence" in a "constitutional process"?

Are there no limits on the authority of a churchwide assembly? Here is the full text of section 12.11 of the ELCA constitution:

> The Churchwide Assembly shall be the highest legislative authority of the churchwide organization and shall deal with all matters which are necessary in pursuit of the purposes and functions of this church. The powers of the Churchwide Assembly are limited only by the provisions of the Articles of Incorporation, this constitution and bylaws, and the assembly's own resolutions.

In theory, a churchwide assembly should be limited by section 2.03 of the ELCA constitution: "This church accepts the canonical Scriptures of the Old and New Testaments as the inspired Word of God and the authoritative source and norm of its proclamation, faith, and life." On the particular matter of homosexuality, since the Scriptures consistently and clearly proscribe all homosexual behavior, in theory an ELCA churchwide assembly ought not have the authority to decide that homosexual behavior is not sin. Just as a churchwide assembly ought not have the authority to decide that Jesus was not the Son of God or that he wasn't physically raised from the dead, body and all, on the third day.

However, the basic assumption from day one in the ELCA is that a churchwide assembly does have the authority to decide if homosexual behavior is sin.

Given this assumption, ultimate authority in the ELCA has shifted from the external Word of God to a process and an assembly. The irony of this shift is that the ELCA has reverted to a position essentially the same as the position of the Roman Catholic Church in the 16th century. The difference is that instead of the Pope and his advisors claiming authority over God's Word, the ELCA gives that authority to a legislative body. Either way, sinners take matters into their own hands and tell God what He is saying or what He meant to say, but just didn't do it clearly enough when He inspired the writing of the Scriptures.

Is there no fear, or at least a little caution or hesitancy, in granting so much authority to a human institution? Apparently not and perhaps one of many possible contributing factors for the absence of fear is that Christians in denominations and traditions that use a common lectionary are shielded from some of the most discomforting words that God speaks in the Scriptures.

A Lectionary That Avoids Some Troubling Texts

THE REVISED COMMON LECTIONARY (RCL)—the three-year cycle of appointed Scripture readings for worship in many churches—is an international and ecumenical project of the Common Consultation on Texts, whose web site—<www.commontexts.org>—documents the history of the lectionary. Representatives from Catholic, Orthodox and Protestant churches have been involved in developing the lectionary. Though the RCL was produced for North American churches, there is growing interest in the lectionary in other parts of the world. This means that it is not just ELCA members or members of mainline Protestant denominations in North America who may not be hearing some discomforting words in the Scriptures.

In addition to the widespread use of the RCL, it and its predecessors have been used for more than 30 years in North America. The catalyst and original basis for the RCL was the new three-year Roman Catholic lectionary issued in 1969, *Ordo Lectionum Missae*. An ecumenical team issued a trial lectionary in 1983 that was based on the Roman lectionary. It was revised and issued as the RCL in 1992. However, before the trial lectionary was issued, a number of denominations used the Roman lectionary as a basis for developing their own three-year lectionaries, including Lutherans in North America. The Inter-Lutheran Commission on Worship (representatives from The American Lutheran Church, The Evangelical Lutheran Church of Canada, the Lutheran Church in America and The Lutheran Church-Missouri Synod) used the Roman lectionary to develop their three-year lectionary for their new hymnals in the 1970s, *Lutheran Book of Worship and Lutheran Worship*.

There is much to commend about the RCL, with its discipline of reading through much of the Gospels and New Testament epistles. There are advantages to having many Protestants and Catholics hearing the same Scripture texts on most days of the Church year. The RCL includes much of the heart of the Scriptures. The weakness is what is not included in the lectionary. A number of readings cut out verses in the middle of the selection. The excluded verses speak discomforting words and reveal a living God who ought to be feared.

I have not looked in detail at the books of the Bible that have no passages in the RCL—four in the Old Testament (1 Chronicles, Ezra, Obadiah and Nahum) and three in the New Testament (2 and 3 John and Jude). Nor have I looked at whole sections of books that are excluded from the lectionary or what the lectionary excludes just before or after a text.

However, I think an analysis of these excluded texts would show the same tendency to avoid some of the most discomforting words in Scripture. For example, Hebrews 10:31, the verse quoted at the beginning of this essay is excluded from the RCL. Or consider the three excluded New Testament epistles, which all have very discomforting words. Who wants to hear these words from the beginning of Jude?

> Beloved, although I was very eager to write to you about our common salvation, I found it necessary to write appealing to you to contend for the faith that was once for all delivered to the saints. For certain people have crept in unnoticed who long ago were designated for this condemnation, ungodly people, who pervert the grace of our God into sensuality and deny our only Master and Lord, Jesus

Christ. Now I want to remind you, although you once fully knew it, that Jesus, who saved a people out of the land of Egypt, afterward destroyed those who did not believe. (Jude 3-5)

Or why would the RCL exclude the introduction to the story of Noah and the great flood?

The LORD saw that the wickedness of man was great in the earth, and that every intention of the thoughts of his heart was only evil continually. And the LORD was sorry that he had made man on the earth, and it grieved him to his heart. So the LORD said, "I will blot out man whom I have created from the face of the land, man and animals and creeping things and birds of the heavens, for I am sorry that I have made them." But Noah found favor in the eyes of the LORD. (Genesis 6:5-8 ESV)

Are people not supposed to hear that God finds "only evil continually" in sinful human hearts and that He truly grieved that He had made humans and almost did away with the human race?

It would be worthwhile to do a more extensive analysis of what is not in the lectionary. However, I will focus only on the RCL readings that intentionally cut out middle sections of a passage. I will not examine readings that cut out middle verses for other probable reasons— abbreviating long passages; eliminating lists of names; eliminating lengthy descriptions; and using the beginning of a section to set the later verses in context. These exclusions seem warranted and necessary to fit as much Scripture as possible into a three-year lectionary and they do not significantly alter or slant the meaning of the overall passages.

However, there are twenty places in the RCL where middle verses are cut out and the absence of the verses significantly changes the reading. Most of the excluded passages are just a few verses or less, so the reason for excluding them cannot be to limit the reading to a reasonable length. In a few cases the same passage is cut out of the readings for more than one day in the Church year, which looks all the more as though the RCL avoids some troubling readings.

If all churches used pew Bibles some people might take note of the missing verses. However, since many lectionary churches use missals and Scripture inserts with only the RCL texts printed, many people will never even notice that words in the middle were cut out. Unless they read through the Bible on their own or attend a Bible study that works through an entire book of the Bible, it is likely that many people will never hear or read the excluded verses.

I begin with the last book of the Bible, because it was the RCL's exclusion of middle verses from a reading from Revelation that first piqued my curiosity to look at the other excluded middle verses. It also may be the most significant exclusion and illustrates a serious weakness of the lectionary.

Revelation 22:12-14, 16-17, 20-21 (ESV) (7 Easter C - the three years in the lectionary are designated A, B and C): The whole passage with the three excluded verses inserted in bold is:

> "Behold, I am coming soon, bringing my recompense with me, to repay everyone for what he has done. I am the Alpha and the Omega, the first and the last, the beginning and the end."
>
> Blessed are those who wash their robes, so that they may have the right to the tree of life and that they may enter the city by the gates. **Outside are the dogs and sorcerers and the sexually immoral and murderers and idolaters, and everyone who loves and practices falsehood.**
>
> "I, Jesus, have sent my angel to testify to you about these things for the churches. I am the root and the descendant of David, the bright morning star."
>
> The Spirit and the Bride say, "Come." And let the one who hears say, "Come." And let the one who is thirsty come; let the one who desires take the water of life without price.
>
> **I warn everyone who hears the words of the prophecy of this book: if anyone adds to them, God will add to him the plagues described in this book, and if anyone takes away from the words of the book of this prophecy, God will take away his share in the tree of life and in the holy city, which are described in this book.**
>
> He who testifies to these things says, "Surely I am coming soon." Amen. Come, Lord Jesus!
>
> The grace of the Lord Jesus be with all. Amen.

The first exclusion (vs. 15) might lead some to hear that everyone may enter the city gates and plays into the tendency that many people want to believe in universalism, that all are saved no matter what. The clear and frightening word that some are kept outside the city is missing from the lectionary.

The second exclusion (vss. 18-19) is astonishing to say the least. No doubt the people who worked on the RCL worked carefully in choosing which texts to use, but did anyone on the committee raise questions about cutting out words that specifically warn not to leave anything out? Was there apprehension in the minds of the committee about cutting out those two verses? What about the many Christian churches that use the butchered text? Do clergy take note of the missing verses and if so, are they at all apprehensive about not reading the verses aloud in worship?

Here are the other nineteen readings with missing middle verses with brief comments about the key missing verse or verses.

Exodus 15:1b-11, 20-21 (ESV) (Proper 19 A; Vigil of Easter A, B, C also excludes vss. 14-16): The excluded verses reveal an awesome God who caused the other nations to tremble in fear when God delivered His chosen people out of bondage in Egypt.

Deuteronomy 4:1-2, 6-9 (ESV) (Proper 17 B): The three missing verses remind the Israelites that God had destroyed many of them at Baal-Peor because of their idolatry, that is worshiping the local baals, gods, in the region of Peor.

1 Samuel 2:18-20, 26 (ESV) (1 Christmas C): The missing verses report how the priest Eli's sons were having sexual intercourse with women by the entrance to the Tent of the Meeting. The exclusion of verse 25 in particular is troubling. Eli confronts his sons, saying, "If someone sins against a man, God will mediate for him, but if someone sins against the LORD, who can intercede for him?" The narrative reports, "But they would not listen to the voice of their father, for it was the will of the LORD to put them to death." We do not want to hear that it is the will of God to put some to death, but should we not hear that word?

2 Samuel 6:1-5, 12b-19 (ESV) (Proper 10 B): The missing verses report that God got angry with Uzzah and killed him on the spot when he touched the ark of God as they were transporting the ark back to Judah. The oxen pulling the cart stumbled, so Uzzah presumably reached out to steady the ark on the cart. David "was afraid of the LORD that day, and he said, 'How can the ark of the LORD come to me?'" (vs. 9) He was so afraid he refused to take the ark home with him.

1 Kings 8:22-30, 41-43 (ESV) (Proper 16 B) / **1 Kings 8:22-23, 41-43** (Proper 4 C): The missing verses from Solomon's prayer of dedication for the temple include his request that God forgive the sins of His people if they turn toward the temple, confess their sins and ask for forgiveness. The key missing verses are the verses (39-40) at the end of the section, in which Solomon prays that God hear His people when they turn toward the temple in times of drought, famine and pestilence:

. . . then hear in heaven your dwelling place and forgive and act and render to each whose heart you know, according to all his ways (for you, you only, know the hearts of all the children of mankind), **that they may fear you all the days that they live in the land** that you gave to our fathers. (emphasis mine)

Job 42:1-6, 10-17 (ESV) (Proper 25 B): In the missing verses God speaks to Eliphaz, one of Job's friends, "My anger burns against you and against your two friends . . ." The exclusion of verses 7-9 is also odd in that they explain why Job prayed for his friends, which is mentioned in vs. 10.

Psalm 92:1-4, 12-15 (ESV) (Proper 6 B, 8 Epiphany C and Proper 3 C): This selection cuts out all of the words of judgment in the middle, making the psalm appear to be just a psalm of praise and thanks, and about the righteous. The key missing verse is 7: ". . . though the wicked sprout like grass and all evildoers flourish, they are doomed to destruction forever; . . ."

Psalm 104:1-9, 24, 35c (ESV) (Proper 24 B) / **Psalm 104:1-9, 24, 35b** (Pentecost A, B, C): For two different Sundays in two different ways the lectionary cuts out the first part of verse 35: "Let sinners be consumed from the earth, and let the wicked be no more!"

Jeremiah 14:7-10, 19-22 (ESV) (Proper 25 C): Strong words of judgment are excluded and perhaps the most significant are verses 11-12, in which God tells Jeremiah, "Do not pray for the welfare of this people. Though they fast, I will not hear their cry, and though they offer burnt offering and grain offering, I will not accept them. But I will consume them by the sword, by famine, and by pestilence."

Lamentations 3:1-9, 19-24 (ESV) (Saturday in Holy Week A, B, C): The beginning verses of this selection are surely discomforting words, but the excluded verses drive home the point all the more that God has turned against the prophet like a bear or a lion on the prowl, and like a hunter in search of game.

Joel 2:1-2, 12-17 (ESV) (Ash Wednesday A, B, C): The beginning verses of the selection speak of the approaching day of the Lord, "a day of darkness and gloom," but the frightening description of the day, an invasion of locusts, is excluded. Why not let people hear a few more verses on Ash Wednesday, when there should be no rush to finish a worship service, and in particular the end of vs. 11: "For the day of the LORD is great and very awesome; who can endure it?"

Matthew 11:16-19, 25-30 (ESV) (Proper 9 A): Here are the excluded verses:

> Then he began to denounce the cities where most of his mighty works had been done, because they did not repent. "Woe to you, Chorazin! Woe to you, Bethsaida! For if the mighty works done in you had been done in Tyre and Sidon, they would have repented long ago in sackcloth and ashes. But I tell you, it will be more bearable on the day of judgment for Tyre and Sidon than for you. And you, Capernaum, will you be exalted to heaven? You will be brought down to Hades. For if the mighty works done in you had been done in Sodom, it would have remained until this day. But I tell you that it will be more tolerable on the day of judgment for the land of Sodom than for you."

This exclusion is astonishing. Jesus' condemnation of two towns in which he spent much time, did many mighty works and presumably had many friends occurs only in Matthew 11:20-21 and the parallel passage in Luke 10:12-15. Both are missing from the RCL (see the next item). In deleting these sections, both Gospel texts are significantly altered. The readings explicitly avoid the need for repentance by those who know Jesus the best. Is it any wonder that the 2007 ELCA churchwide assembly objected to using the language that God uses Scripture to call "sinners to repentance"?

Luke 10:1-11, 16-20 (ESV) (Proper 9 C): See above and note that vs. 12 ("I tell you, it will be more bearable on that day for Sodom than for that town.") is the conclusion of vss. 1-11, making the exclusion all the more inexplicable, unless of course we are not supposed to hear too many reminders of God's fearful judgment against Sodom.

John 6:35, 41-51 (ESV) (Proper 14 B): Here are the excluded verses (in brackets) beginning with vs. 35:

Jesus said to them, "I am the bread of life; whoever comes to me shall not hunger, and whoever believes in me shall never thirst. (But I said to you that you have seen me and yet do not believe. All that the Father gives me will come to me, and whoever comes to me I will never cast out. For I have come down from heaven, not to do my own will but the will of him who sent me. And this is the will of him who sent me, that I should lose nothing of all that he has given me, but raise it up on the last day. For this is the will of my Father, that everyone who looks on the Son and believes in him should have eternal life, and I will raise him up on the last day.")

Why exclude these verses, when it significantly changes the reading? Is the notion of a God who chooses to give some sinners to His Son that objectionable or frightening?

John 13:1-17, 31b-35 (ESV) (Maundy Thursday A, B, C): This exclusion is troubling. There are no time constraints on Maundy Thursday, so why not hear the entire story? The missing verses provide the details of the depth of Judas' betrayal. Particularly on this day in the Church year sinners need to hear the whole story. Judas' betrayal is alluded to in vss. 1-17, so it makes all the more sense to hear the whole story. Perhaps though, these words (vss. 26-27), in response to the beloved disciple asking who will betray Jesus, are too frightening for sinners to hear:

Jesus answered, "It is he to whom I will give this morsel of bread when I have dipped it." So when he had dipped the morsel, he gave it to Judas, the son of Simon Iscariot. Then after he had taken the morsel, Satan entered into him. Jesus said to him, "What you are going to do, do quickly."

2 Thessalonians 1:1-4, 11-12 (ESV) (Proper 26 C): The exclusion of these verses significantly changes the beginning of Paul's letter, by omitting strong words of judgment, including:

. . . God considers it just to repay with affliction those who afflict you, and to grant relief to you who are afflicted as well as to us, when the Lord Jesus is revealed from heaven with his mighty angels in flaming fire, **inflicting vengeance on those who do not know**

God and on those who do not obey the gospel of our Lord Jesus. They will **suffer the punishment of eternal destruction, away from the presence of the Lord** . . . (emphasis mine)

2 Thessalonians 2:1-5, 13-17 (ESV) (Proper 27 C): For two consecutive Sundays the RCL emasculates Paul's letter. The full text of the excluded verses is worth noting:

> And you know what is restraining him now so that he may be revealed in his time. For the mystery of lawlessness is already at work. Only he who now restrains it will do so until he is out of the way. And then the lawless one will be revealed, whom the Lord Jesus will kill with the breath of his mouth and bring to nothing by the appearance of his coming. The coming of the lawless one is by the activity of Satan with all power and false signs and wonders, and with all wicked deception for those who are perishing, because they refused to love the truth and so be saved. Therefore God sends them a strong delusion, so that they may believe what is false, in order that all may be condemned who did not believe the truth but had pleasure in unrighteousness.

Paul refers to the "man of lawlessness" and "son of destruction" in vss. 3-4, so why not hear all that Paul has to say about him? Is it too frightening to hear that Jesus "will kill with the breath of his mouth" the man of lawlessness? Perhaps it is most frightening to hear that God sends a "strong delusion" upon "those who are perishing."

Hebrews 13:1-8, 15-16 (ESV) (Proper 17 C): The exclusion of these verses is unfortunate. Their exclusion significantly changes the reading and they are powerful words about Jesus' suffering for sinners outside the city. Furthermore, the beginning ("Do not be led away by diverse and strange teachings . . .") and ending ("For here we have no lasting city, but we seek the city that is to come.") of the excluded passage are words that sinners in every time and place ought to hear.

James 3:13-4:3, 7-8a (ESV) (Proper 20 B): Why omit three short verses that speak the truth about all sinners?

> You adulterous people! Do you not know that friendship with the world is enmity with God? Therefore whoever wishes to be a friend of the world makes himself an enemy of God. Or do you suppose it is to no purpose that the Scripture says, "He yearns jealously over the spirit that he has made to dwell in us"? But he gives more grace. Therefore it says, "God opposes the proud, but gives grace to the humble." Submit yourselves therefore to God. Resist the devil, and he will flee from you.

Should not sinners hear that they cannot be both friends of God and of the world? Is it too frightening to hear that the devil is assailing sinners?

I cannot read the minds of the people who prepared the RCL. I am sure they were well intentioned and I appreciate the many strengths of the lectionary. There certainly are passages in the lectionary that reveal God as one whom we should fear. However, I think the effect of the lectionary in some ways is to present a tame God and a tame Jesus. People want to hear that God is love, not anger and judgment. People want to hear a nice Jesus.

I am reminded of the first talking doll, Chatty Cathy. Pull a string and Chatty Cathy said such nice things. In this digital age, there are far more sophisticated talking dolls and creatures that can say much more than Chatty Cathy. The maker of the talking toy decides what it will say and has authority over the words.

The RCL can be used in ways that essentially present a "Chatty Cathy" Jesus who says nice things that we want to hear. In other words, the RCL can be used to fashion an idol. The idol, fashioned when lectors and preachers read selected texts, will certainly speak Jesus' words and God's words, but like all idols, it is not the living God and the risen Jesus. The maker of the lectionary decides what will be heard and therefore assumes authority over the Word.

I should add that non-lectionary churches are just as much at risk of fashioning a "Chatty Cathy" Jesus as the lectionary churches. I suspect that when preachers in those churches "pull the string," that is choose the texts for worship and preaching, there is a tendency to choose the same kinds of texts and fashion a God and Jesus that they want to hear and want others to hear.

Furthermore, anyone can fashion a "Chatty Cathy" Jesus in their devotions and personal Bible study by tending to read and study the same books of the Bible. There is no monopoly on this form of idolatry, hearing only what we want to hear.

Conclusion

I have cited two indications that people in North American churches might not be all that fearful of assuming authority over God and His Word—we assume we can vote on what God says and we limit the words that we hear from God. More indications could be cited. All humans are idolaters and there are many ways to fashion the god you want. The point is that the question, "By what authority . . .?" only gives pause to people who genuinely fear God and His judgment against idolaters, and perhaps there is not enough fear of God.

Let the living God and the risen Jesus Christ speak all that they have to say. Read all of Scripture and trust that the Holy Spirit will be at work in the hearing of the Word to bring sinners to repentance and salvation in Jesus Christ. Trust that the Holy Spirit will use the most frightening words in Scripture always in conjunction with the most comforting words in Scripture. It is "a fearful thing to fall into the hands of the living God," but better to fall into His hands than our own hands or the hands of a "Chatty Cathy" Jesus. There is no hope if we fall into any other hands than His.

Ole Hallesby's final words in 1937 in his devotion on Luke 12:5 are a fitting conclusion:

> Those who fear God do not need to fear people; nor need they fear misfortune, illness, or death.
> God, give us grace to fear and love Thee above all else!
> Amen.

Steven E. King serves as Senior Pastor of Holy Cross Lutheran Church in Maple Lake, Minnesota. He is a graduate of Luther Seminary, and has served his years of ministry in Southwestern Minnesota Synod of the ELCA. Among his broader pastoral duties, he has had a particular focus on Christian education, for both children and adults. He has produced a number of Bible Studies on various theological topics and books of Scripture, and has written and illustrated educational materials for Sunday School and VBS. One of his most recent projects is a children's paraphrase version of Luther's Small Catechism.

Pastor King has been active in the leadership of the WordAlone Network, on both the synodical and national level, and was a voting member at two ELCA Churchwide Assemblies. Until 2007, he served as the national coordinator for the congregational mission and ministry association LC3 (the Lutheran Churches of the Common Confession). He recently joined the staff of the WordAlone Network to serve part-time as Education Director, producing educational materials for the network's new ministry, called Sola Publishing.

Pastor King and his wife Becky are involved in music and theater. They have written a number of songs together, as well as a full-length musical based on the biblical story of Ruth. They have two teenage children, Brandon and Molly.

❧ 21 ❧

The Practical and Functional Authority of Scripture

Steven E. King

THROUGHOUT MY SEMINARY YEARS, I was fortunate to have as my faculty advisor the late Professor Donald Juel, who was also the instructor for some of my first New Testament courses. I remember a particular occasion when Professor Juel had asked the students in my class to write an essay on the authority of Scripture. Though I don't remember exactly what I wrote; I do remember his response. He wrote at the bottom of my paper: "Your description of the biblical text is fine—but would the Bible have this same authority if it were sitting dusty and unused on a shelf?"

Dr. Juel's simple question had an important point: What we say about the Bible is one thing, but the real authority of Scripture lies in how it actually functions in our lives—when it is heard, read and studied. That is to say, Scripture has not simply a static authority, but a functional and practical authority, demonstrated when the Word God, in law and gospel, is used by God to speak and act upon us.

I've always found this to be an important point to remember. Too often in discussions of biblical authority, we tend to focus on the text itself, with arguments about the Bible's veracity and clarity, or of the limits of its context and translation. We use terms like "inerrant" on the one hand, or "historically conditioned" on the other to describe the words on the page, but we neglect to make any statement at all about how God uses those words of Scripture to address our lives. Speaking words about the text is very different from making a confession of what God is doing with the text. It is in the latter where God exercises the authority of his Word.

In the same way, when we speak of different approaches or methods for 'interpreting' the Scriptures, we are placing ourselves in the position of the user, rather than seeing Scripture as the instrument that God uses to act upon us. In such cases, the discussion tends to focus on how we address the text, or how we understand and apply it to our context, rather than focusing on what God is doing to bring us to repentance and faith in the One who is the living Word, Jesus Christ.

Ironically, a static view of Scripture's authority can be found both on the theological right as well as the left, in what might be called the "traditional" and "revisionist" approaches to Scripture.

When it is the quality of the text that determines its authority, the Bible itself becomes little more than an object of human scrutiny. Whether we see the Bible as an ancient artifact to be disassembled and reconditioned for the times, or one written in stone to be enshrined under glass on a marble pedestal, the Bible is treated as if it were static and inert, rather than "living and active" as Scripture describes itself. Without a sense for how the Scripture actually functions upon us, our appreciation for its real authority is lost.

In the Small Catechism, when Luther discusses the meaning of the second petition of the Lord's Prayer ("Thy kingdom come . . ."), he explains when and how this happens. Luther writes:

> God's kingdom comes when our heavenly Father gives us his Holy Spirit, so that by his grace we believe his holy Word, and live a godly life on earth now and to eternity.

Luther understood that the Word of God has power because the Holy Spirit uses it to create faith in us. By the gracious gift of God, the

226

Holy Spirit makes us to trust in God's Word which includes both the spoken message and the written text of Scripture.

We see this same thing in the Small Catechism when Luther describes how God works in the promise of Baptism. In answer to the question "How can water do such great things?" Luther teaches that the power and authority in the sacrament is found in the function of God's Word:

> It is not the water that does these things, but God's Word with the water and our trust in this Word. Water by itself is only water, but with the Word of God it is a life-giving water, which by grace gives new birth through the Holy Spirit.

Comparing the function of God's Word in Baptism with the function of God's Word in the Scriptures, one might make the statement that it is not the ink in the words on the page that gives Scripture the authority to create faith, but the fact that the Holy Spirit uses the words of Scripture to speak the Word of God. The power and authority rests in the function of the Word, and God's actual use of it in our lives.

An illustration of this functional authority of Scripture is found in the eighth chapter of the Book of Acts. It is the story of when the Holy Spirit sent the Apostle Philip to walk the wilderness road, where he found an Ethiopian soldier in a chariot, reading from the prophet Isaiah. When Philip asked if the man understood what he was reading, the Ethiopian said: "How can I unless someone guides me?" (Acts 8:31 NRSV) It was then that Philip took upon himself the role of teacher, and as the story says, "starting with this Scripture, he proclaimed to him the good news about Jesus." (Acts 8:35) Philip did not simply teach about the text from Isaiah, but through that text he spoke the message of Jesus Christ; and in that teaching moment God did something to the Ethiopian. God brought about faith in Christ.

As one who has focused much of my time and energy as a parish pastor in the teaching role, I have witnessed the functional authority of Scripture often revealed in just such a way. By means of the simple earthly practice of reading, studying, and discussing the Scriptures, God has used his Word to impact human hearts.

While such a phenomena could be discussed in abstract, theological terms, I would rather focus on the practical implications of the use of Scripture in the life of the Church. For example: I have found, in terms of the Bible's functional meaning and significance in the average lay-person's life, how a person describes the Scriptures is far less important than whether they actually participate in a Bible Study group. In the same way, among my clergy colleagues, I have found that the best indicator of a pastor's view of the authority of Scripture is whether or not they actually teach and lead Bible studies in their churches.

I believe this is where my own denomination faces a great challenge. If one were to take a casual poll of congregations in the Evangelical Lutheran Church in America (ELCA), it would not be uncommon to find churches where the only regular Bible study that meets throughout the year is the monthly women's group. Many pastors will admit that teaching the Bible is low on their list of priorities, and hard to fit into their busy schedules. The result is that even though the Lutheran Confessions speak of Word and Sacrament as the center of the church's ministry, a regular focus on the Word in teaching is often treated as if it were irrelevant to a congregation's ministry, outside of a fifteen minute sermon each week in worship.

Even in cases where groups do meet for adult education in our churches, too often it has little or no connection with the Word of the Scriptures. Consider how many educational materials produced by our denominational offices are referred to simply as "studies" as opposed to "Bible Studies." (When did the word "Bible" get removed from the phrase Bible Study?) Whether it be examples like the 'study' published to introduce the ELCA's new hymnal, Evangelical Lutheran Worship, the "studies" produced by the ELCA Task Force on Sexuality, or even the many single page "studies" included in recent issues of *The Lutheran* magazine—all these have the outward appearance of what used to be called "Bible Study," without having any intentional, central focus on the reading, teaching, and discussion of Scripture. In a time when biblical illiteracy is recognized as rampant in the church and culture, it is amazing to see how little practical emphasis is placed on the Bible in creating educational materials for use in our congregations.

This says far more about how the ELCA understands the authority of Scripture than any constitutional statement of faith. Regardless of what we may say about the Bible, in most cases, it sits dusty and unused on our shelves.

No denominational institution can claim to be a "Bible-based" Church, unless its members as individual Christian believers have a foundation (a "base") in the reading and study of Scripture. This is no abstract, ethereal proposition, but a matter of everyday, practical usage of the Bible, and the priority we place on the ministry of biblical instruction. Congregations—and especially pastors—must take up their role as teachers of God's Word, if we hope to recognize, appreciate, and experience the real authority of Scripture in our churches.

I offer here just a few suggestions to be considered for how this might happen. Each pastor and congregation faces different challenges, as well as different practical circumstances. However, there are ways that people's exposure to the Scriptures—and the opportunity for people to be able to receive instruction in the Bible—can be greatly enhanced.

1) Reclaim the Coffee Hour

IT HAS OFTEN BEEN JOKED that the third Lutheran sacrament is the coffee hour. Many congregations already have time set aside every Sunday when people gather between worship services. Often, even when "adult forums" are scheduled, they are limited to single-session topical presentations or to guest speakers. Such a time could be used (or created) as a regular teaching time for the congregation. Instead of a random series of informational talks, an Education Hour can become an opportunity for continuous in-depth Bible study series, led by the pastor or by a trained lay leader. And there is no need to take away the coffee!

2) Use Real Bible Studies

IT IS IMPORTANT NOT TO WASTE the precious and limited time we have for education in the church on instruction that might be done just as well in community education at the public school. When people of the church gather for study, let it be study of the Scriptures. In many cases, even when we do engage in Bible Studies, we end up reading more "about" the Bible, than we do of the Bible itself. Those who lead instruction, whether pastors or laity, should look to see if the materials being used actually focus on biblical texts, or if they are simply designed for the sharing of personal opinions. Often, what passes for "Bible Study" is simply a conversation or book review, which may be fine in itself, but not an experience of the authority of Scripture.

3) Pastoral Study and Leadership

IF THERE IS ONE THING I WOULD encourage of all pastors, especially those new to the ministry, it is to develop the regular habit of writing their own Bible Studies, just as they develop the regular habit of writing sermons. It is a skill learned by experience and practice. To write one's own materials does not necessarily require the writing of elaborate manuscripts and handouts, but can be as simple as a sketched outline of related Bible texts, and a list of some questions for discussion. Some of the most simple studies to produce are chapter-by-chapter discussions of a book of the Bible, although topical studies based on a variety of biblical texts can work just as well. As for the time it takes to prepare such studies, in my experience, I have often found it easier to produce an hour-long presentation, than to write a fifteen minute sermon. In addition, the simple concordance work and planning of a study does wonders for one's own familiarity with the Scriptures.

4) The Continuous Story of Scripture for Children

ONE WAY TO INCREASE THE BIBLICAL LITERACY of both children and adults, is to use a "Children's Sermon" time in worship for the simple telling of Bible Stories. Instead of searching for a cute object lesson each week (which often rely on abstract symbolism young children are developmentally unable to understand), try starting with the first chapter of Genesis, and simply tell a successive Bible story each week until you reach the last chapter in Revelation. It not only allows the opportunity to give all listeners a better sense for the over-arching story of Scripture, but it provides what amounts to an automatic twelve-year plan for Children's Sermons.

These are just a few things a pastor or congregation might want to consider, as ways of seeking to experience the practical authority of Scripture by allowing God the opportunity to use his Word in the life of the church. Through simple habits and planning, the study of God's Word can be given a priority in the church, which in itself will serve as an expression of Scripture's authority.

In the Small Catechism, when Luther wrote about the meaning of the Third Commandment, ("Remember the Sabbath Day, to keep it holy"), he wrote about our attitude toward the Word, and the practical habit of studying the Scriptures, saying: "We should fear and love God, so that we do not despise his Word and the teaching of it, but gladly hear and learn it."

Luther's wisdom and advice applies to both the student and the instructor. To recognize and appreciate the true authority of Scripture, we must not despise the Word of God, but actively engage in the hearing and learning of it. It is in this that we experience the power and promise of Christ, the Word become flesh, in whom we believe.

Paul Varo Martinson was born in China of missionary parents, coming to the States when two and one-half. His grandparents went to China in 1902, working with the Lutheran Church in Henan Province. In late 1946 the family returned to China, and from 12-17 he attended boarding school first in Henan, and then in Hong Kong after 1948.

Finishing high school in California, he attended one year of the Lutheran Bible Institute in Minneapolis, after which he studied at St Olaf College and Luther Seminary. In 1962 he married Ida Marie Sather, after which they studied intensive Chinese at Yale and served with the Lutheran Church in Hong Kong from 1963-1967.

Returning to the States Paul and Ida both did their doctoral studies in Chicago; Paul at the University of Chicago in Religions and Chinese Studies. In 1972 he began teaching at Luther Seminary, retiring in 2001 as the Fredrik A Schiotz Professor of Missions and Religions. Over the years Ida Marie taught nursing in Minnesota, California, and Hong Kong. Over the years their careers intertwined in numerous ways, always connecting in some way with China. Paul wrote articles for various journals, and published his second book in 1999 on *Families of Faith*, a theological reflection for lay readers, responding to questions frequently asked by Christians.

Upon retirement, he, Ida Marie and several others established China Service Ventures, which he currently serves as vice-president.

During his many years as a teacher of missions and religions, it was his commitment to give an honest presentation of all sides while also facing the tough questions about truth. Currently, it seems, a large segment of the Christian community in North America places an emphasis upon tolerance, with an over-riding focus upon multiculturalism, with a hesitancy to recognize the distinctives of the Gospel. He also finds in the area of mission, a strong emphasis upon humanitarian work combined with a hesitancy to be open in the public space about the story of Jesus. He, with

so many others, prays for renewal in our faith and life as we follow our crucified and risen Lord into God's future for us all.

232

≈ 22 ≈

Mission: By What Authority?
Ponderings from China Service Ventures
Paul Varo Martinson

China Service Ventures is a Lutheran based mission initiative, formed as a non-profit organization in late 2001. Who are we in faith? Who are we in action? We begin with a theological reflection on our understanding of authority and mission. We follow with comments on our work and its undergirding principles.

A. Authority?

NONE OF US INVOLVED IN SERVICE and witness dare claim an autonomous authority. Whence does it come?

In the second of a package of articles articulating the ELCA's approach to dissent, an affirmation on authority was put forward—see *The Lutheran*, July 2006, p. 14. In Matthew 18:15-20, Jesus talks about the church empowered to loose or bind the sins of an individual. Jesus also states that those who disobey the church in its decisions are to be treated as gentiles and tax collectors, that is, people to be "regained" from unbelief to faith. *The Lutheran* writer makes this affirmation: "God's judgment respects the church's decision no matter what the outcome. So even if the com-

233

munity fails to discern God's reforming work accurately and leads a person to sin, disobeying the church is itself sinful."

Wow!

It may be that a rather different view of authority emerges from scripture. We believe there is. *The Lutheran* article tries to clarify how it can be said that disobedience to the institution was sinful and unjust even if possibly right, apparently even for Jesus. The question is then posed, "What do we do when both obeying the church and disobeying the church are sinful?" The answer given is "to sin boldly" and take the consequences. But, is disobeying the church when it requires one to do something that is sinful, really sinful? Jeremiah, Jesus and Luther all disobeyed the "church." Was that disobedience in and of itself sinful? When Jesus violated the food and Sabbath laws of the "church" of his day, was it sinful? To declare, or even imply, that it is, despite Jesus' words in Matthew that "the Son of Man is lord of the Sabbath," is a stretch indeed. What sort of authority is at stake in each case? Perhaps we need to re-ask the question—By what authority? and, For what is that authority given?

Perhaps that authority, and the authority given to the church in the Gospel to bind and to loose, was an authority for the proclamation of law and gospel. Perhaps it was not a politically construed and then divinely sanctioned ecclesiastical power over the community of faith.

So then, what do we mean by mission?

B. Mission as God's Identity?

MISSION—SENDING, IS GOD'S WAY of being God. How? It is the three-fold life of Father, Son and Spirit, with its eternal giving and receiving, sending and returning. God is always in relationship. Relationship is enacted in the creating, redeeming and consummating work of God. The Spirit sent forth from God moved over the waters. God sent forth a word and a world came into being. The Spirit inspired the prophets. The whole life of Jesus, from birth through death and beyond, was God's incarnating way of being God—"God sent His only Son." Thus also Paul speaks, reciting a confession of the earliest church: "who, though he was in the form of God . . . emptied himself . . . became obedient to . . . death on a cross . . . Therefore God exalted him . . . so that at the name of Jesus every knee should bend . . . and every tongue confess that Jesus Christ is Lord." And consistent with mission, this was for the other, the glory of God in all God's fullness, not for himself. This giving and receiving, sending and returning, constitutes the divine life of Father, Son and Spirit, and is a relational dynamic without end, that embraces the world within its dynamic.

So also, then, through the Son God sent the Spirit, creating a new community of faith. Baptized into Jesus Christ and nourished by his Body and Blood, the church is called to a participation in this life of giving and receiving for the sake of the world and to the glory of God. This is the divine apostoling--sending. This participation in God's way of being God becomes the church's way of being the Church. This is our identity.

C. Justification: The Concurrence of Authority and Mission

HOW SHALL WE UNDERSTAND JUSTIFICATION? It is God's free action that makes sinners right with God, transforming a broken and false relationship that disrupted the trust and faith intended in creation. This action of God, which becomes effective for us in faith, conveys to us all the riches of Jesus' life, death, and resurrection, including forgiveness, the fullness of Jesus' own righteousness, and rebirth into a new life, a new life of community with God and others. It is the "joyous exchange" in which we give God our worst and God gives us God's best. It is rightly described in these words: "We . . . become righteous before God by grace, for Christ's sake, through faith." There is no growth beyond this, only into it.

Now, how do authority and mission fit in with this?

Not surprisingly, we will turn to Paul. The question of authority lies at the heart of Paul's turning to Jesus Christ. So also does the question of mission. He makes this very clear in these words: "But when God . . . was pleased to reveal his Son to me, so that I might proclaim him among the Gentiles, I did not confer with any human being, nor did I go up to Jerusalem to those who were already apostles before me." Eventually he did, but not with the option of adjusting "the truth of the gospel" but to make sure that he and the church were on the same page, "that I was not running, or had not run, in vain." Indeed, he refers to "false believers secretly brought in," who in fact were not on the same page.

Well, what happened in Paul's turning to Jesus, the "false Messiah" he devoutly opposed and whose believers he persecuted? Acts gives us some hints on that. As he approached Damascus to ravage yet another church, a light flashed from heaven and he fell to the ground, hearing words directed to him. "I am Jesus, whom you are persecuting," he learns, in response to his desperate question, "Who are you, Lord?" It was only a few days later that Paul was proclaiming in Damascus' synagogues that, "He is the Son of God."

This encounter of Paul with Jesus was clearly an encounter about authority. The one he denounced he now pronounced "Lord." What has happened? The Torah and its interpretation of scripture, which till then was at the heart of his understanding of authority, was completely thrown into disarray. The event he deemed a sure sign of God's curse upon Jesus as a false messiah, namely the crucifixion, was now discovered to be the basis for Jesus' exaltation and lordship. The Torah is unable to exegete the cross, it is the cross that exegetes the Torah. This event, the cross, and the God of this event, who has announced to Paul its meaning as forgiveness and redemption, is the final authority for faith and life. At one and the same time, this event, through this encounter, becomes the mission, the sending, of Paul to proclaim amongst the Gentiles the redemption of God. Authority and mission are an inseparable unity.

Paul is so clear on these matters that there is little room for doubt. Paul, as all believers, has been crucified with Christ and been joined with Jesus' resurrection life. Neither the ecstatic visions of some, nor the alleged authority of human assemblies granted by others, can compromise this final authority. The loosing and binding granted to the assembly of believers is the right and duty to proclaim this Word of the gospel. It is no *deus ex machina*. It is not some sort of divinely sanctioned political authority. It is a living Word that calls the dead to life while confirming the continued death of the one who rejects, who is then to be called back to faith. As Paul makes clear, "we have come to believe in Christ Jesus, so that we might be justified by faith in Christ, and not by doing the works of the law," including the work of obeying human assemblies. But this is hardly a license to individualism. It is the creation of community, a community bound to this Word and its gift of proclamation, a community bound to this Word and its fruit of service to others.

No wonder the Gospel of Matthew concludes with this pronouncement: "All authority in heaven and on earth has been given to me. Go therefore and make disciples of all nations." Authority and mission are one.

D. From Theology to Practice

SO, WE HAVE DISCOVERED A PROBLEM—a miscast view of authority that defines it institutionally. We have explored a theology, a theology seldom broached by many church leaders today—and discovered by repeated instances that authority and mission are one. We now explore a solution—one that embeds service in proclamation, without division, no matter how complex the situation. And such service embedded in proclamation impels us forward into relationships between and amongst people, rather than upward into the dizzying heights of hierarchy and structure.

For example, this proclamation is set forth as the underlying principles that guide China Service Ventures in its work.

China Service Ventures (CSV) is a mission initiative rooted in the Lutheran confessions and formed in late 2001. With the formation of the ELCA, China quickly disappeared from congregational awareness. One obvious reason was the political situation created by a Communist China. But another was, however unintentionally, self-made. A system of synod to synod relationships was established with synods in this country and Lutheran churches in Asia, Africa and Latin America, described in terms of companion synods. This helped synods to focus their attention upon highly specific relations, something good in itself. But it also removed an active sense of involvement and responsibility for worldwide mission. China, for example, was excluded since no longer could a church declare itself Lutheran. Overnight China seemed to fall into a black hole so far as our congregations and synods were concerned.

The year 2002 was spent by CSV in research and investigation as to work and service opportunities in China. This research led us to Henan province in central China, not much larger than Minnesota, the most populous province in China, with one hundred million and counting, and one of the most poverty-stricken. It also happened to be the largest center of former American Lutheran work in China. Only now, in this initiative, have we Lutherans in North America begun to restore relations with this large and widespread and isolated Christian community in Henan that has suffered so much and is now growing with great rapidity, as we work in service amongst the far vaster general population. High level Chinese friends in Beijing, in the government as well as in the areas of Health and Education, did the initial investigation that led to our service there. In March of 2003 our work commenced, as we were welcomed by the Mayor's office of Xinyang, Henan, China, and initiat-

ed our first support project for the schooling of impoverished rural children. Soon we will be completing our 5th year of service. Remarkable
developments have taken place, which we can only allude to. Our mission? To foster mutually beneficial relationships between Christian communities in North America and communities in China, including
Christian communities, through service to the community and witness
to the gospel of Jesus Christ.

E. Underlying Principles Governing CSV Work

HOW DOES CSV SEE ITS WAY FORWARD in a ministry of service and witness given the kind of situation described above? Certain principles
underlie our mode of operation, and we believe they are valid in a wide
array of circumstances in China.

1. We do not simply come in on our own as a foreign entity or
foreign persons, but work with and through Chinese counterparts.

For example, in January of 2002 I accompanied Ida Marie to
Hong Kong where she was head of a School of Nursing at The Hong
Kong Polytechnic University. The newly formed Board of CSV asked us
to find a way to begin ministry in Henan Province, a place that was a
former center of Lutheran work. We had no idea how to proceed. While
flying to Hong Kong we pondered this. The first thought was to connect with a couple of our Lutheran missionaries in Hong Kong who had
a special responsibility for connecting with China and frequently trav-
elled there for this purpose. But further pondering suggested that we
might better work through a Chinese counterpart. This we did. Once in
Hong Kong we contacted Jin Qiao in Beijing, a close friend of ours, and
a nurse in China with a stellar national standing. She came to Hong
Kong, met with us and the PolyU, and agreed to lead an investigative
trip to Henan. Upon return from Hong Kong to Beijing, she contacted
the Henan Provincial Representative Resident in Beijing. He in turn
contacted the local authorities in the Xinyang Administrative region

where he, as well as I, was born. He Jinming, Jin Qiao, and David Du an associate of Jin Qiao, then joined in an investigative visit. On the basis of information gained on that visit, Jin Qiao made a recommendation, coming personally to the US by invitation from the Board to make the presentation (she speaks no English). Thus, from the start we had local government support for our coming and work.

2. We are open and public about our Christian identity, while doing so in ways that foster trust, not suspicion, and are appropriate to the local context.

3. We are consistently committed to give priority in our work to the least advantaged, especially the rural communities, in a way that enables community involvement in contrast to institutional specialization and isolation. At the same time we engage in urban activities that can enhance this commitment in helpful ways.

4. Our primary involvement and accountability is to the government and government entities such as schools, hospitals, and various administrative offices. We deliberately avoided a primary relationship with the Church. Had we done so, we would have come under the supervision of the Religious Affairs Bureau which would have significantly inhibited our relationship with the wider community.

5. In so far as we relate to the Church, we do so by relating to the local Church first, not at the national or even provincial level first. As the relationship develops, it is the local Church that initiates the process of negotiating necessary matters with the provincial and national bodies. This has been exceedingly effective in the development of the Bethel Bible program. Now, for the first time, the Bethel Bible Program is authorized for use at several sites in China.

6. Our relation to the Church begins through participation in worship, mutual acquaintance, and establishment of trust. We deliberately avoid first asking the Churches how we might help them, but await their own initiative in asking us for assistance in one way or another if they so desire. A variety of illustrations can be given of this, and its effectiveness.

7. We also take continual opportunity for witness to the gospel in our various interactions in the normal course of things with local people, whether government people or citizens. Those who are there on a long term basis have the most numerous, richest and deepest opportunities. Significant results have come from this including several baptisms.

8. Everything presupposes that we act in a way that fosters trust.

9. We recognize that the needs of the least advantaged is not simply a material, educational or political lack, but has important roots in attitudinal deficits. It is therefore our intent to always open up those we work with to wider horizons.

The very fact of serving others without any evident advantage to ourselves (though we are rich beneficiaries in many ways) is a most obvious example. Such an attitude is not characteristic of Chinese society. In fact, just the opposite, self advantage, pertains in the public sphere.

Acceptance of one's fate is also typical, especially of the disadvantaged, so we seek to open up minds and hearts to new opportunities. The rural/urban divide with the attendant prejudice against the rural peoples is also characteristic. Our work calls this into question in a direct way and serves to enhance the value placed upon rural peoples. One example of this last point is the establishment of an "Unbounded Love" (bo-ai) class of 40+ rural students by and in an urban high school, to which they have assigned a special responsibility for CSV, thus giving rural students educational advantages enjoyed almost wholly by urban kids for primarily economic reasons.

Our first on-site developer couple, John and Betsy Gronseth, currently studying Chinese in Beijing with three of their children, will be the first feet on the ground there. They will initially supervise this class. As other on-site developers arrive, they will move into a community center to be rented or built by CSV, providing many useful activities for local residents, including the young, parents, and the elderly. Local authorities at different sites are competing for this opportunity.

10. We affirm shared responsibilities in our activities. This is negotiated at every step without arbitrarily putting forward our own

requirements as the norm. Rural and urban settings have very different potential in such matters.

11. We work as much as possible by way of networking. This applies to our way of operating in the US and internationally, as well as in China at all levels. Our relation with World Mission Prayer League is one example, as mentioned earlier.

12. Finally, countless church related organizations and non-governmental organizations engage in impressive humanitarian work. For this we can only be grateful. Yet, for many church organizations, such work is devoid of public witness to Jesus Christ. Deeds are not yet words. The church does something that nobody else can or will do. And that is to bear witness to the life, death and resurrection of Jesus Christ. If it is to be trustworthy before the world with what has been uniquely entrusted to it, it not only can, but must speak these words, especially among those who have yet to hear. We believe the crucified Jesus is the most complete expression of trustworthiness to be known. To introduce this One, is the richest contribution that those called to mission alone make.

F. Concluding Comment

THIS IS THE FIRST TIME I'VE BEEN GIVEN an opportunity to focus on the important underlying question of all mission, and that is the relation between authority and mission. The attempt to make the decisions of human assemblies as receiving a priori divine sanction, even to the extent that to obey and disobey are both sinful, makes a parody of the authority that God has unequivocally given to the church, the authority to proclaim law and gospel. Do denominational assemblies have the high authority so attributed? Or is it the church council of every congregation? Or is it the Papal office above all that is intended? Is this a return to the role of tradition that Luther struggled so hard to address? Is this to reinvent the legal structures of Pharisaic Judaism or parallel the role

242

of sharia in Islam? It is a strange conversation. All the instances of authority that we have looked at in this essay connect authority and mission, authority and proclamation.

It is this that fills our hearts and minds. It is this that inspires. It is this that builds community. It is in the failure to achieve all of this that we find our disobedience and sin exposed. What a gift this is, authority for mission.

David Lahren spent his boyhood years on a farm in the Red River Valley of eastern North Dakota. He remembers living in a farm house without electricity or indoor plumbing. He also recalls Norwegian worship services once a month at Walcott Lutheran Church where his mother was the organist and his father often played solos on his carpenter's saw. Luther League and the Walcott Hustlers 4H Club were both major social and family events each month in the community of 300.

He was one of six classmates to graduate from Walcott High School in 1954.

Lahren went on to earn a BA in English, with a minor in mathematics, from Concordia College in Moorhead, Minnesota; an MDiv from Luther Seminary in St. Paul, Minnesota; an MS in Mathematics from North Dakota State University in Fargo, North Dakota; and a DA in Mathematics from the University of Northern Colorado in Greeley. He taught mathematics for thirty-eight years, thirty-five of them at St. Cloud State University. He and his wife, Elouise, are blessed with two children, Paul and Emilie, and son-in-law Mark Olson.

Since retirement in 2001, the Lahrens continue to live in St. Cloud, Minnesota, and enjoy walking, biking, traveling and studying many of the great issues of the faith, such as the authority of the Bible and the Word of God, the Christian Worldview, Christian apologetics, and Intelligent Design.

Dave has served on the Steering Committee of the Mid-Minnesota chapter of the WordAlone Network in St. Cloud since its inception in 2004.

❧ 23 ❧

Inerrancy Is Not a
Four-letter Word

David Lahren

SOME WORDS, WHILE POTENTIALLY very useful, come wrapped in so much emotional baggage that they fall prey to two types of abuse that are poles apart. Some people, on the one hand, abuse the word by unscrupulously using it as a springboard to grand pronouncements that a careful definition would not permit. Others, on the other hand, abuse the word by timidly shunning it completely. Thoughtful and fruitful dialogue is ill-served by both.

Two such words are "evolution" and "inerrancy." The former is a scientific term which is quite readily, though not simply, defined; but is most often used (and it is profusely used) and abused, unfettered by careful definition. The typical result is meaningless pontification and unsupported extrapolation, unworthy of good science. Other folks avoid the word entirely because they believe it, undeservedly, to be threatening.

The latter word, inerrancy, is generally used, when it is used, in the context of discussions relating to the authority of the Bible. This term also is open to careful, though not simple, definition; but is most often used carelessly as a pejorative, implying that those who affirm it are uneducated and unaware of modern methods of scholarly criticism. Other folks shun the word, not because they are in conflict with its

245

meaning, but rather because they sense it would be an academic or personal liability for them to publicly affirm it.

We focus our attention on inerrancy. Although the word is of more modern currency, the concept is rooted in the biblical witness and was embraced by the likes of Augustine, Aquinas, Luther, and many other Christian scholars throughout the history of the Church. In 1960, the constitution of the newly formed American Lutheran Church decreed: "As the primary condition of union, we declare our joint unanimous and unreserved acceptance of all the canonical books of the Old and New Testaments as a whole and in all their parts as the divinely inspired, revealed, and inerrant Word of God."

For the first 1800 years of its existence, the Church had great confidence in the Bible as the Word of God (in its possessive sense), not simply as a word about God. (See Paul's use of the phrase, 'gospel of God' in Romans 1:1). The crisis of confidence in the authority of the Bible has evolved primarily in the last 200 years, a period in which our Western culture has experienced a general distrust of authority. Some people reveal their lack of confidence by attempting to show that the Church has for 2,000 years misunderstood what Scripture is saying about an issue. Others agree that the Bible is clear in what it is saying, but assert that it was addressing a different culture in a different time; and since the cultural context has changed, the import of the original words no longer applies to ours. The Holy Spirit is doing a new thing.

A case in point is Luke Timothy Johnson, a professor of New Testament at the Candler School of Theology at Emory University. In "Scripture & Experience," published in *Commonweal* magazine, June 15, 2007, Johnson wrote regarding homosexuality: "I think it important to state clearly that we do, in fact, reject the straightforward commands of Scripture, and appeal instead to another authority when we declare that same-sex unions can be holy and good. And what exactly is that authority? We appeal explicitly to the weight of our own experience and the experience thousands of others have witnessed to, which tells us that to claim our own sexual orientation is in fact to accept the way in which

God has created us. . . . We are fully aware of the weight of scriptural evidence pointing away from our position, yet place our trust in the power of the living God to reveal as powerfully through personal experience and testimony as through written texts. . . . (I)f the letter of Scripture cannot find room for the activity of the living God in the transformation of human lives, then trust and obedience must be paid to the living God rather than to the words of Scripture."

Albert Mohler, president of Southern Baptist Theological Seminary writes in response in his blog, dated August 29, 2007: "If we are to trust human experience as an authority superior to that of the Bible, whose experience are we to trust? (Johnson) can only mean his own experience and that of others whose experience he chooses to privilege. . . . (T)he Bible cannot be the Word of God if God must oppose His own Word. We are no longer to submit our experience to the authority of the Bible but instead are to submit the Bible to the authority of experience. . . . Professor Johnson's argument leads to disaster. Indeed, it is a disaster in itself, justifying what the Bible condemns as sinful."

In an earlier blog, dated March 22, 2006, Mohler writes: "If the very words of Scripture, in the original languages, are not inspired of God, and thus precisely the right words for the church throughout all time, then we are left in a constant battle to negotiate the meaning of the biblical text. Its meaning in one generation might be very different from its meaning in another, and generations to come might actually reverse the interpretation settled upon by Christians living in our times. In other words, God seems to be leading His people in many different directions over time, and the biblical text becomes a fabric that can be stretched in any number of different directions, all claiming to be led by the Spirit of God."

Gerhard Forde, former professor (now deceased) at Luther Seminary in St. Paul, seemed to concur. In *The Preached God*, a collection of essays by Professor Forde, edited by Mark Mattes and Steven Paulson, he wrote, "(I)f we are to honor Scripture all we have to offer finally is not loopholes but absolution. If that is not the end of our conversation, I fear it has no end at all."

So we see, most assuredly, that we are faced with a very real issue. It is not hypothetical. At this point we pause to consider what those who affirm the inerrancy of Scripture understand it to mean. We will then go on to see how that understanding undergirds the concept of authority. Most who hold to inerrancy acknowledge that it should not be seen as a test for salvation or a litmus test for a genuine Christian. They do, however, treat it with the utmost seriousness.

It is commonly acknowledged that inerrancy is affirmed only for the original autographs of Scripture, the original works of the inspired writers. And, although the original autographs are not extant, there does exist a very extensive collection of copies of the autographs from which scholars seek to determine what was originally written. The science of textual criticism seeks to reconstruct the original text from these copies. It is also acknowledged that there do remain some apparent discrepancies in the texts that are still being carefully scrutinized. A great many apparent contradictions, however, have been resolved satisfactorily, some in the early church and others more recently. New knowledge about the ancient manuscripts and the meaning of language used in biblical times and new archeological finds give reason for optimism regarding the future resolution of remaining difficulties. In the relatively few cases where uncertainty about the text remains, no doctrine of faith is impacted. It should not be surprising that a collection of 66 books written over a period of approximately 1400 years by about forty different authors in three different languages on three different continents would present us with some harmonization challenges.

R.C. Sproul says that inerrancy does *not* mean that there aren't grammatical crudities in the text, nor does it mean that it speaks with modern scientific precision. However it does mean that the text always tells the truth, as the New Testament defines the truth. Rudolph Bultmann says that the Greek word for truth in the Bible means that it is without deceit, it is without fraud, and it communicates real states of affairs. Thus we could say that the Bible makes no assertions that conflict with objective reality, whether historical, factual or spiritual.

In 1977, a group of some 200 biblical scholars constituted the International Council on Biblical Inerrancy to study the issue of the inerrancy of the Scriptures. In its formal statement, issued in 1978, the council said: "We affirm that canonical Scripture should always be interpreted on the basis that it is infallible and inerrant. However, in determining what the God-taught writer is asserting in each passage, we must pay the most careful attention to its claims and character as a human production. In inspiration, God utilized the culture and conventions of His penman's milieu, a milieu that God controls in His sovereign providence." The full text of this statement, and much more, can be found in a booklet entitled *Explaining Inerrancy* compiled by R.C. Sproul, which is available from Ligonier Ministries.

Inerrancy essentially asserts the complete truthfulness of Scripture, that all its affirmations correspond with reality. What is at stake here is whether we understand Scripture to be the word of men or the Word of God. The question is not about who penned the words. They were penned by human beings. But the question really is about the source, the author, not the writer. II Timothy 3:16 (ESV) declares: "All scripture is 'breathed out' (*theopneustos*) by God." Paul is here making a very clear statement about the source of scripture. It is God Himself. II Peter 1:21 (ESV) asserts that "men spoke from God as they were carried along by the Holy Spirit." Thus men wrote the text of scripture under the inspiration, the superintendence, of the Holy Spirit.

It is not claimed that the writers were automatons with the Spirit moving the pencils. Nor is it claimed that the writers were secretaries simply taking dictation, writing down the words that the Spirit whispered in their ears. The mode of inspiration is not spelled out in scripture, but it is asserted clearly that God Himself is the *author* of the text and therein lies ultimate *authority*. Some charge that those who hold the Scriptures in such high regard are guilty of bibliolatry, the worship of the Bible. Surely that is unfounded. If my wife speaks those very special words, "I love you," to me, I cherish those words simply because I hold in very high regard the one who spoke them to me. I consider the source. To believe a message, we must trust both the message and the messenger. In a somewhat similar way, we cherish the words of the Bible because it is God Himself who "breathed them out."

When people begin to lose confidence in the authority of scripture, they inevitably begin to look to human opinion and reason for guidance. Consequently authority is claimed for fallible human reason and experience, resulting in serious confusion and a cheapening of the biblical concept of truth. When anyone claims that the Holy Spirit is "doing a new thing", it must be remembered that the Spirit always works in concert with the Word of God, never against it.

R.C. Sproul defines authority as the right to impose obligation. When someone says, "You ought", you may well respond with, "Says who?" or "By what authority?" When Martin Luther was asked to recant his writings at the Diet of Worms, he declared, "My conscience is held captive by the Word of God." The authority he was bound by was the Word of God, sola Scriptura.

According to J.I. Packer, the problem of authority is the most fundamental problem we ever face in the Church. That is because Christianity is built on truth, on the claims of Jesus Christ, on the resurrection as history, on the content of revelation. If that content were found to be fraudulent and untrustworthy, then the veracity of the one who is reported to have declared, "I am the truth," would be seriously in doubt.

In Matthew 4:4 (ESV), Jesus rebuked the devil in the wilderness by saying, "It is written, 'Man shall not live by bread alone, but by every word that comes from the mouth of God.'" In John 17:17 (ESV), Jesus in His High Priestly Prayer addressed His Father in these words: "Sanctify them in the truth; your Word is truth." And in John 18:37b (ESV), Jesus proclaimed to Pilate, "(F)or this purpose I have come into the world—to bear witness to the truth." Our high regard for Scripture reflects the very high view that Jesus Himself has. The issue of the authority of Scripture ultimately depends on the teaching and authority of Christ Himself. Who do we say He is?

The cartoon, *Non Sequitur*, recently hit the nail on the head. It depicted a Political Science 101 classroom in Cable News University. The confident professor is up front in the classroom looking somewhat sideways at his students with an air of disdain and is pointing to the gem he has just written on the blackboard: "It's not *what* they say. It's the context in which you misinterpret it."

Let us endeavor to interpret the Bible as it was written, rather than interpret it as we would like it to have been written, justifying the prejudices of our own desires. In his biography written by Alister McGrath, J.I. Packer says, "The conservative evangelical differs from his liberal brother, not by committing himself to interpret the Bible in a different way, but by committing himself in advance to believe whatever the Bible turns out to be saying."

Gary Diers and his wife, Linda, are forgiven sinners who serve the Lord Jesus as dairy farmers in Waverly Minnesota. Gary is the oldest of nine children, eight boys and one girl. One brother was killed in a farm accident shortly before the age of twelve.

Gary and Linda have five grown children and eleven grandchildren with another on the way. Gary farms with a brother in a family farm corporation. The farm was homesteaded by his great-grandparents in 1874. Dairy cattle, about two hundred twenty-five, are the principal enterprise along with all the young stock, dairy beef and crops grown to keep them all fed.

In addition to farm activities, Gary enjoys carpentry (remodeling) and is an avid reader of fiction. His formal education is high school. While in school, Gary was a 4-H member and a FFA member. Gary and Linda's children were all 4-H members and they, along with others, received training and instruction from Gary.

Gary has also been a member of the Dairy Herd Improvement Association (DHIA) all of his adult life, and served on the Wright County board of directors for seventeen

years, the Minnesota DHIA board of directors for twenty years and attended many national

DHIA functions for twenty years before retiring from those activities in 2002.

Gary and Linda are members of Trinity Evangelical Lutheran Church of Watertown Minnesota where Gary has been active in many leadership roles for the past twenty-five years.

❧ 24 ❧

No Middle Ground

Gary Diers

"All Scripture is God-breathed and is useful for teaching, rebuking, correcting and training in righteousness so that the man of God may be thoroughly equipped for every good work." (2Tim 3:16-17 NIV)

First I need to say that I do not try to live my life according to God's will as defined in the Holy Scriptures or to do good works to gain God's approval, but I do it with the full understanding of His unbelievable love for me shown by His dying on the cross in my place. I can do no other.

I suppose even as a layman having read and studied the Holy Scriptures I could go into some lengthy discourse on "By What Authority," but that might not be very helpful for anyone, and in my case, probably wouldn't even be honest. Being someone who walks and talks with the Lord Jesus all day long every day, it simply has never occurred to me that the Holy Scriptures are not authoritative. They are God's Word or they are not, there is no middle ground. So in answering the question "by what authority" I want to tell the story of Chuck and his family.

About twenty-five years ago we got to the point in our dairy operation where we needed a full time non-family employee. We did not advertise, but through contacts among fellow dairy farmers heard that Chuck was looking for a job. Chuck, it turns out, had been employed at many area dairy farms. He had everything that a dairy farmer could be looking for. He was on time, did an excellent job, was easy to get along with, and he had that rare natural ability of working with livestock, especially milk cows. I think he could literally communicate with them and he felt they were his best friends. Chuck also loved to fish in his spare time and was the most successful fisherman I have known. He kept himself and all of us supplied with all the fish we wanted and then some.

Chuck however had one evil from which, until his death, he was unable to completely escape. He was a mostly recovering alcoholic and as a result he had very little in the way of material blessings. He and his wife and two young children lived in a mobile home we provided on the farm. One time, after he again did not show up for work after his days

254

off, I had already decided before even seeing him that this time we would need to terminate him, but the Lord had other plans.

I was in the barn, preparing to do his chores when he walked in and before I could say anything he broke down in tears saying that he had let us down, he had let his family down, and most of all, he had let himself down and that he understood that he needed to go for treatment again. He did that, and for the next month we got along without his help while his family continued to live on the farm. At that point the Lord was clearly telling us that because of the kind of job he did and the effort he was making in dealing with his alcoholism that we needed to do whatever was necessary to keep him as a very important part of the farm operation.

The mobile home he was living in was small and not suited to a growing family so we knew something had to be done. We had a small piece of land by a lake that could have a house built on it. In talking about that with Chuck he agreed that he would like us to do that. We decided to divide off that parcel of land and build a house on it, then sell it to Chuck and his wife. Chuck was a veteran and could finance it with a VA loan. Chuck didn't feel that he had any ability to do any of the paperwork himself in order to get this done, so a brother I farm with and I did everything for him. I need to say here that Chuck lacked the confidence to do any of this himself, but he was really a very intelligent person. He also did not believe in using banks, doctors, insurance or government programs.

We were able to get all this done one summer about fifteen years ago. Chuck and his family moved into their new home in September that year and he told me he never had anything like this, nor had he ever expected to. All of this pointed out to me that Chuck and I had a very special relationship that went well beyond that of employer and employee.

Although I knew he had no use for insurance companies, I suggested to him one day that to protect his family, a wife, a daughter who was now five and a son age three, he ought to get enough life insurance to at least cover the mortgage on his new home. I told him of an insurance agent where we did all our business. He came to work one day sometime later and told me he had gotten the insurance policy and had given it to his wife and told her to put it in a safe place. He never told her what it was nor did she even figure it out at the time. She just put it away.

One evening about six weeks after he moved into his new home —his weekend off—a sheriff's deputy came to the house and asked if I was Chuck's employer. When I informed him that I was, he told me that Chuck had been killed in a single vehicle accident. I told you earlier that Chuck and I had a special relationship. I realized at that point that I had just lost my best friend. There was also something else that I now understood, but had been fearful of telling anyone. For most of the year before Chuck's death I had the fairly regular occurrence of a feeling that I would not live out the year. When Chuck died, that feeling went away and I have never had it since.

Chuck's wife did not handle any of this very well at all, and she did not have much supportive family so we all stepped in to help as much as possible. She, among other things, now understood that she would have to find another home, but the insurance agent going by the death notice in the paper did what was needed to get the proceeds of the life insurance policy Chuck had gotten. He took that check to her one day, and she still did not know it was coming, and as a result she and her children were able to remain in their new home, fully paid for.

She still lives in that home today and she and her two children are like a part of our family. Her daughter, once she was old enough, was a regular babysitter for a couple of our granddaughters here on the farm. She graduated from the local high school three years ago and was salutatorian of her class. She is attending college and is planning on becoming a teacher. Chuck's son, Robert, once he was old enough began spending all of his free time at the farm. He has all the wonderful abilities of his father. He learned over the years how to operate nearly every piece of farm equipment we had and did it whenever he had a chance. He also has his father's abilities with livestock.

My own children worked on the farm and with the livestock and were just a little older than Robert and they became his mentors along with my brother's children. When he was old enough, he joined 4-H and learned to show dairy and beef animals of his own. He was also an FFA member while in high school. He was one of the captains of the football team his senior year and graduated as an honor student. Two years ago he exhibited the Reserve Champion beef animal in the 4-H Show at the Minnesota State Fair. The animal sold at auction after the show for $6,000.00 that went into a scholarship fund for him. He exhibited the Reserve Champion dairy animal in the FFA show at the State Fair the same year. He was always paid for working on the farm and along with the sale of the beef animal and other scholarships was able to attend the University of Minnesota College of Agriculture in St. Paul, Minnesota. He comes home every weekend and helps out on the farm, much like any other family member.

I look at the Lord working in the lives of these two children that Chuck left and see how the Lord has used something very devastating for so much good and imagine often how proud Chuck would be. This is for me living out the authority Jesus gave us with His death on the cross for us and finally His triumph over death which is the hope of our faith.

I want to close with the beautiful doxology Jude gives us in his very timely letter for today.

> "To him who is able to keep you from falling and to present you before his glorious presence without fault and with great joy to the only God our Savior be glory, majesty, power and authority, through Jesus Christ our Lord, before all ages, now and forever-more! Amen." (Book of Jude, NIV)

Rich Melheim grew up on the plains of North Dakota but never did own a pick up with a gun rack. An entrepreneur, author, speaker, playwright, songwriter, family counselor, business systems consultant, amateur complexity theorist, log cabin builder, cartoonist, and student of the human brain, Melheim has appeared on fifty network television news shows from WNBC-NY to KTLA to CNN consulting on family issues.

Rich is also an ordained ELCA Lutheran Minister with a specialized call from the St. Paul Area Synod to experiment with family-connected Christian education systems.

Rich is the founder and initiating force behind Faith Inkubators, a Christian education systems design think-tank and resource provider dedicating to "incubating faith every night in every home." He serves as Chief Strategic Officer and Chief Creative Officer of two non-profits and his one tithing-for-profit publishing company that make up the Faith Inkubators family.

Rich holds a BA in journalism from UND where he graduated summa cum laude in three years and was chosen Outstanding Graduate of 1977. With an MDIV from Luther Seminary, Rich served parishes in Owatonna and Stillwater, Minnesota (1981 to 1993). In the fall of 1993 Rich left salary, pension and parish life for a sabbatical, threw his wife and babies in the back of a borrowed Winnebago, and hit the road as a faith entrepreneur to speak about changing the educational paradigm of the church. The restless pastors and frustrated Christian education pioneers who heard him speak in seventy-five cities that fall started the national think tank

and learning organization that has become Faith Inkubators. 275 churches joined the movement that first year. A year later there were 540. A year later 1,000 churches were members. A year later 1,500. A decade and a half later, tens of thousands of churches and millions of families have been impacted by this ministry.

Needless to say, Rich is still on his sabbatical.

Melheim has counseled parents on CNN, Donahue, Leeza, Rolanda, and Montel. He has two children, Kathryn Elizabeth, eighteen, and Joseph Martin, fourteen. Rich is married to his Bible Camp sweetheart, Arlyce Joy, who has put up with him for twenty-eight

ꙮ 25 ꙮ

Word Alone: Every Night
in Every Home

Rich Melheim

URING THE SIEGE OF LENINGRAD, THE CITY ELDERS HAD a difficult decision to make. The Nazi's had cut off most supply routes
to the city. The few remaining truck routes across the frozen lake
were bombed daily. It became clear that there was only one-third
enough wheat to get them through the winter. What would they do?
Cordon off two-thirds of the city and feed only one-third? They could-
n't bear to make that decision. Instead, they mixed their bread with one-
third wheat, one-third saw dust, one-third manure.

That winter tens of thousands of children went to bed every
night starving to death on a full stomach.

I have spent the last twenty-six years of my ministry focused on
youth and family ministries. In that time I've come to observe something
that haunts me when it comes to our American life-style and the poverty of
the rich: We have full houses and empty homes. We have full schedules and
empty lives. Our kids are watching twenty-seven hours and fifty-three minutes of television a week and are spending 37.5 minutes a week in one-on-
one conversations with their parents (excluding scolding and commands).
By the time a child reaches kindergarten, she will have already spent more
time with the television than she will with her dad for the rest of his life.

We are bombarded by consumer messages that promise personal fulfillment, economic riches, popularity, sexual prowess—you name it —all in a bottle, a can, an investment strategy or a pill. Our cell phones ring at all hours of the day and night, connecting us to work, to friends, and to the inescapable business of post-modern life. Our laptops and wi-fi connections follow us home and into bed, nagging us to finish the work we didn't get to during the nearly extinct nine to five of our parents. From the moment the alarm goes off in the morning to the time we hit the pillow and drift off to Leno or Conan or Ferguson, we are bombarded by noise, commercial images and the least-common-denominator of our current excuse for humor.

We are completely full. And we are completely empty. We are starving to death on a full stomach. Sawdust and crap. All the while, the fresh, nutritious bread sits in the wrapper on the counter. "I am the bread of life," says Jesus.

HERE I SIT

"The B-I-B-L-E, yes that's the book for me.
I sit alone on the Word of God
The B-I-B-L-E!"

What's wrong with this song? It's all too true, that's what's wrong with it. We are a church that used to stand on the Word of God. Now it sits neatly under our pews, unopened. We print it conveniently in our bulletins so no one actually has to pick up the book. We cut out three of the four texts for Sunday so we have time for more announcements and another sappy "Hold Me Close" (i.e. "I want Jesus to be my boyfriend") sentimental song. We have abandoned personal morning devotions in favor of five extra minutes of sleep. We have abandoned family devotions in favor of television, iPods and the Internet. We have abandoned Bible study in favor of reading groups dedicated to Oprah's latest pick. We have abandoned the Bread of Life in favor of Twinkies and Starbucks.

And we wonder why we've lost our moral compass as a nation. And we wonder what's gone wrong with the next generation. And we wonder why nothing seems to fill us. And we wonder why "get more" isn't enough to satisfy. (The only thing we don't have is "more".)

We sit on the Bible in church and leave it neatly on the dusty top shelf at home, tucked conveniently out of reach of the children and away from our lives. And we wander from one guru, one talk show host or shock jock, one "Secret" or "Da Vinci Code" to the next, looking for the "truth" of the moment or a self-service 24-7 god who will give us what we want when we want it.

"I am the way, the truth and the life," says Jesus. "No one comes to the Father but by me."

Starving Our Children

It's one thing to starve yourself. It's quite another to starve your children.

The most recent studies show that one-third of American children are obese. Their over-indulgent "never say no" parents have set them up for a life of physical, mental, emotional and spiritual pain. We're happy to fill them full of sugar and carbs. We're happy to fill their rooms with computers, flat screen televisions, iPods and the latest video game players. We're happy to fill their schedules full of traveling sports teams, private music lessons and a dizzying array of extras that keep them busy from dawn to dusk.

Their lives are completely full. And, in many ways, completely empty. There is no time for family meals, no time for Christ in the schedule, virtually no faith talk or prayer in Lutheran homes. There is no room in the inn. It's been turned into a time-share, and it's booked from now until never.

"Lord, to whom shall we go? You have the words of eternal life."

Counterfeit Bills and Temple Prostitutes

How do they get bank tellers to recognize counterfeit money? They saturate them with the good stuff, the right stuff, the real stuff. If you know the truth, the false is easy to spot.

The Children of Israel had wandered in the wilderness for forty years. Finally on the edge of the Promised Land, God gave Moses a final teaching to prepare the people: "Keep these words which I command you this day in your hearts. Recite them to your children, and talk about them when you are at home, when you are away, when you lie down, when you rise. Bind them as a sign on your hands. Fix them as an emblem on your forehead. Write them on the doorposts of your house and on your gates."

God wanted Israel to saturate her children with the will and Word of God. Why?

The Promised Land wasn't empty. It was filled with people who practiced a strange, alluring, and dangerous religion. There was child sacrifice in that land. There were temple prostitutes at the core of the religion. In the official temples, and out in the countryside on top of the high hills and under the greenest trees, they called to the inhabitants to have sex with them to keep the gods happy and cajole them into sending fertile rains and crops.

The only way to protect their children in this dangerous land was to saturate their minds and hearts, homes and gates with the true things of God.

Now, you might object: "This is America in the 21st Century. We don't have child sacrifice anymore. We don't have temple prostitutes enticing our children away from worshipping the one true God."

Guess again.

We sacrifice our children on the altars of consumption, materialism, and business. There are thousands of voices calling "come and lay with me" on billboards, magazines, television advertisements, and, scary to say, in our own homes on the new computer we bought them innocently masquerading as other thirteen-year olds chatting with your children every night.

It's not just counterfeit. It's not just sawdust. It's not just crap. It's poison.

Gene Therapy and the Future of the Church

We buried my CEO's fourteen-year-old son last summer. Alex was full of cancer. They did everything they could to save him, but his whole body was under attack. The cells were sick, and the body could not survive.

The body can be no healthier than the cells.

The ELCA lost 80,000 members in 2005. We've lost 275,000 members in the last five years. Why? There are many reasons, but let me suggest one underlying, systemic truth. We are dying because the body can be no healthier than the cells.

Imagine this: You are a new bishop, freshly elected to a Synod with 270 churches. You take a quick survey of the congregations under your care and you find out that 265 never opened a Bible last year. 260 of them don't have a Christian education program. 255 of them didn't bother to pray all year. 250 of them didn't do a single act of Christly service for anyone outside of their walls.

What would you think of such a synod? You'd certainly have your work cut out for you. The body (your synod) would have no future if the cells (the churches) were not healthy.

Now imagine this: You are a new pastor, freshly installed in a church with 270 families. You take a quick survey of the families under your care and you find out that 265 never opened a Bible last year. 260 of them didn't mention God's name aloud last year. 255 of them didn't bother to pray all year. 250 of them didn't do a single act of Christly service for anyone outside of their home.

What would you think of such a church? You'd certainly have your work cut out for you. A church cannot be healthy if the cells are not healthy.

Our homes are the cells of the church body; and most of them are sick, malnourished, and starving for the bread of life. How might we change that? How might we change that sooner rather than later?

God's Word in the Home

I have been passionately (and sometimes obsessively) focused specifically on youth and family ministry for my entire ministry. In that time I have come to understand one thing clearly: The home is the main incubator of faith.

Parents have been, are, and always will be the most influential faith teachers in a child's life. Parents are teaching faith every day—no question about that. The only question is: "What faith are they teaching?" When they give the kid twenty dollars for a movie on Saturday night and a buck for the offering on Sunday morning, what faith are they teaching? When they drop the kid off for Sunday School and go out to Starbucks to read the paper, what faith are they teaching? When some vague institutional memory kicks in and they suddenly force the kid into confirmation with a "just get through this and then you can decide for yourself if you want to go to church!"—what faith are they teaching?

Parents ARE the main faith teachers. The home IS the most important incubator of faith. Luther called the parents the bishops of their little churches. Yet, we continue to perpetuate systems in the church that let parents off the hook. How much better would it be to call parents to do and be what they once promised to do and be in baptism, then give them the tools and systems to fulfill their promises?

I've got a simple little experiment I'd like you to consider to equip them to do just that, and I'd like you to consider implementing it this fall from the start of Sunday School right up to Reformation Day.

Five Nightly Faith Practices (Gene Therapy)

I believe the Lutherans in America have one last best chance to fight this cancer that is killing our future. It won't come from institutions. It won't come from seminaries. It won't come from on high in the form of edicts, statements, or studies. The only chance we have for our church to survive as a body, is to attack the cancer at the source—cell by cell—and do significant gene therapy.

We must splice God's Word into the genetic make-up of the cells —the homes—and we must do it as quickly and pervasively as humanly possible.

To do this, I am calling on pastors and teachers, professional church workers and parents to commit to ask parents to bring the Word of God back into the home, and surround it with five simple faith practices "every night in every home."

SHARE: Highs and lows of the day
READ: A verse of Scripture, either from Sunday's text or your kids' curriculum
TALK: About how the highs and lows relate to the Scripture (Is God saying something?)
PRAY: For one another's highs and lows
BLESS: One another before turning out the lights on the day

I'm asking congregations to challenge families this fall to commit to six weeks of this kind of genetic engineering for our families for five minutes every night. Turn off the television, put down the newspaper, log off the computer. (There will be plenty of time for all that when the kids are grown and gone). Take five minutes to bring caring conversations, active listening, God's Word, prayer and blessing into the heart of the nightly routine.

A few years ago the American Family Research Council did a study on how much conversation was going on between parents and teens on a normal week. They set homes up with microphones to record the chat, then compiled the stats, excluding scolding and commands. What they found was the average parent and teen are talking 37.5 minutes a week!

If you simply add five minutes a night to the conversation, you are nearly doubling the amount of talk between parents and kids. If you use the five steps above, you're also bringing God into half of the conversations.

Question 1: What happens to a family over time if they engage in these simple faith practices for five minutes every night?

Question 2: What happens to a church over time if even a third of their families are engaged in these faith practices?

266

You may just bring health, love, faith, compassion, communication and God into the nucleus of each cell. You may just change the DNA of the family. You may just give them something that can keep them together in a world that could tear them apart.

Bring God's Word, care and prayer back into the center of the family, and you may just change a family. Change enough families and you may just change a church. Change a church and you may just change THE church. Change THE church, and you may just change the world.

Join me this fall in calling ALL of your homes to bring God's Word into the core of their conversations for five minutes a night from Rally Day to Reformation Day. (See Afterword to learn how.)

Afterword

Last year I designed a series of "verse a night" living journals for parents and kids to use to record their nightly highs and lows and prayers. For elementary kids, these journals include 120 Bible stories in cartoons and Bible verse songs. For confirmation aged kids, they includes songs and games, plus short devotions. Check out the Living Journals at <www.faithink.com>. and let me know what you think of the concept of a reflective tool that puts God's Word into the heart of the nightly caring conversations.

Louis M. Hesse is a Lutheran layman with a life-long interest in history and theology that has brought him to the point where he has been termed a "lay theologian." The oldest son of a dairyman, Lou was baptized, confirmed, and married at Trinity Lutheran Church (LCMS) in Hillsboro, Oregon. After high school, he attended Iowa State University, receiving a Bachelor of Science degree in Animal Science in 1976. He returned home to continue farming with his family, this time with a focus on hogs rather than dairy cows. The farm operation was moved from Oregon to Central Washington in 1987. Lou, his father, and son, Ben, grow approximately 900 acres of grain and silage corn, and market over 8,000 hogs each year.

Lou's interest in reading and studying European history began early and expanded into Christian history as an adult. He has traveled to Europe several times, including Wittenberg and other Luther sites. After the family joined an ELCA congregation in 1990, Lou served as a voting member at several synod assemblies before being appointed to the ELCA's Human Sexuality Task Force in 2002 as the "middle-aged conservative white lay male who is not afraid to speak his mind." When the final report of the Task Force was released in January 2005, Lou's dissenting position was included. The connections and friendships he made while on the task force, from seminary professors and students to

WordAlone pastors and laymen, have helped Lou deepen and strengthen his understanding of Lutheran theology and his own faith. He currently serves as Executive Chair of the Augsburg Lutheran Churches.

Lou and his wife, Debbie, have been married twenty-nine years and are the par-

ents of three married children and two grandchildren. They are founding members of Living Word Lutheran Church in Moses Lake, Washington, an independent Lutheran congregation that formed as a "house church" in 2006 and recently moved from the home environment to donated space at the local Christian Academy.

☙ 26 ❧

The Lord Found Me

Louis M. Hesse

M Y THIRTIETH HIGH SCHOOL REUNION in 2002 was an interesting gathering. Held at a local country club near the old home town, it was a chance to reconnect with people that we had lost sight of and remember some of the things we had in common. Old friends whose lives had taken a turn for the better or worse . . . a chance to show off photos of children and even grandchildren . . . an opportunity to remember those who had died or had problems so severe with drugs or whatever that, sadly, they had been institutionalized.

Near the end of the evening I spotted an old classmate I hadn't seen in years coming towards me. "Hi, Lou, remember me?" Sharon asked as she approached. "Of course I do, Sharon. What's new with you?" I responded as I remembered how we had had a social studies course together our senior year called American Problems. We had spent most of that senior year in a mostly friendly contest of arguing about the nature of man and human problems. She was a secularist who believed a just society would result by good education, teaching people to do the right thing. I was, and still am, a Christian arguing from a belief in original sin, the innate fallenness of man, and the inability of people to do the good without Jesus Christ. It was a strong discussion that tested both of us.

269

"I just wanted to let you know the Lord found me." With these words Sharon simply left me speechless (a very rare thing for me as anyone who knows me can testify). This was an electrifying moment. I knew immediately I was talking to a sister in the faith. She smiled and said, "Yes, I know—who would have thought?" We talked awhile about all the mundane things but we also have a connection now that can't be broken.

Authority in the church is like Sharon's statement, "The Lord found me." You know it when you hear it, and a number of assumptions are immediately in play. Authority has some things in common with unity. You know when it's present and you know when it's absent. Sharon and I have unity in the faith because Jesus speaks to us—that is also authority. Just as the surest sign of disunity is scheduling a vote on unity, so also the surest sign of a lack of authority is debating what is authoritative.

Jesus said, "I am the way and the truth and the life. No one comes to the Father except through me," (John 14:6 KJV) and "All authority in heaven and on earth has been given to me." (Matt. 28:18 KJV) "In the beginning was the Word, and the Word was with God, and the Word was God." (John 1:1 KJV) At the baptism of Jesus, a voice from heaven declared, "This is my beloved Son, in whom I am well pleased" (Matt. 3:17 KJV); at the transfiguration of Jesus, a voice from a cloud declared, "This is my beloved Son, in whom I am well pleased; hear ye him." (Matt. 17:5 KJV).

If you have ears to hear, this is authoritative; if you don't have ears, no amount of cajoling, debating, or haranguing can change that. Only one person can change that—as my sister Sharon said, "The Lord found me."

Ordering Information

This publication and others are available from WordAlone's central headquarters in the United States at the address below. While WordAlone is a reform and renewal group within the Evangelical Lutheran Church in America some of its materials may well cross over to other mainline churches, both Protestant and Catholic, seeking reform.

Bible studies, women's and men's groups, parish libraries, pastors and laity will find among these printed materials a storehouse of information often withheld or ignored by mainline churches today who have turned their backs to the Word of God.

WordAlone Network
2299 Palmer Drive, Suite 220
New Brighton, MN 55112-2202
Tel: (651) 633-6004   Toll Free: (888) 551-7254
Fax: (651) 633-4260   Email: wordalone@popp.net
Website: www.wordalone.org